LAYING IT ON THE LINE

THE BORDER AND BREXIT

LAYING IT ON THE LINE

THE BORDER AND BREXIT

JUDE COLLINS

MERCIER PRESS

MERCIER PRESS
Cork
www.mercierpress.ie

ISBN: 978 1 78117 744 0

A CIP record for this title is available from the British Library.

Printed and bound in the EU.

To Hugh and Maureen Taggart,
life-long and valued friends.

CONTENTS

PREFACE

While the border in Ireland has its roots in the centuries-earlier plantation of Ulster, its modern emergence can be more easily traced to 1912, when hundreds of thousands of Northern unionists, opposed to Home Rule for Ireland, signed the Ulster Covenant. This committed them to resisting Home Rule, by physical force if necessary.

Over the decade that followed, three major events combined to culminate in Ireland's partition. The first was the Great War of 1914–18, which drew thousands of Irish recruits to fight in British uniform. From the South came those Irish Volunteers convinced by John Redmond that after the war Britain would fulfil its promise of Home Rule. From the North came the Ulster Volunteer Force (UVF), formed to oppose Britain's planned Home Rule and now intent on proving its loyalty to the mother country. Despite sacrifice of life on a massive scale, both Irish groups were doomed to have their trust in Britain betrayed.

The second historic event with bearing on the border was the Easter Rising in 1916. Militarily this was a failure, but when the leaders of the Rising were executed, Irish public support swung behind the insurgents and the War of Independence erupted.

The third, and conclusive, event was the Anglo-Irish Treaty of December 1921. The Treaty led to civil war between former republican comrades: some accepted that it allowed for the copper-fastening of a Northern state and some saw this as the ultimate betrayal.

Northern unionists had grudgingly accepted this new six-county state, even though it left hundreds of their fellow unionists stranded in the new Free State to the south. In the new Northern Ireland, hundreds of thousands of nationalists felt similarly abandoned.

When King George V opened the parliament of Northern Ireland in June 1921, he spoke optimistically of a better tomorrow for all Irish people:

> I speak from a full heart when I pray that my coming to Ireland to-day may prove to be the first step towards an end of strife amongst her people, whatever their race or creed. In that hope, I appeal to all Irishmen to pause, to stretch out the hand of forbearance and conciliation, to forgive and to forget, and to join in making for the land which they love a new era of peace, contentment, and goodwill.[1]

The monarch's commitment to forgiving and forgetting was not widely shared.

Northern republicans felt trapped, left behind by their Southern countrymen, unwilling subjects in a six-county state with which they felt no identification.

For their part, unionists felt under siege. To the south lay the Irish Free State, whose constitution explicitly laid claim to Northern Ireland. Within Northern Ireland's tortuous boundary, one-third of the population resented the very existence of the state and its institutions.

And so unionists set about securing their new home. Discrimination against the Catholic population in jobs and housing became systemic, and electoral gerrymandering (the manipulation of electoral boundaries) was used to minimise nationalist representation. Derry city, for example, had a two-thirds Protestant/unionist corporation elected by a two-thirds Catholic/nationalist population. Northern Ireland's first prime minister, James Craig, stated the obvious: Northern Ireland was now 'a Protestant parliament and Protestant state'.[2]

Over the following decades the IRA mounted sporadic attacks on border posts with little success or support, and it abandoned its efforts in 1962. Constitutional nationalists, committed to non-violence and politics, were equally ineffectual, their political representatives impotent in the face of the unionist majority.

In the late 1960s the civil rights movement emerged. Its leadership was composed of young men who had benefited from Northern Ireland's education system and now had sufficient confidence to confront, not the border, but state injustice. Modelling itself on the black civil rights movement in the US during the early 1960s, the Northern Ireland Civil Rights Association (NICRA) held mass rallies against discrimination in jobs and housing, demanding for Catholics the rights accorded to other British citizens.

Northern Ireland's unionist government found peaceful protest hard to cope with, and the Royal Ulster Constabulary (RUC) responded to demonstrations with baton charges and tear gas. Eventually the British army was called in to support the RUC. At first welcomed, the British soldiers soon became targets in armed conflict. The IRA grew in strength, and what became known as the Troubles lasted for some thirty blood-soaked years. The IRA called a ceasefire in the early 1990s, and in 1998 the Good Friday Agreement (GFA) established the power-sharing Assembly at Stormont.

But like the Northern state itself, the Stormont Assembly suffered for two decades from internal and external tensions. Suspended four times, it collapsed in 2017 amid charges of corruption and fiscal mismanagement by the Democratic Unionist Party (DUP). Stormont was put in cold storage, where it sits at the time of writing.

A year earlier, in 2016, in an effort to resolve divisions within his Conservative cabinet, Prime Minister David Cameron had called a UK referendum on Britain's membership of the European Union (EU). To widespread surprise, the Leave side won by a 4% majority. Cameron resigned, leaving Theresa May, at the launch of her bid to succeed him, to declare on 30 June 2016 that 'Brexit means Brexit', which was of limited help. Astonishingly it appears that, before the EU referendum, no one had considered the implications of a Leave majority for the border in Ireland.

Since the GFA in 1998, the border between North and South had become 'invisible'. Socially and economically, the line between the two jurisdictions had faded as movement and business had developed and integrated on both sides. The GFA had seen the Republic of Ireland abandon its constitutional claim on Northern Ireland; in return, the militarised border of the Troubles had been removed, and cross-border commerce and interaction, with both states within the EU, had flourished. With the approach of Brexit, fears of a new 'hard border' returned.

There was also the uncomfortable fact that, although the DUP, Northern Ireland's biggest political party, had campaigned to leave the EU, 56% of Northern Ireland's population had voted to remain. Clearly, if the UK (including Northern Ireland) were to leave the EU, this would damage the GFA, which had assumed continued membership for both jurisdictions. It began to look as though the Irish border that lightly marked the division between North and South would now become the line between the EU and the UK.

The DUP declared itself in favour of maintaining the invisible border but was adamant that the border between the Republic of Ireland and the UK mustn't be transferred to the Irish Sea, arguing that this would make trading relations between Northern Ireland and the EU different from those between the rest of the UK and the EU – even when the distinction would be in Northern Ireland's favour.

After two years of negotiation, Theresa May's Conservative government agreed a withdrawal bill with the EU, which included what would become known as the Irish backstop. This guaranteed that the existing arrangement of an invisible border, with trade and traffic flowing freely between North and South, would continue until some better arrangement was agreed on. In practice, this meant that Northern Ireland would have access to the UK market *and* the EU single market – the best of both worlds. But the bill was opposed by the majority of MPs, including the ten DUP MPs, and it proved impossible for Theresa May to gain the backing of Parliament for her deal.

At the time of writing, the DUP face two major difficulties. The first is that, as a number of interviewees note, the party is out of step with its electorate. The DUP's Leave policy and its refusal to support Theresa May's withdrawal bill put it at odds with farming and business in Northern Ireland, both sectors that are keenly aware of the economic destruction that Brexit and a hard border in Ireland would bring.

The second difficulty for the DUP is an existential one. The DUP favours UK withdrawal from the EU, but the price of that withdrawal, in the view of some commentators, will be the disintegration of the UK. By insisting there is no trade impediment between Northern Ireland and Britain, the DUP may create conditions in which a hard Brexit is unavoidable. This will mean economic hardship for all of the UK, particularly Northern Ireland and Scotland – both of which voted to remain in the EU. Brexit may well lead to a second Scottish referendum for independence, and a hard border in Ireland may well lead to demands in Ireland for a border poll on Irish reunification (as provided for in the GFA). The price of Brexit may be UK disintegration, Irish unity and an end to the 100-year-old border.

* * *

In conducting these interviews during the first half of 2019, I have been aware that the rapid pace of events may render some of the views expressed out of date. With that in mind, the interviews have been arranged in chronological order, reminding the reader that all thinking is shaped by what is happening at that particular time.

I have tried to gather as wide a range of views as possible. American influence has long played a part in Irish history, most recently through the contributions of President Bill Clinton and Senator George Mitchell to the GFA. With that in mind I have included several interviews with prominent Irish-Americans.

Similarly, the views and values of unionism were an essential component of the GFA in 1998. This collection of interviews includes the voices of the RUC, the British army and loyalist paramilitarism.

As political parties are central to the present momentous events, I am pleased that former and current politicians from Sinn Féin, Fianna Fáil and Fine Gael are also included. I had hoped that the DUP and the Ulster Unionist Party (UUP) would be part of the conversation, but despite repeated written requests to the leaders of both, neither party responded. The significance or non-significance of this I leave to the reader to decide.

To all those who did give of their time to share their thinking in this collection, my sincere thanks.

A special word of gratitude to Patrick O'Donoghue, Wendy Logue and Deirdre Roberts of Mercier Press, who defied the laws of time to produce this book, and to Alice Coleman for her vivid cover design.

1

MARTINA ANDERSON

8 FEBRUARY 2019

Martina Anderson was born in the Bogside area of Derry in the 1960s and grew up amid the civil rights campaign and the unfolding political situation that led to conflict. She was active in republicanism from the late 1970s and spent over thirteen years in prison, mostly in English jails, for republican activities. She was released in 1998 under the terms of the Good Friday Agreement and went on to serve as a Sinn Féin MLA and a Stormont minister. She is currently an MEP.

I recall one time my father got a new car – new to us, that is – and my mummy took my younger sister Sharon and me out of school early, and we got into the car and went across the border to Buncrana. It was like a big adventure – I was around six or seven. At the border we were just curious – why were they stopping the car? There was talk of smuggling butter and bread – it was something we always did. And for us as children, there was a certain nervousness, because Mammy and Daddy were doing something bold and they might get caught with their sugar or butter or whatever! And later, as I was growing up, there was the story of this girl who had her wedding dress confiscated at the border. So not everybody got waved through even then.

This maybe sounds contradictory to everything I now know and believe, but we had a sense that when we crossed, we were in Ireland. We had no relationship with the state in the North, so it did feel when we crossed the border as if we were going into another country. There was a sense of belonging. Comparing Portrush in the North to Lisfannon or Buncrana, there was something bright and Irish about Lisfannon and Buncrana.

Then I remember people talking about the military installations going up at the border. I came from a particular family, a particular area, a particular community, which meant that, before my arrest at sixteen, I had been pulled out of the car at the border hundreds of times. The car was stopped and searched, you were taken into a hut, you'd see people you knew at the side of the road. After militarisation of the border, I don't remember ever crossing without there being that sense of aggression. So from crossing to something bright and beautiful, it was now more that you felt a sense of relief when you had crossed the border. On the Donegal side, there were no British soldiers on the streets, there were no Saracens, there were no helicopters.

Our day-to-day living in the North and the South was markedly different. When they divided our country and created partition, they didn't just divide the country's landscape. It was deliberate that they had two health systems, two education systems, two agriculture systems, two of everything, in all cases markedly distinct.

I think the people in the twenty-six counties, for all its faults, had a connection with the establishment of that state and with those who were in government, despite the damage done by the Civil War and all of that. Growing up here in the North, our community never felt any kind of connection with the various branches of the state. For people in Donegal, like them or loathe them, the police came from the community. They were John and Jane who lived round the corner. Somebody would have known the guard, someone knew the civil servant, somebody knew the judges and solicitors and all that. We didn't.

The border is invisible because Europe made it clear that funding through Interreg [a series of programmes to stimulate cooperation between regions of the EU] was not for back-to-back projects, it was for projects that had to be truly integrational, across the border. Today we have somewhere in the region of 170 areas of all-Ireland cooperation.

In the withdrawal agreement there was this 'backstop'. It was there to prevent physical infrastructure on the border in Ireland ever emerging again. We had to ensure that Europe understood the three strands of the GFA. The fact was, neither the European Council nor the MEPs understood the GFA and all of its parts. But we finally got them to understand that if you're going to have an all-Ireland economy, you cannot have a regulatory system that is different in the North and the South.

I think the EU would have tolerated the hardening of the border in Ireland if they hadn't understood the conflict, the peace process, the political process. It has taken a lot of hard work to get the EU to understand the damage that would be done if the GFA were torn apart – which is what Britain is doing.

No one talked about Ireland before the referendum. Everyone was talking about Scotland. But now they are realising that Ireland is the only successful peace process that Europe has.

Europe needs that to be able to help war-torn places. They cannot protect the GFA in all of its parts and operate the all-Ireland economy while saying, 'We will put in an EU border.'

[*In March 2017 Martina Anderson made an angry speech in the European Parliament telling colleagues, 'Ireland is told "Get over it – it's going to be a frictionless border" – whatever the hell that means. Let me put the record straight to everyone here: no border, hard or soft, will be accepted by the people of Ireland. What British armoured cars and tanks and guns couldn't do in Ireland, twenty-seven member states will not be able to do. So, Theresa – your notion of a border, hard or soft – stick it where the sun doesn't shine, because you're not putting it in Ireland.'*[1]]

I was quite disturbed going back to Brussels, having heard people tell me that Brexit is already here, in our purses, in our wallets, the bottom's falling out of the pound. So to tell you the truth, it was just exasperation with all of it that led me to let rip. I hadn't actually expected it to go viral, but for forty-eight hours, I couldn't cope with the demand across Europe. We got international attention in a way we hadn't before. Italy, France, Greece, TV, radio – I couldn't cope with the demand. But nobody said anything about my having been bold in the chamber. They were all starting to get an understanding of partition, of the border, why we needed to be in the customs union and the single market to preserve the GFA.

I think the backstop debate has accelerated a conversation we've been having for years. I've wanted to see this country reunited since I was able to understand the damage partition was doing. In Europe I was on the Brexit Steering Group and I urged protection of the GFA in all of its parts. And in the Council meeting on 29 April 2017, the Council sent its first signal: in the event of reunification, the North will still continue to be a member of the EU.

There are a growing number of people who like what they see in metropolitan Dublin, for all of its faults. If they had a choice of which union they wanted to be a part of, the union with the EU with all its deficiencies or the union with a UK which is breaking up, it would be an easy choice. Some are coming to realise what we have known all our lives: that the British establishment doesn't care about them. There are people in the Protestant/unionist community who are progressive, who don't want their children or their grandchildren to be living in a backward place. They want guarantees, and rightly so, that their identity and their culture will be protected. It's very important to plan and prepare. I don't want the North just bolted onto the South.

There's a role for Europe to be able to say, 'What will that mean, compared to if you're not in?' And I think we need a white paper from the Irish government. This is not a Sinn Féin-driven process. Progressive nationalists are turning their backs on Westminster and even Stormont – although I think we need a place where we can go during transition.

I think the economic argument for unification was won a long time ago. Farmers have for some time been operating on an all-Ireland basis. There is £1.2 billion of trade every week across this island. There are 200,000 jobs dependent on it. Every day, 32,000 people cross the border.

The backstop is not enough. The backstop is not going to uphold our rights. The Irish government, at the stroke of a pen, could provide people here in the North who are Irish citizens with the opportunity to vote in European elections [the EU has re-allocated the exiting UK's European Parliament seats, giving two of these to the Republic of Ireland]. There are twenty-two member states out of twenty-eight who afford their nationals the opportunity to vote. The Irish government can give us those two extra MEP seats. Do I think they will? Absolutely not. When the Taoiseach said, 'No Irish government will ever again leave you behind', we welcomed the warm words and it was great that an Irish Taoiseach [prime minister] realised that we had been left behind.[2] But I was with the Department of Foreign Affairs in Dublin last week, and I told them, 'You have an opportunity to send a signal to the people of the North that you will stand over what you said.'

The first right to go and the only right to go during the transition period is your democratic right to vote in a European election. That's forty years after our campaign for 'One "man", one vote.'

But it's not just having MEPs. The rights that are going to be stripped away as a consequence of Brexit affect us all. An example: part-time workers got their right to holiday pay only because speech and language therapists took Britain to the European Commission and the Commission acted. So part-time workers in the Protestant/unionist community are having their rights upheld only because of Europe. The British government wouldn't have facilitated that. So representation is one aspect of it, and we find it precious because we had to fight for that right. But people who are British are entitled to the same rights as all of us.

Mary Lou McDonald, the president of Sinn Féin, was invited into a conversation in Derry, and the loyalist bands were part of that. Jeffrey Donaldson of the DUP was on the podium with a few others. Jeffrey said, 'You know, nobody is talking about Irish unity. When I talk to people, they're talking about the Assembly up and running.' And this guy stood up and said, 'Jeffrey, we in the loyalist bands are talking about it. And Mary Lou – I want to know, how are you going to protect our rights?' I didn't think I would have heard that – a challenge to Jeffrey Donaldson about the need for rights to be protected.

The plates have shifted, and people want to know if their rights will be protected. People want to be able to make an informed decision.

It's not going to work unless all sides are happy. I'm not saying every person, but we all have to try to arrive at an accommodation. I don't think it'll be just the economics – it'll be social, it'll be political. Sometimes you don't know what you have until it's gone.

2

AODHÁN CONNOLLY

11 FEBRUARY 2019

Aodhán Connolly is the director of the Northern Ireland Retail Consortium, a leading trade body for retail in Northern Ireland covering everything from the smallest bookshops to the largest multi-nationals. He has worked in the political process for over twenty years and lobbied on issues such as young people not in employment, education or training, the environment, trade regulation, commercial rates and public health.

I was brought up in Annakera, a wee place outside Portadown, thirty miles from the border. When we went over the border we knew we were going on our holidays, and the stress on my dad lifted. But on the way home, it always came back. You'd often be taken out of the car and searched – not always, but it did happen. This was particularly the case when we were five or six – the time of the hunger strikes. [Between March and October 1981, republican prisoners went on hunger strike to back their demand that they be recognised as political prisoners. Ten men died on hunger strike.] I was always frightened of the soldiers. When you're that age and you see guys with guns, you know what they are but don't understand why they're there. There was fear in us and you could also feel the stress in the car from both my parents, but especially my dad.

Even now when I'm coming back over the border from the South, it's not a nice feeling. I live in the North but there's a twinge, a memory that's ingrained each time I drive across that line.

I'm dealing with the legacy of life when I was growing up. But my thirteen-year-old, who's never known a physical border between North and South – his idea when we go over the border is still 'Yeah, we're going on holidays.' But does he see a boundary that marks a different country? I don't think so, although he identifies himself as Irish or Northern Irish depending on who's asking the question.

The backstop in the UK–EU withdrawal agreement is an insurance policy. It's there so that if everything breaks down, there'd still be no hard border. Northern Ireland would still have unfettered access to the GB market, and also to the Southern and therefore the EU market. We here in the North would be part of the single market of the UK as well as part of the single market of the EU.

In considering this matter I put my political views to the side and looked at it purely in terms of economics. That's been the problem – people have been looking at this in terms of ideology and not economics, in terms of politics and not people. I'd go further and say there are people concerned with jingoism and not jobs – people such as the European Research Group (ERG) [a pro-Brexit group in the UK's Conservative Party]. They're making this into a constitutional issue. They say they don't want a border in the Irish Sea. But the figures show that, while a border in the Irish Sea would mean slightly more paperwork for trade coming from GB to Northern Ireland, we would have alignment with the UK and so there'd be fewer checks needed. The fact is we already have checks on some things coming from GB to Northern Ireland – animals and animal products, for example. It happens at Larne, at Warrenpoint, at Belfast. We've done the figures. It would mean nine lorries a day would have to get checked – out of almost 9,000 lorries that would have the potential to be checked.

People say, 'Oh, your members must be very mad at this.'

No they're not. Slightly increased checks as opposed to a hard border? I think not.

With a hard border, you're talking about the systematic disintegration of the supply chain in Northern Ireland.

One of the things I, along with other trade-body leaders, have been saying is that we're not doing the amount of negotiating work that we should be doing. What we are doing is breaking down lies – shooting unicorns. You had Gerard Batten, the party leader of UKIP, coming out and saying on 30 January that there were only 100 lorries on the border and half of those were Guinness. In fact there are 13,000 lorries which go over the border every day – and very few are Guinness lorries.

We really do have to question our media on this – the amount of time that they're giving to people like Batten and the fact that they're not challenging statements they make. It's the old point: someone can say it's not raining, but, before printing, it's up to the journalist to stick his head out the window and see.

We have also allowed people to turn this small economic and regulatory issue into a constitutional issue. But the biggest barrier to a united Ireland was never the unionist population –

it was middle-class nationalists who were afraid they'd be hit in the pocket. If we have a hard Brexit and the GB economy tanks and the Northern Ireland economy tanks, you've removed one of the biggest barriers to a united Ireland.

Thirty per cent of Northern Irish milk goes across the border to be processed. A lot of that comes back as goods. If we have a hard border, between VAT and duties on it, the milk will be worthless.

We're not talking here about an economy that's been built over twenty years of peace. We're talking about an economy that's been built over forty years in the EU. The [Northern Irish] Brexiteers always say, 'Oh, but we do £11.5 billion [in trade] with GB and only about £5 billion with the Republic of Ireland and the EU.' But we can't have an either/or. We need both to be prosperous – it's that simple.

If you look at any of the trade bodies that we're working with – the Confederation of British Industry (CBI), the Institute of Directors (IoD), Freight NI, Manufacturing NI – they're all in agreement. If you'd told me two years ago that I'd be standing with freight, farmers, processors – all of us shoulder to shoulder – I wouldn't have believed you. The two big things we're asking for are one, a deal, and two, no border in Ireland. I don't think in my lifetime there's ever been a time when business has been so forthright about what it believes, but also so united in the course of action that it wants to take.

The DUP has taken a stance which reflects what its core demographic feels. But that stance is at odds with the economy, with what business people and people with jobs want. The majority of people here voted to remain. There are a lot of people in Northern Ireland – check social media and you'll see – who think that the backstop is a weakening of the union. I have to look at this in economic terms and I don't agree. It could be argued that securing the economic position of Northern Ireland secures that union, whereas economic chaos would make the Republic of Ireland more enticing to some people.

I met with Prime Minister May last week, and she was full of reassurances and full of commitment to a smooth Brexit. I wouldn't want her job – she's not just going up against the EU but going up against her own party, the ERG and the Labour Party – so fair play to her. I don't know how she finds the tolerance and the energy for it. We're pretty sure there will be a deal done by 30 March on aviation – but what you can carry on those planes, as far as trade and goods are concerned – that is going to change overnight.

This is a point that I don't think is expressed enough. The British government say they don't want a hard border. The Irish government say they don't want a hard border. The EU says they don't want a hard border. But there's going to have to be a hard border from one side or the other – the path to hell is paved with good intentions.

The UK needs to protect its single market, but this is an existential problem for the EU. The UK can say all it likes, 'We don't want to pay the £39 billion.' I'm sorry, but you have to if you want to be taken seriously as a trading nation. You can't have no border – it sets a hugely damaging precedent for the 200-odd borders the EU has to the east.

Brexit is a sliding scale. No Brexit would be good. If the withdrawal bill were to go through, there would be cost increases but things would continue largely as normal. The supply chain would continue; haulage would continue. A transition period would help work out the kinks. There'd be a little bit more admin added on – some of that would be passed on to the consumer. But compare that to the absolute shitshow of a no deal – and it's not often I'd use that word. Your checks, your delays – what are known as non-tariff barriers can be up to 29% of the value on food items.

And it's not just what we export to the EU. We export a lot of stuff we don't use to Asia. Because we do that, the nice bits that we get – your steak and pork loin, for example – are actually cheaper, because the suppliers are getting more money for the rest. If they don't get that extra money, it'll have to come from somewhere. And they won't get that if we're not part of the EU.

Brexit will hit the smallest businesses first; it'll hit the most vulnerable households first. That's just not acceptable. A hard Brexit means a hard border.

Again it's shooting unicorns. Technological solutions could cover the border, but I don't know of any right now – we're ten or twelve years away from that. If they did exist, do you not think there'd be a company out there shouting, 'Please, give me your billions of pounds and I will solve the problem'?

I don't have a crystal ball, but what I can say with some certainty is that Brexit – no matter what kind of Brexit we have – will make things harder all over the UK. But a hard Brexit will make things intolerable here in Northern Ireland. And that is more of an economic undermining of the union than anything that's happened here in the past 100 years.

3

IAN MARSHALL

11 FEBRUARY 2019

In 2018 Ian Marshall became the first Ulster Unionist senator elected to Seanad Éireann. In conjunction with the Seanad, he currently works at Queen's University Belfast in the Institute for Global Food Security. He has vast experience and extensive knowledge of farming and all aspects of the agri-food industry, enhanced by his completion of a Master of Science in agri-food business development at Ulster University and Babson College, Boston, USA. He is a former president of the Ulster Farmers' Union (UFU), a member of the Agri-Food Strategy Board and at the time of writing a professional member of the Institute of Agricultural Management.

I grew up in South Armagh, maybe six or seven miles from the border. It was close, but all through my early childhood it seemed very far away. For us as a Protestant Presbyterian farming family in South Armagh in the midst of the Troubles, the border region wasn't all that inviting a place. So most of our travel went northwards – to Portadown, to Armagh and other towns and villages to do our shopping. And our holidays would have been northwards – places like Portrush, Newcastle and Bangor.

Through the lens of a child, I saw the military and the soldiers' presence as protection. My father and before him my grandfather were both farmers and would have traded a lot across the border, but the Troubles curtailed that. I remember asking my father, who's now eighty-seven, about Crossmaglen pre-Troubles, and he described it as a friendly, ordinary village where everyone worked together.

I laugh now when I hear people talking about 208 crossing points at the border. I think there are 22,000 crossing points at the border. There were all those paths and tracks where the old people would have told you no one would ever bother you. But from my childhood, concrete is the thing I remember at the border – steel, barbed wire, concrete.

I spoke to people who came from the South to play Gaelic football matches in the North, and there was a nervousness about that – a sense that they were moving into this different jurisdiction. I was twenty-five years of age before I visited Dublin. That was probably the case with most country people – you lived and worked in your own locality.

On a horrible, wet, black afternoon in January of last year, here in Queen's University, I took a phone call from the EU agriculture commissioner Phil Hogan – I had worked with him when I was president of the Farmers' Union in Brussels – and he said, 'Expect a call from the Taoiseach, he'd like to nominate you to run in a Seanad by-election.' So in a couple of hours the Taoiseach rang and asked if he could nominate me.

He invited me to Dublin for a coffee and I was very nervous about it. I was born into an Ulster Unionist family. We talked for an hour and a half in his office. I said, 'What's happening – am I some sort of token unionist to fit the picture at the moment?' He said, 'When I was made Taoiseach I addressed gender inequality in government. I took males out of my cabinet, put in females. I've done that and I want to have a balanced Seanad. When the Seanad was set up in 1921, there were sixty senators – thirty Protestant and thirty Catholic, and that was for balance of opinion. We still have Protestants and Catholics in there, but no Northern unionist voice. I would like to have a Northern unionist voice to give perspective in debate.'

In the Seanad in Dublin, I don't feel in a foreign environment at all. I know I'm in another country – that's a statement of fact, not a political statement – but I certainly don't feel any issue of being different or not welcomed. As we sit here today, my office in Queen's University is 105 miles from the office in Leinster House. But it's light years apart in understanding.

My first time in Leinster House in Dublin, I had lunch with some of the admin staff. They'd just come back from Belfast on a hen weekend. The girls were saying they'd had a lovely weekend and the people were lovely – and it was the first time for many of them in Belfast. 'What did you expect from Belfast people?' I said. 'Did you think they wouldn't be nice people?' The thing that blew them away was that people would ask them their names and what schools they had gone to in order to find out what religion they were. For these girls from Dublin, that was completely alien. Protestant or Catholic is an irrelevance for them in Dublin. They don't know in their group of friends who's Protestant and who's Catholic, and they don't care either. I think the Catholic Church has relinquished its grip on society: what I see now is a very progressive, forward-looking society.

And I see young people very engaged in the South. A couple of days after I arrived in Dublin, I had to go up to Grafton

Street to get my phone contract. The young guy who spoke to me in the Vodafone store was Brazilian-born but an Irish national. He was tattooed from head to toe, had stretchers in his ears, piercings in his lips, nose and cheeks, his head was shaved and the small piece of hair he had was bright red. So he was filling in my details and he said, 'Oh – you're a senator in Leinster House.' I said, 'I am,' and we had a twenty-minute conversation on politics that would have blown your mind. This was from a lad who couldn't have been more than nineteen or twenty.

When I came out of the store my personal assistant said, 'What did you think of that?' I said, 'That was impressive – that young guy is really engaged in politics.' He said, 'Ian, they all are here. The referenda have brought these things to the fore, whether it's same-sex marriage, LGBT rights, abortion – they're engaged, they're being taught about politics and they're better informed.' I was really impressed.

There's no doubt that the North is lagging behind in that respect. I love the North to bits, but it's a goldfish bowl of politics. When you take people out and you look back in, it does appear a bit crazy.

I heard only one disrespectful comment made among the farming community here, through a third party, and apparently it was 'Ian Marshall has gone to Dublin for twenty pieces of silver.' My wife, who's much sharper than me, said, 'For goodness' sake, Ian wouldn't go for twenty, he'd go for a hundred and twenty!'

There's a private side and a public side to this. When I speak to some of our elected public representatives, Members of the Legislative Assembly (MLAs), very influential people in unionist or loyalist circles – when I ask, they say, 'We're supportive of you. It's the right time, you're the right person, and you actually represent 99% of unionists.' But when I say, 'Well, could you tell your people that?' they say, 'Couldn't do that, Ian.' That's disappointing, from my perspective. In our society, it only takes a small number of disgruntled people who are very vocal and very influential on social media.

What I ask such people is, what makes them better unionists than me? And I fail to get an answer. My argument is that it makes me a stronger unionist: I'm prepared to sit down with anyone and have a mature, grown-up conversation, and I don't feel that compromises my situation. I've always believed that any dispute has to be resolved through dialogue.

At the micro level, there are lots of farming businesses that straddle the border. That creates complexity, with different sets of forms and papers needing to be presented to Belfast or London or Dublin, different herd records. That was a nightmare for such farmers. At the macro level, it provided huge opportunities in trade. People could use the price differential to be good businessmen.

Post-1973, the border became a notional idea. What you have in Ireland is an [agriculture] industry that's been inextricably linked for generations. That all happens pretty seamlessly. So agriculture presents a unique set of problems for the Brexit conundrum. For most of the other industries, there are solutions to the problems. Agriculture and agri-food – we still have failed to find the technological solutions that people talk about to deal with this. If you have a dairy cow milked in Armagh today and her milk goes to Monaghan, it's processed in Monaghan – produces liquid milk, yoghurts, cheeses, creams. It then comes back North and could go on to England or to Dublin or France. All that movement isn't unique to dairy products: you have it for red meat and other commodities too. Your tanker of milk is perishable – it can't afford a delay. You can't afford a disruption to that supply.

Our biggest market is the UK. But equally important is the EU – a market of 500 million people. If, for example, you produce a pig or a chicken, you can sell a portion of that into the UK. But to make a profit, you've got to sell *all* of the pig or the chicken. With a chicken, the premium end is the white meat – the breast. We in the UK don't like dark meat; we don't like the feet, the head, beaks or whatever else. But there are markets out there, and we have to have access to those other markets.

The Dutch are particularly good at this. What they do is they put their chicken or their pork into the UK because it's a premium market, but they've carved out very lucrative markets for the other components of those animals. It's the same with your beef and your cattle – you've got to sell the whole animal, including the offal. So you can't be completely dependent on the UK market. And that's why continental Europe is extremely important for us.

All this started two years ago with ideology. And the ideology was that the UK would click its fingers and carve out trade deals and boundless opportunities around the world. I think that was an ideology that was more akin to 1918 than 2018. In the intervening two years we have found that this separation isn't as easy as we imagined. We're sitting here today in Queen's University – the academics are telling us this doesn't make any sense, business people are telling us this doesn't make any sense. I was at a meeting of the Law Reform Commission in Dublin and the legal profession are saying this doesn't make any sense. This forty years of linkage with Europe, on a legal basis, with regard to law and the courts and the judiciary: it's a bit like trying to take the yolk out of the scrambled egg. It's very hard to do, it's virtually impossible to do.

I'm critical of both sides in this discussion, because I think there were a lot of lies on both sides. All the dividends that were promised to the British people in 2016 have simply vanished like snow off a ditch.

If we go back to 1957, when the European Economic Community (EEC) was set up it had two ambitions. First, to ensure there were no more European wars. Other than occasional flare-ups, it has done that. The second thing was to feed European people. At this moment, 550 million people have safe, good-quality, traceable food. For all intents and purposes, the EEC has delivered that too.

The Common Agricultural Policy (CAP) was brought in to make sure farmers obtained a living from their work. There is a reality check we have to bring everyone back to. If you continue to produce food with prices below the cost of production, you've only two options: a) you pay farmers a support mechanism to keep them in business, or b) you pay more for food. Governments have found time and again that one thing which is unpopular with the electorate is to see food inflation – and that's why governments have resisted it at all times.

I would say that about half of farmers are dependent on that support mechanism from the EU. The British government has committed to retaining support until 2020. But the reality is that the British government will quite simply have to support farmers beyond that. By supply and demand, market prices will not sustain the industry unless there's a huge inflation in the price of food. So I think the British government will be compelled to continue support.

A report I got out of the House of Commons Library showed how many UK laws were influenced by EU laws: 4,514 out of 34,105 UK laws were influenced by EU laws. And out of the EU laws that influenced the 4,514, it was discovered that seventy-two were forced on us against our will. The commissioner told me that the UK got 77% of things they asked for from the EU. I don't think that's a bad strike rate, as one member of twenty-eight.

I think for the DUP, this was about having the bond to London, the bond of the union, cemented. To ensure that the place for Northern Ireland within the union was secured. The interesting irony is that the link has probably been weakened as a consequence of this. The Scots are looking on with interest to see what happens in Northern Ireland; Sinn Féin has dropped a hand-grenade into this called unification – that has been unhelpful. I think the Brexit discussion should be treated separately. And then whatever comes out of that discussion will form part of another discussion about unification. But I think to play to the fear and insecurity within unionist circles isn't helpful. It actually complicates and confuses the issues.

If you wanted assurance that your cultural identity or civil liberties weren't infringed, then being part of Europe was the place to be. In Westminster, we actually have a much smaller voice than we had in Europe. The charges are that the EU is top-heavy, unwieldy. Actually, there are about 1,000 members in both houses in Westminster and there are about 750 in Europe. So you have 1,000 managing business for 62 million people and 750 looking after 550 million people.

Britain's position in the EU has always been that it wants to be at the party but not really to be at the party. Had we, in 1973, truly embraced this European project, we would still be the number-one strongest economy, a position now held by the Germans.

I look at things now and I'm very nervous that the UK is a completely divided society over Brexit. Communities divided, families divided – husbands and wives divided over Brexit. If the UK is to leave [the EU] in that situation, I think it'll be in a pretty precarious place. Because for anything negative that happens to the UK in the next ten years, I as a Remainer will say, 'I told you so, I warned you that this would happen.' And for anything that's positive, the Leavers will say, 'Look at the opportunities we have.'

I think Theresa May is going to come back with nothing. They've had two years, and all the concessions have been made during those two years. Any tinkering around the edges will be minimal. The backstop is there – whatever form it takes, a backstop is necessary.

No votes in Parliament have brought a decisive majority. If we're in a position where Parliament can't decide, the only way to bring the UK back together as one nation is to go back to the people.

Why on earth enter a situation where we're going to be bound by the rules and regulations of Europe yet have no say?

I think a hard Brexit will deliver a serious shock right across the border counties. Will that extend to the rest of Ireland? I think it could. People who are not exposed and quite comfortable will have a different experience from those exposed.

This is not about Project Fear – this is about Project Reality. When I listen to academics and economists, business people – where have the opportunities in Brexit gone? 'Stiff British upper lip – we've got through harder things.' Hello?

The economic unity case doesn't have to be made simply for Ireland – it is made for Europe. There is no logic in a hard border or a border throughout Europe. It's been demonstrated for the last thirty years how beneficial [not having such a border] is.

I was asked at a recent meeting how, as a Northern unionist, I felt about unification. My response was, 'Wars have been fought historically over land and territory. Wars in the future will be fought over data and information. Wars may be fought over water, who knows. But for me, unification isn't about land, it's about people. What I see north and south of the border are people who are so, so similar. To quote the late MP Jo Cox: "There's more that unites us than divides us."'

I think the focus needs to be on unifying the people across the North and South – and for that matter between Ireland and England and the rest of the UK. I see huge advantage in the global economy functioning as a unit, working together. I have faith in democracy – I'm a democrat – and I think good will triumph over evil. There are dark forces playing in Brexit, and I think people haven't realised that. History will reveal it: there are people who are set to benefit from a hard Brexit. There's a right-wing populism emerging across Europe, and there are people set to gain personally from this. There are very influential people who, if we had a separation and a clear-out, it could benefit them.

4

GLENN BRADLEY

14 FEBRUARY 2019

Glenn Bradley was born in 1967 in unionist West Belfast. A former British army infantry non-commissioned officer, he became an officer of the UUP and participated in the negotiations that led to the GFA. Today, he is recognised as an ethical trade pioneer, engaged in international trade using global supply chains. He is chair of the Northern Ireland Business and Human Rights Forum and is a member of the IoD (Ireland).

I was born and raised in Woodvale, which is the unionist area of West Belfast. I was raised in a traditional unionist family, so talk of the border, talk of partition, would have been very much part of our history. My grandparents would have felt that the three Ulster counties which weren't included in Northern Ireland were betrayed.

The family was very into rugby, as I am, so trips down to Dublin to see Ireland playing were commonplace. And I was raised with a sense of respect for the Irish national flag. Indeed, my uncle Hugh Smyth, the former head of the Progressive Unionist Party (PUP), would have taught me that the orange of the Irish national flag was us. But he was still pro-union, pro-UK.

I always saw the border as something separating people who were essentially the same. Once over the border, you noticed road signs and so on in Gaelic. At the time, that made me feel alienated, although at the same time I never had a problem with being Irish but also being loyal to Britain. I do love rugby and the Irish national anthem being played. And I'd no problem with the flag. But I had with the IRA, who used that flag as a means to assault and insult the community from which I came. But that was later in life.

At the age of sixteen I joined the army. I served for a couple of years in different parts of the world, but my first tour on the border came in 1987. I was attached to an English regiment. We operated the vehicle checks and manned the towers. Then my second border posting came in 1988–89 and my third in 1990.

As a teenager I had joined the army to get the best training possible to then come back here and take the war to the IRA. That was my motivation. I could have joined the UVF, but certain loyalists convinced me to join the army, get the best possible training and then come back where, if need be, I could utilise that training.

I wasn't afraid, being posted on the border. I was coming at it with an appetite. I was a professional soldier; I was in the business of kill or be killed. Make no mistake about it – infantry soldiers are trained to kill. They're not trained to shoot weapons out of hands, they're not trained to shoot people in the legs, they are trained to put rounds into a target until that target is no longer a threat. So I was enthused about coming here. I also thought, 'When I get there, I'll teach these limeys a thing or two about what they're doing wrong!' Underlying all was the thought that I'd now taken the fight to the IRA.

On the border, we were sleeping on three-tier bunk beds, with eight men or even up to thirty men in the room, depending. Conditions were cramped, they were antiquated, they were pretty shit. But that was part and parcel of what you'd signed to put up with.

I lost friends on the border. At Clonoe, in 1990, the IRA drove a car bomb by proxy into the vehicle checkpoint. My friend Cyril knew immediately what it was – he shouted a warning to the boys in the tower and they warned us. Cyril then released the civilian who had been tied into the vehicle to die, and he was getting the man out of the way when the bomb went off. So you can picture him running away from the vehicle, pushing the driver. The bomb detonated and Cyril took the main impact.

A month later, on the same tour, my uncle, Detective Constable Louis Robinson, who had been fishing in Dingle Bay, was kidnapped on the border. He was held and tortured by the IRA for four days before being summarily executed.

That was all happening when I was working there as a soldier. So you could say the border has made a significant impact on my life. At one point the IRA engaged an army unit with an M60 machine gun and a firefight ensued. I was on duty at the time, although it wasn't actually my half-section that was under fire, but we came to the aid of those soldiers who were. Most of the armed action for me was on the border tours. In fact, any time I found myself in Belfast, it seemed a relatively relaxed place to be, compared to a border tour.

I get irritated when I hear unionist politicians spouting about the border of old – particularly if they're young. There are a lot of young unionist politicians now, in their twenties, who have absolutely no experience of the conflict, let alone the border. When I hear them spout, I get annoyed and angry.

What the border means to me now, as a man in my fifties, is free movement. The border for me doesn't exist. I'm a businessman who operates across this island. I can go from Belfast to Limerick, to Cork, to Donegal – the border means absolutely nothing to me, despite my experience of it. I've moved on.

I believe political unionism and the Tory ERG are making the border a point of contention. Some in political unionism would like to refight the war, the conflict. Some in political unionism, whose only contribution to society here has been to flag-wave, want to flag-wave more. Some in political unionism believe in religious supremacy. They believe that all of those in Protestantism are better than those in Roman Catholicism. One of the things I remember from growing up, and recently I've started hearing it again, is 'We were never raised to hate Catholics.' And that's true. But some unionists were raised to believe that they were better than Catholics. As for the ERG, I believe it's just living in a right-wing fantasy, with this notion that Britain can once again rule the waves. They see Northern Ireland as the place to put the flag-marker in.

I am happier with no border, and most of business is in agreement with me. If you look at every commercial and trade body in Northern Ireland – Northern Ireland Retail, CBI Northern Ireland, Northern Ireland Chamber of Commerce – every one of those trade bodies that have massive membership are in a sizeable majority against a border. I'm talking upwards of 75–80%. The backstop, if Brexit must proceed, is essential to maintain the well-being and the economy of Northern Ireland.

If we're talking about the DUP, I believe that Arlene Foster [party leader] has huge difficulty getting over her past. Many of us in the conflict were hurt. That scar over my right eye [*points to it*] was caused by an IRA no-warning car bomb at twenty minutes past eight on a June morning in 1972 when I was walking to school. Any of us could sit and fester over what happened to us in the past, and I believe Arlene Foster, as a human being, sits and festers over the attempted assassination of her father and a bus bombing that actually happened during the time I was serving. I believe she lets that permeate her rationale. She has surrounded herself with a little cabal of predominantly Orangemen – if we look at Lee Reynolds, if we look at William Humphrey – they're all senior figures within the Orange [Order]. I'm someone who was in the Orange and the Black [the Royal Black Institution, similar to the Orange Order] because it was a family tradition, and I believe in many of the positive things the Orange and Black do in my community. But the reality is, part of the membership are about religious supremacy, about 'Oh, I was never raised to hate Catholics, but I was raised to believe I'm better than Catholics.' And that is their driving force: the inability to adjust to a post-conflict society, and the practice of supremacy by any means possible – including the use of the petition of concern in Stormont [a cross-community veto intended to prevent discrimination but used to block decision-making] and how it was employed to vent religious prejudice against the LGBT community or against women.

I think the DUP had their best outing at the general election of 2017. They used Project Fear of a united Ireland and they rallied the loyalist paramilitaries around them. I don't believe they'll get that size of vote again. I believe the allegations of corruption [regarding the awarding of public contracts], like the renewable heat incentive [a DUP scheme which overspent massively and is the subject of an inquiry], like Red Sky [a company awarded contracts with the Northern Ireland Housing Executive which were then cancelled over concerns about work practices] and so on, have absolutely disgusted many in working-class loyalism. Within the business community, I think all this will increase apathy. Among unionist business people, it'll be 'I can't vote for them, but I'm not going to go out and vote for anybody else.' I think we'll have increased apathy, which in itself is a major problem already. I'm aware of businessmen who have funded the DUP, or who give an annual donation, whether that be £250 or thousands of pounds. Sitting here, I know of three businessmen who will no longer do that. That's because the DUP has shown complete and utter disdain for the trade and industry bodies of Northern Ireland.

All of us, post-GFA, had to become persuaders for whether we wanted to remain pro-union or whether we wanted something constitutionally different on this island. Unionism has utterly failed to grasp that, at any level.

The pro-union cause was never solely about the loyalist or unionist communities. It was always reliant on that professional silent minority. They are a minority, but a minority that can swing in favour of a new constitution in a united Ireland or of remaining in the status quo, in the union. The DUP has completely alienated that 10–15% of people who silently acquiesced to British rule, the British institutions that existed here. When I talk to people within the business community, it's that group that has switched off completely from the DUP and the pro-union cause.

A tumble-out to World Trade Organisation tariffs is not acceptable to businesses across Northern Ireland. If it happens, the well-being of the economy here will collapse within weeks. If we think of foodstuffs, if we think of the pharmaceutical and retail sector, the effects of a no-deal Brexit will come within six to eight weeks. It will be that quick.

The politicians who don't understand supply chains don't get this. To sizeable sections of our community, sizeable sections of business, a no-deal is just a non-starter. There will be so many people alienated against the imposition that Britain is putting on us here that a border poll and ultimately a change in the constitution is inevitable. Those favouring a united Ireland would have with them that section of unionists; they would have that business backing.

Don't get me wrong – I still believe there'd be that 20–24% who would vote pro-union. But with a hard Brexit, there would be a surge of people who would wake up and say, 'This imposition is going to damage me, it's going to damage my grandchildren, and it's simply happening because of the force of numbers of English people who don't live here. I don't want to be a part of that.'

Brexit is going to damage things no matter what form it comes in. But the withdrawal bill and the backstop will protect

Northern Ireland's well-being and its economy from the annihilation that would follow a no-deal Brexit.

There will be casualties among smaller firms. Companies
that solely import or export to Europe – they will be damaged. Take the business I'm in – I import stone. We process
stone that is used in the public realm. For example, all of the
stone around Belfast City Hall is stone that I supplied, all the
stone in Corn Market is stone I supplied, the stone outside this
building [Belfast's Linen Hall Library] is stone I supplied – so
I'm a stonemason who does big public-realm projects. Most of
my stone comes from Europe – I import it. We joint-venture
operations in countries like Portugal, and the reality is, any
type of Brexit will affect that. Even with the withdrawal bill,
it is highly likely that we'll all need to start using certificates of
origin, all need to use C88 forms [the main customs form used
in international trade]. There'll be all sorts of inconveniences
which can still be managed. But a no-deal Brexit? Nobody –
not even the British government – is prepared for a no-deal
Brexit. So when I use terms like 'annihilation' and 'Armaged-
don', that's what the no deal is. And unless and until someone
in the no-deal camp can come to me and show me that it won't
be that, as a practising businessman in international trade that's
what I believe. The backstop is essential. With a hard Brexit
and a hard border, I see a border poll within two years and I see
Britain's political presence gone within five years.

If we have the soft option, I see the ongoing campaign to
persuade people of the benefits of a united Ireland continuing,
and I certainly see it happening within my lifetime. Within
maybe ten to fifteen years. The demographics are changing,

and those demographics will eventually trigger the consent principle [the guarantee in the GFA of a united Ireland should that be the wishes of the majority in Northern Ireland]. Where I believe political unionism has made a huge, huge error is that they're focused inward, and incestuously, with their own. And they are utterly abandoning if not infuriating that silent acquiescence that has always maintained the union.

When I was a soldier I worshipped at the high altar of violence – and was exceptionally good at it. But it was a period of my life and I've now moved on. I could be sitting up the Woodvale still – on the brew [dole]. I had a choice. I could take my experience and use it to better myself and my family. Or I could wallow in bitterness and hatred. I chose the first.

The lasting legacy of the GFA means that the status quo that I inherited is not set in stone. It is only there by the consent of the people here, and that consent is changing. As someone who is pragmatic and open-minded, I say if it's good for our diverse people, then I'm happy enough with it. And if that brings about constitutional change on this island, that's fine. Whether it's the union flag flying over me or the Irish national flag, it won't really make much difference, as long as it's come about by consent.

By some, I'm seen as a maverick. If you go to the good people of the Woodvale Road, I would say 50% of them see me as a maverick, 50% see me and say, 'Yeah, he's got it.' That 50% would agree with me, providing change is brought about by consent. But the problem is, within the 50% who'd see me as a maverick, there is an element that believes in supremacy, that believes in the absolute right of queen, country, empire and all that false myth that has got nothing to do with Irish people with allegiance to Britain. Yes, I'm seen as a maverick; but the more things change, the more people are saying, 'Bradley's got it.'

I'm a proud Irishman. Specifically from Ulster, specifically from Belfast. I hail from the pro-union community. I've no qualms about saying that. That's who I am. But if events change and that birthright of being British in any new constitutional Ireland is respected, I have no problem with that. Where we are having problems is with these people who think they're uber-British – more British than the English, the Welsh, the Scots. I don't understand where that mythical, delusional utter denial of reality comes from. But there'll always be that element. Whether we go to a new constitutional position or whether we stay where we are – there'll be that element that will be about supremacy and violence.

5

MICHAEL PATRICK MacDONALD

18 FEBRUARY 2019

Michael Patrick MacDonald grew up in South Boston in the neighbourhood with the highest concentration of white poverty in the United States. After losing four of his eleven siblings and seeing his generation decimated by poverty, crime, addiction and incarceration, he became a leading activist, organiser and writer. He is the author of the *New York Times* bestselling memoir *All Souls: A Family Story from Southie* and *Easter Rising: A Memoir of Roots and Rebellion*. He was awarded a fellowship at the Rockefeller Foundation's Bellagio Center and a 2019 Fulbright Scholar Award to teach at Queen's University Belfast.

When we were having our busing riots in Boston in the 1970s, the images coming out of Boston were often compared to the images from here in the North of Ireland. My grandfather is from Kerry, my grandmother is from Donegal – I was very close to her. Donegal is a place that was strangled by the border.

But proximity is everything. I came over to Europe in the summer in 1984. I was travelling around with some friends and I ran out of money. My mother had no money – we were from the project [a social housing area in South Boston] – so I called my grandfather and asked if he could loan me a couple of hundred dollars. He couldn't believe I was travelling around Europe and had no intention of going to Ireland.

I was trying to escape Southie in Boston and all the things I associated with Southie, like the racism and a kind of closedness. So I begrudgingly went to Ireland, to get the $200. I was eighteen. My cousins were in Donegal, so I got on a bus in Dublin. When we got to the border, nothing had prepared me for the checkpoint and soldiers fully armed. They got on the bus, and since I was an American, they asked me to get off, asked for my passport, where I was going. This held things up, which pissed off all the people on the bus who'd been shopping in the South. So I got on the bus again, and the first thing I hear as we're rolling away is someone calling the soldiers 'black bastards'. That confirmed everything I'd thought about the Irish: they're racist even when there were no black people around! [*Laughs*]

But that was the start of my education, including learning what 'black bastards' really meant in this context. And then I discovered my cousins, from Donegal, although their lives were more in Derry. They worked in Derry, they shopped in Derry, so they were very opposed to the militarised border. When they would ask about racism in America and racism among Irish-Americans, I was surprised that they themselves were so anti-racist – and surprised again when they told me they identified with the black struggle in the US.

We were going back and forth to Derry a lot, so I was at least getting a lesson in what it meant to be from that part of Ireland. I was seeing the same dynamics at work as at home, except that here everyone was white. The mentality of resistance that at home I would have associated with black communities was associated here with my cousins and their community.

Derry has that open skies feel to it – it's not all that different from Donegal in a lot of ways. But crossing the border, there was always a kind of tension, with everyone going quiet. And I had a sort of unnecessarily guilty conscience – they're going to get me, even though I haven't done anything! [*Laughs*] My cousins and the locals would tell me just not to talk, because that would hold them up. It was really all about people not wanting to be delayed.

Now in the places where I've been working, such as Leitrim and Manorhamilton, there are all these spots where you're passing through the border multiple times and wouldn't know it. But back then the air was thick with it. On every corner there'd be soldiers on bended knee, and that was something I wasn't used to.

I saw no difference in the people on either side of the border. There was a freer feeling in Inishowen, in Donegal, and that was different. But then it was August as well, so people were coming from London and other places, back home on holiday, and that helped. But there was just more a sense of freedom there that was more than I'd experienced in the rest of Ireland.

Crossing the border now? A little buzz goes off in my pocket. I'd been staying up in Manorhamilton and Leitrim, working on a Men's Shed project there. In that whole area your pocket would be buzzing all the time, indicating that your phone company is communicating with you that you've crossed the border. The absence of anything else now kind of blows my mind. Although there is a little kind of shift you feel, in Enniskillen more than Derry. It feels just a little more … British. It depends on what part of Enniskillen, I'm sure, but it does feel more middle-class than Derry.

The Men's Shed thing involves men over fifty, often over sixty, often in rural areas. Some are dealing with loneliness, some with mental health issues, some with alcohol and substance abuse, some just looking to be part of a community. Men gather and don't just do woodwork and things men do in a shed, but have conversations and build a community. So I was asked to come over and do a curriculum I do back home in Boston. It's a trauma-related curriculum, working with survivors of various things. The part of the brain that's concerned with speech and words tends to close down in the face of trauma. So you have to exercise that part of the brain with words, tell your story, be in charge of your narrative. It's not about collecting stories, it's about people gaining control of their own stories. People can rip their story up, they can keep it to themselves, they can walk away. But in the group they share it, and what happens is that, in telling your story to people you think you don't have a lot in common with, you find you actually do have a lot in common.

So when I came over here and did it, some stories would just be around farming life, some would be around memories of the old market days and things like that, the way things used to be. But once one person goes to a memory of the Troubles – a bombing, for example – then others will tell their stories. And this being Ireland, on both sides of the border the stories contain a lot of black humour. That cultural sameness applied to people from Catholic/nationalist backgrounds and Protestant/unionist backgrounds. That's a cultural trait throughout the whole of Ireland, in fact, and we have it in Boston too. It's a survival mechanism.

Another similarity that I find at home in Boston, too: divisions of class are more important than false divisions of race or religion.

Post-Troubles stories tended to involve Brexit and their fears of what's to come. And their fears are rooted in their memories. They fear a border coming back, soldiers coming back and responses to those soldiers. And they have economic fears, what Brexit might do to the economy, which was loosened up some by the border going away.

I was doing this project over a number of years, and initially there was denial – 'Oh, it won't happen, it won't happen' – until more recently. Now people are pretty pessimistic about what may happen. There's a lot of mistrust of Britain. Most of the people in the Men's Sheds programme would be from Catholic/nationalist backgrounds, but any participants from Protestant/unionist backgrounds seemed to me as mistrustful of the British as the Catholic population.

I'm always shocked when I discover the common ground people have, knowing how contentious the past is. Even here in Belfast, people hear the American accent and they want to talk to you. A lot of taxi drivers I've had would be unionist, from Protestant backgrounds like the Shankill [a loyalist area of West Belfast]. Now I don't know if this is just to me, but they're saying they're not afraid of a united Ireland. That's how they put it: 'That's not something we should be afraid of.'

These are hard-working people who have lives and families and kids.

The other thing I'm struck by is people from unionist backgrounds calling themselves Irish – I think that's changed a lot. Every time I come back to Ireland I see more and more change from people of unionist backgrounds.

I bring twenty students from the States over here every year. We meet with various people and look at the history of this place, including all nine counties of Ulster. We spend time in Gweedore, spend time in Derry, in Belfast. We meet with people who identify as British, but they also say that they're Irish.

Crossing the border with students, I have to get up and make a big announcement about how we are now crossing the border. They'll look up and say, 'Huh?' They really don't get it. The first time I came to Ireland [with students], we went through the border at Belcoo, and I had to tell them what it was like that first time for me. Being from the States, borders are on their minds, and they do associate them with negativity.

I think the backstop is crucial. It's terrifying to think of what could happen if the border came back. When we heard recently that a number of British police were mobilising to man the border – that gave me chills, a physical reaction. Hard loyalist groups may be penetrated by British intelligence, but they could wreak havoc with the assistance of the state. To be honest, the car bomb that went off in Derry in recent weeks – I had to wonder why anyone who'd call themselves nationalist or republican, right now when we're probably closer to seeing the reality of a united Ireland than I ever imagined we could be, why would these people go blowing stuff up? I would be on the lookout for those who want to see a hard border instigating some dissident violence. Why blow stuff up when we're so close to a united Ireland? I didn't think I'd see it in my lifetime, but now I think I will.

The reason we're closer to a united Ireland is that the border went away. The border being gone gives the space. If nationalists and republicans are at the forefront of discussion and negotiation, they're only there because they were given the space to be there. The border going was like dealing with a wooden splinter. You have to take it out first, so you have room for the healing and can create a healthier future. It's taking away the aggravation of the border.

Bringing students over here who are nineteen, twenty, allows them to interact with young people here who are the same age. They've gone out to nightclubs and so forth with young people here who are Catholic and Protestant and who are envious of the social justice rights that exist in the South, and indeed in the rest of the UK, but don't exist here. LGBT rights, choice and so forth – that's a big deal for them too.

A couple of my students at Queen's University who'd be most progressive in terms of rights are from loyalist working-class backgrounds. In fact they were so progressive that, coming in with my own preconceptions, I had assumed they were Catholics. I had assumed they were these young Bernadettes from the Falls Road [Bernadette Devlin was from a Catholic background and a leading figure in the civil rights movement in the late 1960s and early 1970s]. But no, they were from the Shankill. So that's a change, I think, that's come about by making space, opening up the border. It's a very small island, and down the road there's a fiscally conservative but socially progressive state. And the young people are really envious of that.

I'm here on a Fulbright scholarship, but I'm really here to get away from Donald Trump for a while – or maybe forever. If there were a united Ireland, I could see me living here because this is one of the rare places (knock on wood) that doesn't have a burgeoning fascist movement happening. Fascist populism is burgeoning everywhere and this place doesn't have it. I think it has a lot to do with the history – that Ireland never had an empire.

I used to tell people in the States about my experience in the 1980s where Irish people were anti-racist, and they'd say, 'Oh yeah, that's because they don't have other races.' When different nationalities did start coming here, Polish people and so on, that's when you saw racism, but it really did settle down. I think it's partly the cultural obsession with hospitality and welcoming. In Dublin if there's an attack on a black family, within hours people will mobilise and organise, hold a vigil outside their house. That's something you don't see in the States, or France, or other places.

I've heard here in Belfast about an Iranian family that was relocated to Beechmount and was totally embraced. That's something that's more likely to happen in West Belfast than in other parts of Belfast, sadly.

I'm living on the Upper Ormeau Road in Belfast now. When I was coming here in the 1990s, I was coming over as an international observer on the Garvaghy Road [a Catholic area near Portadown – annual attempts by Orangemen to march down the Garvaghy Road led to serious violence, and some

100 observers, mainly from the US, were invited to witness what happened], and then with Gerard Rice on the Ormeau Road [the Lower Ormeau Road is a Catholic area where Orange marches also resulted in rioting during the 1990s]. Then we were observers in the Short Strand [a Catholic flashpoint area of East Belfast] and so on, leading up to the GFA and after. But we would be down in the Lower Ormeau Road and we were always told, 'Do not cross the bridge into the Upper Ormeau Road.' But that's where I'm living now. And I walk past the Orange Hall there every day. The presence of Orangeism has really diminished – if anything, there's an increase of Catholic yuppies living up there now.

When I was an observer back then, we were tending to wounds a lot – people hit over the head and so on. I don't think that raw loyalism is gone, but it's not as prevalent. I rode my bike here to meet with you [in the Falls Road Cultúrlann], and five years ago I wouldn't have taken the Donegall Pass [a loyalist area] to get here. I walk it now and I cycle it as well. Knock on wood, nothing will happen to me on the way home. But going through there I find it sad. I identify with it, being from a poor Irish-American Catholic area in Boston. The housing projects there had a siege mentality in a poor white way. You're of the ascendancy – in the States we call that 'white skin privilege', here they call it 'Protestant ascendancy' – but at the same time you don't have a pot to piss in. You have nothing to show for it and you're clinging to the notion that it might pay off someday, and it's not going to pay off, ever. It's sad to see that clinging to something that's no longer there. The ascendancy's gone, but you still have people who are hostage to the leadership or lack of leadership in their communities. To see the murals, the UVF with the balaclavas, that just says, 'This is a no-go area if you're not one of us.' That's sad for all the young people growing up there, who are not benefiting at all from clinging to an identity which some of their leaders have.

In this town, other than the peace walls where you can't pass through, the dividing lines, the bordered areas that did exist, such as the Donegall Pass, are diminished. And the people who live there are often ignored, as they are at home, by progressive-minded people; they're even feared by them. But it's two-way: they're not opening up to others either. The physical presence of the peace walls prevents any possibility of opening up. Places like Donegall Pass are opening up long before you'll have it with places where there are physical structures.

I think physical structures are everything. And that's going to be the aggravating factor that will cause a response.

6

DECLAN FEARON AND DAMIAN McGENITY

20 FEBRUARY 2019

Declan Fearon and Damian McGenity are spokespersons for Border Communities Against Brexit (BCAB), an organisation formed to protect people living close to and on both sides of the border from the negative effects of Brexit. It is composed of people from business, farming and other professions who believe their livelihoods will suffer severely in the event of Brexit. Declan Fearon runs a small business and Damian McGenity is a cattle farmer.

DECLAN: Where we're sitting now [in the Carrickdale Hotel, Co. Louth], we're just over 100 yards from the border. And my home is another mile and a half after that. We're both born and bred here, right on the border. I remember in the early to mid-1960s, as a young lad, serving Mass up the road. The old priest would send me down for his newspaper (across the border) and I'd bring it back up to him after half-past eight Mass.

There was an economic border at that time – the roads were closed and spiked. Smuggling would have been of a very minor nature: people smuggling butter and tea and items like that.

We never considered ourselves as moving from one jurisdiction to another. In fact the parish that we come from here is 80% in the North and 20% in the South.

DAMIAN: My memory when young is slightly different. I don't remember those spikes on the road. I was born in 1973, and my mum had a sister in Dundalk, and I'd have travelled up there as a child. My main memory is of the militarisation growing in this area. There was a huge amount of British army patrolling.

DECLAN: Most of the people living in this part of South Armagh would have looked at Dundalk as their home town – we were more a hinterland to Dundalk than to Newry. My father worked as a bus driver with Córas Iompair Éireann (CIÉ) [Irish Transport System] in Dundalk, and he drove the bus from Newry to Dundalk every day for thirty-two years. There would have been a bit of hostility with the border even before the Troubles, in that it stopped you moving freely and trading freely across it.

DAMIAN: I remember relatives getting stuff posted to us in the North, and then we'd try to jump it across the border for them, because they didn't want to pay the duty on it. Those kinds of stories are very prevalent.

DECLAN: When the Troubles began in the early 1970s, the British customs posts became targets for the IRA, and the post just down the road from us here was the first attacked. Then they fortified it, and that was attacked again and blown up. Bit by bit, a lot of policemen came in to try to protect it, with patrol cars and patrol jeeps. Then they were attacked, and then the army came, and helicopters and lookout posts. And suddenly you were living in the middle of the most militarised area in Western Europe.

DAMIAN: People really resented it. They mightn't have shown it – there was always a fear factor when you were going through, whether it was a spot check or a fixed installation. They had X-rays, they had bollards that rose up out of the road, so you were effectively trapped there until they decided you were free to proceed. So there was huge resentment.

DECLAN: The first manifestation of that resentment I saw was when the border roads were organised for opening by the local people – in our case, I think it was the parish priest who organised it. The spikes were there and the concrete blocks were there closing the road, and I remember one instance, up at the back of the railway there. It was a Sunday morning just after Mass. The people were there and the army came and attacked them. They beat a lot of people, and some were bitten by dogs. Three or four of them were dragged off and they put them in a helicopter. That was the first time that I saw real resentment. That became a weekly event, with local people trying to get these minor roads opened, and the army would come and try to stop it.

DAMIAN: I'm forty-five. People who are thirty-five do not remember any of that stuff. They were too young at the time. They have grown up in a peaceful country in which they can travel where they like, they can work where they like. Most people in the border communities perceive themselves as Irish, living in Ireland. While there would be a massive economic fallout with a hard Brexit, a bigger risk is the social unrest, where people will see that we are being divided again.

The jobs thing is enormous. Five miles from where we sit, you have the second biggest animal pharmaceutical company in the world – Norbrook Laboratories. They employ over 2,000 people in Newry. They've said in the last few days that they will have to relocate. Big companies like Bombardier, who employ 6,000, another 12,000 sub-contracting jobs supplying them; the factory on the Beersbridge Road; the Guinness bottling plant employs 1,500; you've Coca-Cola in Lisburn; you've Almac in Portadown, which employs I think 2,800 people. And then there are all the other, smaller companies.

We fervently believe there would be tens of thousands of jobs lost in those pharmaceutical and manufacturing supply chains very, very quickly. As an example: Norbrook are stockpiling the product they make in the EU, but that product will only supply those EU markets for maybe six or eight months. The workers in the factory will be saying, 'If we make this product today, the owners will be saying, "We can't bloody sell it!"' Which would mean they'd have to close, and I think that would happen very quickly.

DECLAN: Companies like Almac have already invested and opened up in Dundalk – a company from Portadown opening in Dundalk.

DAMIAN: I think the North is looking at – let's give a conservative estimate – 50,000–60,000 jobs lost. There are 100,000 people in the agri-food sector alone. There was a meeting of the UFU in the last fortnight, and one of our members was there. A chief policy officer came down from Belfast, speaking about how bad this could be. They talked about the BSE crisis, about the foot-and-mouth crisis, and they agreed they weren't even comparable with this. We're looking at the Second World War here. And in the agri-food sector, you could be talking about 25–30% job losses if there's a no-deal Brexit.

If May's withdrawal bill was passed, that would stabilise things because that would mean we effectively stay in the customs union. So products that are made here can flow into Europe. They could also go unfettered – and this is in the withdrawal agreement – into the UK. The DUP is not fond of telling people about page 313 in that withdrawal deal, where we have unfettered access to the UK market, and total access to the EU market, plus the sixty-three countries the EU has trade deals with.

DECLAN: So what part of that is not the best of both worlds?

DAMIAN: At the annual general meeting of the UFU that was held in Fermanagh, there were seventeen farmers in the room, sixteen of whom were Brexiteers. All of the seventeen are today screaming for the deal to be implemented. That's how big a seismic shift has occurred on the ground. They would be happy with the withdrawal bill, but they think Brexit is going to be a disaster. We don't get the CAP subsidies with the backstop and we're out of common fisheries. Brian Cunningham, one of our members in Kilkeel, will tell you or anyone who will listen that of the fish that are caught in UK waters, 72% of those fish are sold where? In the EU.

DECLAN: So you're going to have all of these extra quotas of fish – and nowhere to sell them. There are some 'unionist' fishermen who have begun to re-register boats in Clogherhead and in Drogheda.

DAMIAN: We lobbied for those same people when we were in Strasbourg last October. The reasons that they voted Leave were, a) they were lied to, and b) the big line was that the quota would be re-allocated, that they would get a 30–40% increase, they could catch more fish; but what they didn't realise was, you can catch all the fish you want, but what if you can't bloody sell them? If they have to pay any tariff on these fish, they're dead.

There's one guy, working out of Kilkeel, who has a boat of £35 million, built eighteen months or two years ago. There's no way that they're going to survive this. No way.

DECLAN: I have a business here employing about twenty people – have done for around forty years. I'm in the high-end fitted kitchens and furniture business. I laugh when I hear people say it will take an extra two minutes or thirty seconds [to carry goods across the border]. My experience from having done this over many years, exporting across the border – and across the border means going to our neighbours three miles up the road – you took somewhere between four and five hours to do that. You first of all had to go to Newry to get your papers initiated; you then came to Cairncar, where you would be stuck in a queue for at least an hour. At this point you got it stamped. This was during the Troubles – pre-1993. Then you went to Dundalk, and that's where you got most of the tracking done – we were heading South. In total, I've never done it in less than four hours. So it'd make much more sense for us to increase the small base we have in the South. My brother-in-law has 250 trucks on the road, maybe more. Brexit would have a major impact on his costs. I would guess he'd have 200 or 300 crossings a day.

DAMIAN: I'm a part-time farmer – I have beef suckler cows. If this crashes, we are out of the CAP – that's a 70% reduction in that payment. For all the farmers around here, it would be unbelievable. More than 90% of the business people want the withdrawal bill voted in. These people have now educated themselves as to what this really means. They do not believe what their leaders are telling them.

DECLAN: I think there's a rift already between the DUP and farmers, from what you hear of those smaller farmer meetings.

DAMIAN: The question is, what will the reaction be to the DUP if its actions precipitate a crash and tens of thousands of people lose their jobs, their farms, their homes?

DECLAN: I was out a few weeks back – myself and the wife went into a local bar up the road. There was a man sitting there with his son. This man's ninety-three years of age. He called me over: 'Declan, I've seen you on the TV and good luck to you on this Brexit thing. And I'll tell you one thing. I've never, ever been on a protest march in my life and neither has any of my family. I tried to keep my family out of trouble all down through the years. But I promise you this: if there's any sign of a hard border or cameras or what have you, I'll be out and I'll give you a hand myself.'

Now that's the thinking on the ground. If you look back to the days of civil disobedience, it began at the start of the Troubles, and I can see that being the start of it once again.

I don't see people here accepting the erection of cameras or customs posts: there'll be a campaign of civil disobedience to block that. It'll be inevitable, I think. Bertie Ahern [former Taoiseach] was right: the local people will tear it down with their hands.

DAMIAN: There will have to be roads closed physically, whether with concrete or whatever. Let's take someone whose parents live four or five hundred yards down the road. He lives in the North, the parents in the South. He wants to go and visit his sick mother, and he has to go and drive fifteen miles of a roundabout route to do that if his road is closed. What's he going to do? I know what I would do in that situation: I'd jump on my tractor and I would tear it down. There's too much talk about what dissident republicans and others might do. That has been blown up far too much. This is how it will impinge on the lives of ordinary people, who will get angry and say, 'I'm not tolerating this.'

DECLAN: It'd probably come as more of a shock to younger people – say, under thirty-five – if they saw a border. The huge question is, and we put it to the EU negotiating teams – these 250 roads that were closed off in the past because there were only seventeen official border crossing points: are they contemplating leaving them open and allowing some chlorinated chicken to head for Antwerp or Paris or wherever? Their answer to us was, 'Whatever it takes.' Now if young people see that closing down of roads, they're probably going to be the first ones to say, 'They're not closing that road on me – that's my friend or that's my football field just over there.' And yes, that's how it starts.

DAMIAN: Young people will feel the loss of identity – they'll feel that they're not Irish, and that feeds into the whole political thing.

Last Friday, there was a checkpoint at Ballymac. A friend of mine was driving a van going to Carlingford, which is on the Southern side. He thought there had been an accident. There were gardaí and customs and health inspectors. They were doing a check. What kind? 'We're checking for food.' And he had to open his van to show he had no food. The gardaí and the Irish army have got text messages to see if they would volunteer for border duty. The Irish government is, unfortunately, having to begin to prepare.

DECLAN: We asked over in Europe who would be responsible for putting up the border. The EU's answer was that it's the member state that has responsibility for putting up the border. Who pays for it? 'Oh, we do,' – the EU pays for it. Now if the members of the ERG say they want to end freedom of movement, will they contemplate leaving an open border for anyone to come in from wherever – just walk up the road here and head over to Liverpool?

DAMIAN: 'Take back control' – where's the control there?

DECLAN: The border which the South would put up would be a physical border, checking people going into the South.

DAMIAN: The EU is currently spending €53 million on a border between Poland and the Ukraine. It's to stop swine fever in wild boar coming from the Ukraine into Poland, infecting the EU. There's a massive fence built between Hungary and Serbia. This is what happens. You need control.

And that's what the backstop, in the withdrawal bill, deletes for us permanently.

Yes, it's unthinkable, but I've come to realise: bad things do happen. Look at the other parts of the world where there is political upheaval in a country that before had been quiet, at peace with itself – and then it takes a change. We know what that's like. Twenty years is not that long ago, and here we are looking at what is potentially change.

If there's not a hard border on 1 April, what will happen if there's no deal is that there'll be a creep border – a border by stealth. Britain will not go in step with the new EU regulation that has come into place. Or some guy or girl will take a load of beef or something into the EU that's against EU rules, and that will make the [European] Commission put pressure on Ireland to create this hard border.

DECLAN: Are politics and economics intertwined here? Of course they are. The economics for people who live here are their daily social lives, and part of daily social life is going down the road to the shop and buying something while you're there, or going into Dundalk and buying a pair of shoes and bringing them back up the road. Or taking your kids into Dundalk to see such-and-such, and while you're there you might need to buy a hammer – that's the intertwining of the politics and the economics of it.

DAMIAN: Over the last few months, I've heard from people I've known my whole life, some of whom are political and some of whom are not and never were. Some in particular might be best described as contrarians. They have all said to me, 'The only solution to this for us is to remove the border.'

We in the Border Communities Against Brexit are trying to be apolitical. The best way we can think of putting it is that people will have to decide what union they want. Do you want to belong to a union that's taking away your jobs, your rights, or do you want to belong to a union that preserves your job, protects your economy and allows you to travel?

DECLAN: The harder the border, the harder the Brexit is and the harder the circumstances of people's daily lives, the more they'll move towards calling for a border poll and the more support they'll get.

DAMIAN: I have sat in a room with unionists who have looked me in the eye and said that if there was a border poll today – this is before a hard Brexit – they've said they would vote for a united Ireland. They don't want any truck with these right-wing Westminster politics. They see their future as being in a more open, pluralist society. You create the loss of tens of thousands of jobs and farms, particularly dairy farms and other farms that are very heavily indebted – that hedge funds or vulture funds will want to repossess. Farmers will see that farmers in the South have the CAP, which gives healthy payments to farmers, has a market of sixty-three global countries that the EU has trade deals with – of course they will want to be part of that.

Now, at the minute, the debate is not sufficient to convince those people, because we haven't yet grappled with how a unionist will feel content in a united Ireland. And unionism hasn't engaged in that. That issue needs to be debated more, and very, very quickly.

DECLAN: It wouldn't take a whole lot of unionists changing their minds. If the GFA says it's 50% plus one [that determines whether or not the North and the South remain separate states], it wouldn't take a lot of them changing their minds to shift the balance.

DAMIAN: You're always going to have a hard core – you're never going to be able to convince all of the people.

DECLAN: Personally, I don't think it's wise to be pushing for a border poll at the moment. We'd do better to wait and see just how Brexit pans out. But definitely, if there's the worst ravages socially and economically, I think there'll be a clamour for a poll very quickly after.

DAMIAN: The backstop cannot be removed because Europe won't agree to it being removed. So the UK has a big decision to make. Is it going to agree with inclusion of the backstop, largely as it is, or are they going to push the nuclear button and crash out with a hard Brexit? The extension of Article 50 is much talked about. It can only be extended either to 15 May, which is before the EU election date, or for a year or eighteen months. You have [president of the European Council Donald] Tusk and [president of the European Commission Jean-Claude] Juncker who are retiring, and that process for re-election will have to happen; you have a new parliament coming that'll need time to settle in. It'd probably be October or November before they'd be in a position to sit down for proper talks again.

DECLAN: For the EU to extend Article 50, it'd have to postpone the European elections. As for the EU going weak on the backstop to get a deal with the UK – I think that would have happened before now. It's been so resolute up to now, with relatively little time left, that the breaking of any ranks in the EU – I don't think you'll see that. I don't think it's going to happen.

DAMIAN: I think Europe is very solid. The Parliament is very single-minded on this, and it has to pass any deal. Before Tusk, Juncker and [European chief Brexit negotiator Michel] Barnier could agree anything, they'd have to get the Parliament's OK. I don't see that happening.

DECLAN: I think at the end of the day there's a reality going to have to kick in in British politics, especially among the Conservatives: that if we're going to have our Brexit, we're going to have to go for the North remaining in the common market and to allow this island to continue to trade as an economic unit. I think somewhere along the line you'll see the British government trying to reinforce the guarantees of sovereignty to the unionist people in some way – however they do it. And it must be done within the realm of the GFA.

DAMIAN: It'll be a bridge. [*Laughs*] There have to be sweets put on every table. They mightn't have to build it but they might promise to build it. Perfidious Albion …

But finally: watch America. We're doing a bit of work with the States. There's a big delegation coming over in April. Democrats have control of the House of Representatives. Richie Neal, who we've met, is the chair of the Ways and Means Committee. Now Ways and Means have the power to slow and bog down or even stop a US–UK trade deal. If the UK crashes out, it's in trouble.

DECLAN: If there's any mention of a border in Ireland.

7

CONOR PATTERSON

22 FEBRUARY 2019

Dr Conor Patterson is the chief executive of the Newry and Mourne Co-operative and Enterprise Agency and a board member of Newry Chamber of Commerce and Trade. He has been actively involved in economic and business development in the Northern Ireland–Republic of Ireland border region since the mid-1990s. He has spoken on the impact of Brexit on the Irish border region in the European Parliament and the French National Assembly, and he has given evidence to the Northern Ireland Affairs Select Committee in the House of Commons and to the Oireachtas Committee on the implementation of the GFA.

I grew up in Barcroft Park in Newry. When we moved into the area in 1969, it seemed a dream house: from a two-up, two-down and an outside toilet to a house with a front and back garden and a bath. Each of the children – the three of us – had a bedroom. But within a year the place became caught up in the insurrection and the community was the focus of intense attention from the British army. We were roughly five miles from the border.

My mother is from Dundalk, my father is from Newry, so my early experience was one of travelling back and forth across the border. Every week our mother took us down to see our granny and the family in Dundalk. For many people in the South, coming North was seen as hassle. Even before the Troubles, my father needed a designation on his vehicle to travel up and down when he was courting my mother.

Sitting at the knee of my grandfather and father, I heard about the Co. Down football team winning the All-Ireland [Gaelic Athletic Association (GAA) Football Championship], about the Sam Maguire Cup coming over the border. Co. Down and most of Ulster took pride in the achievements of the Down team then. There was a very strong sense in Newry that the people wanted to hold on to what they defined as their Irishness.

As to sovereignty in a state, my perspective is that sovereignty is shared at multiple levels. It's a functional thing. For example, it makes sense with energy that sovereignty should be shared east–west. By the same token, there are many areas where, at a functional level, it makes sense for sovereignty to be all-island. And so it has been in commerce.

There are lessons in that for republicans and unionists. There is no totally united kingdom – it's not a real proposition in the modern world. Economic sovereignty is shared right across the globe. A new Ireland must appreciate that there's a concentration of sovereignties within the island of Ireland. But there also has to be the capacity for shared sovereignty east–west – and then wider shared sovereignty within an international framework.

That's what the GFA understood. There were three layers of sovereignty. There was the local sovereignty, then the North–South sovereignty, and then there was the east–west sovereignty. Probably now if you were rewriting it, you'd have a fourth strand that would be international.

When I started my job here in 1995, the two states had largely developed back-to-back since 1922 – partition was pretty deep then. Newry's label was 'the frontier town', with a paper that was the *Frontier Sentinel*; I used to go to the Frontier Cinema, Dundalk was El Paso and South Armagh was bandit country. It was the language of Western movies, and Newry was seen to be on the edge.

When I studied at Trinity College, I had to get off the train at Dundalk and thumb across the border when I was going home. Extraordinarily, there wasn't a train stop at Newry until the late 1980s or early 1990s. The new train station in Newry opened in 2008 – it's part-funded by EU money. The final link between the dual carriageway A1 and the M1 – the plug-in across the border – is 40% funded by the EU. And I know from my own experience of developing five sites in this border region for workspace, probably 50% of investment here at WIN Business Park is from the EU. At Flurrybridge [Enterprise Centre], the first block that was built there was 95% grant-aided. Nobody in the Northern state was interested.

We made a case that should have been embraced: we wanted to take and regularise people who had great talent and who were working in the black economy. They themselves wanted to break out, but they didn't know how or where. We wanted to provide the where: we provided a managed workspace and then gave them a hand, bringing them into a programme where they could get advice on tax, trade and exporting.

What had evolved over the period of partition was a level of non-compliance in the wider community. People who didn't pay their TV licence, who didn't apply for planning permission. When the new road was being plugged in in the first decade of the 2000s and the mapping was being done as to what properties might need to be moved and what compensation would have to be paid, quite a number of them didn't have planning permission. That was part of the culture. There was a culture of contesting partition at some level, and the workarounds in the border area were a form of contesting it.

People here are agile and tough and will find workarounds. It's the extent to which those workarounds have a cost associated with them that is problematic. If we take WIN: most of the businesses here are low-margin businesses, but they've taken people off dependence on the state. They're financially independent and they're paying taxes.

And I'm putting it to the Invest Northern Ireland people, who used to be very snobby (but aren't now) about what is an innovative business: a hairdresser can be an innovative business, a sandwich-maker is a food-processing business. These businesses can be very low margin – we're talking profits of 2–5%. With Brexit, will they be out of business – or will they be out of business here?

The fact is, they will cross the border or they will relocate. Many of them have already put out feelers. The problem they have is that property is more expensive in the South – it's not cheap to move – so they find ways of working around the problem, like collaborating with somebody down South.

If I look at Flurrybridge, most of the tenants there say that, if this goes pear-shaped after Brexit, they will move much of their activity. They will retain a presence here, but in terms of the amount of turnover that is attributable to this jurisdiction – that will fall.

In the past, we didn't have to go looking for partners – they came to us. Now that has completely changed. We don't get emails; nobody calls because of Brexit. We have set up a company in Dundalk called WIN Consultants. The 'N' in 'WIN' is 'Newry' – it's now being located in Dundalk, to be able to bid for EU funding from an EU base. So even we who are a territorially specific entity, dedicated to the development of this territory, are having to move our expertise out of the territory to another area. Our intention, if we generate funds, is to repatriate those funds to support our mission in this territory. But we're only able to do it if we're in the other territory.

This isn't just about trade, it's about public safety. This is about drugs, because there are, as Trump would put it, bad hombres out there. And some of the bad hombres we have on the island of Ireland are very organised. So the smuggling spectre isn't Mum or Dad taking a few pounds of Kerrygold butter home or buying an extra bottle of booze and sticking it under the front seat of the car. If there's a margin, the risk is that criminal elements will fill the space – and they will be organised criminal elements, and the local populations won't get a sniff.

We're told checks won't be near the border, they'll be in Balbriggan. So if a company is trading in Armagh from

Castleblayney, do they have to route down to Balbriggan and then back up? 'Oh no – you see, there's the possibility of a cordon sanitaire.' So are we now talking about a Wild West zone where anything goes? And who fills that space?

In low-margin businesses, the temptation will be there to just not comply, because the cost of compliance could threaten the viability of the business. And non-compliance has a corrosive and corrupting effect. It corrodes the integrity of the Irish Republic as a fully compliant part of the single market. In my experience of growing up here, that tends to roll out across society. Again, it's the TV licence, planning permission history, MOTs and all those things.

What we now have in the nationalist community is a middle class that is very disaffected. A professional business class who feel their aspirations for their kids in terms of study, their potential to study in the Republic, might be interfered with. People who have developed lifestyles and businesses, people who have interacted with European academics: they feel very disaffected with the devolvement settlement. They believe that despite their achievements in a place like Newry, where they have built businesses, paid taxes, built entities that contribute to the Exchequer, where there are low levels of public-sector dependence – they continue to be lectured to, they continue to be disrespected. They feel that their expression of themselves in Gaelic games, in culture, in the language, is at best disregarded and at worst actively disdained.

Why am I talking about the middle class? If you look through the Troubles, you had a professional and business class in the Catholic community that was very much against armed struggle. They tried to differentiate themselves. The Troubles? That's the housing estate. Republicans traditionally drew their support from working-class nationalists.

But now? Take South Down. South Down isn't Turf Lodge, it's not Coalisland. South Down is our stockbroker belt. South Down used to elect Enoch Powell. There was then a lot of hand-wringing when it went out of unionist control and Eddie McGrady [Social Democratic and Labour Party (SDLP)] replaced Enoch Powell. And then it elected Margaret Ritchie [SDLP]. And then it elected in 2017 Chris Hazzard [Sinn Féin]. You cannot explain South Down in any other way than that it is a microcosm of a shift within nationalism.

If you have a middle class that's disaffected from the agents of the state, that to me is very worrying. I'm not saying there's going to be hundreds and hundreds in active conflict. You have people who were complying and were committed to the devolved settlement who have now left it behind – who are zoned out from Northern Ireland. These are professionals and business people. Now those people are turning their sight away from the regulations, from the work and time and bureaucracy involved in compliance. They're shrugging their shoulders at best and are hostile at worst.

During the Troubles, the business class in a place like Newry was as disaffected with the insurgency as was the state and the unionist/Protestant community. This time there will be people – small farmers, young people – required to explain their journey or what's in the boot of their car, and they've never known this before. These are the people who are likely to do the pulling down and cutting down of border barriers. What I hear from people is 'I'm not going to stop! I'm just not going to do it!'

When it comes to the time for a new set of frameworks to be embedded, you need the backbone of the business community, of professional people across sectors, to be compliant. If those people are not complying, you've got a problem.

People are questioning now why they would commit some level of their patriotism to an entity that does not acknowledge their achievements, does not respect their concerns, dismisses them.

You do not seem to get an understanding that partition was imposed and that Northern nationalists were excluded from participation. Many of these nationalists now have family who are participating in the rest of the UK, whose children or grandchildren now populate the green benches of the House of Commons. These people are taking back their experiences in Birmingham, Manchester or London to family here and saying, 'Well, I have a local government vote in Birmingham' or 'I can get married to my partner in Manchester now.' It's this à la carte approach that excluded people on the basis of an assumed identity as Roman Catholics.

So there will be important elements of the population who won't play ball. Will they move to acts of civil disobedience? I don't know. But there will be those in the community who will go down the civil disobedience route. And I'm old enough to have seen how escalation happens. In a hyper-vigilant world of media and social media, stuff is transmitted immediately. There will also be talent that will leave. There are people of my generation who have worked hard who will say, 'I'm gone. I could never go through that again.'

My concern is the issue of enforced differentiation. Currency happens. It takes time to adapt, but it's one thing. Or you change the tax code. It's one thing – it's flagged up in advance. But if this comes in, interlocking, across sectors, across business into private lives, from business to where you want to study, to your health insurance, etc., all rolled into a package of enforced differentiation, and it's enforced against people's will – that's an issue.

I did a talk to members of the Protestant/unionist community and tried to make the point that we live in a world where the biggest variable that correlates with business success is the propensity to collaborate. The idea of the lone wolf, the entrepreneur of Adam Smith fame, is long gone. The Calvinist entrepreneur is dead. It's all about 'Let's have a coffee. What are you doing? Well I'm doing this, we could bolt it together.' Or even if I'm a predatory capitalist, I will buy you out. But it's all about 'I value what you do.'

Newry is ground zero. The metrics don't lie. When I left to teach in the university in Coventry in 1987, unemployment in Newry was 26.5%. When I came back in the mid-1990s, it was 18%. It's now 2%. It's now below not just the Northern Ireland average but the UK average.

Now what lies behind all of that? It isn't public-sector employment; it isn't a big Honda or a big Nissan. It's self-generated. It's the exponential growth of local entrepreneurship and a small sub-set of those local entrepreneurs building world-beating mega-companies that employ thousands. It's a recipe actually for any other area. Home-grown. First Derivatives [a Newry-quartered technology company] are employing AI. They're out hunting. They have a prospects programme where they have young kids in their twenties out in innovation centres throughout the world, from Seattle to Seoul to Paris – you name it. And their job is to go out and find new ideas. This should be celebrated by Northern Ireland.

Nicola Sturgeon [first minister of Scotland and leader of the Scottish National Party] and representatives of the Welsh devolved government were so animated about the backstop; they wanted it too. And I've been active with colleagues from both sides of the community – business and farming and every business organisation – in supporting a Tory prime minister's policy proposition. That's something I never saw myself ever doing. But I was, for that short period when that was government policy. Why? Because Northern Ireland would continue to have free unfettered access into Britain and continued free access into the EU.

We're a month out from the [original] Brexit date and I could be proven entirely wrong. How it looks now is there are too many major figures in the EU ecosystem that have gone on the record time and time again in defence of the Irish position on the backstop, and if they did a complete U-turn, their credibility would be shot. And this is at a time when the EU proposition, which for so long seemed to be apple pie to everybody, never questioned – now the EU is under challenge in so many parts of the EU. So at the political level, I think it would be extraordinary if they shifted. Given the experience with Greece and smaller countries, and given the vulnerability felt not just by those smaller countries but bigger countries like Italy and

Spain vis-à-vis the Franco-German axis, if Ireland was seen to be stuffed, that would undermine the credibility of the Franco-German axis.

A border here in the north-west of the EU would be a 500-kilometre potential hole in the fuselage. I've likened the single market to a pressurised aircraft. You can punch a hole in it and depressurise it – and the stability and safety of that entire aircraft is threatened.

Look at international global crime – the *McMafia* sort of phenomenon. This isn't about bringing in cheap garlic or cheap meat from Brazil or Argentina to destabilise the meat market in the Irish Republic. This has the potential to destabilise the meat market more widely. And then you have the whole issue of safety. European consumers, rightly or wrongly, eschew genetically modified produce – they just don't want it. Nor do they want hormone-injected beef. And those are just two consumer health-and-safety issues. So it's also about consumer health and safety.

In so many different settings, the border poll is in almost every conversation around the politics of Brexit, the politics of the collapse of Stormont and whether it will ever come back, the political implications of all of this and the remaking of relationships within these islands. Does there need to be a commitment to a state-supported consideration of the implications of economic, political and social change? Yes. Is there a need for a New Ireland Forum? Yes. If a border poll is the key that opens that, so be it. But for me a border poll is a means to an end, and the end is the need for a wider conversation about what sovereignty means.

The biggest cheerleaders for Brexit sold off British economic sovereignty to the highest bidder. And what is politics but largely the dialogue around how the income and benefits from assets are shared? Why do you not have a Sheffield steel knife in the cutlery drawer? Why do people not drive British-marked cars? Why is there no such thing as a British airport authority, why is British Rail now in the ownership of asset owners from across the world, why are there British football teams nominally called Manchester but who are actually owned by nobody from Manchester? That's sovereignty. So for me this is really about 'What does a united Ireland mean?' And to understand this, we need to understand what sovereignty means. It's about control over your life and the things that make your life happen.

What populations need to understand is how that equation works. If you invite in anybody from anywhere to buy any bit of your country, they own your country, or bits of it. They have the say, not you.

So Swindon: how sovereign is Swindon, given the presence of Honda? How sovereign is Sunderland given the presence of Nissan? And what if Honda or Nissan leave? What we are trying to build here in Newry is a sense that it's a good thing to have ownership embedded in a community, because those owners have a commitment to that community.

The border is an obstacle to that. It requires that sovereignty be corralled within a tiny zone, irrespective of whether that makes sense functionally or economically. What business has done is traverse that and ignore it.

Republicans in my experience tend to be more open now to considering flux. Many republicans share their cultural sovereignty with the big island to the east. They support football teams located in the big island to the east, they might enjoy music that originates in the big island to the east or read literature, etc. But equally, those who claim to be hyper-British need to understand that there are many people who they would define as Roman Catholics who have more experience of the big island to the east than they do, and that Ireland and places like Newry, which is predominantly 'Roman Catholic', have done extraordinary things in transforming themselves, in embracing change, adapting and rolling with the punches that come with change. The hyper-British can learn from that.

8

PAT McART

25 FEBRUARY 2019

Pat McArt has spent most of his forty-plus years in journalism working between Donegal and Derry. He began his career in Letterkenny with the *Donegal News*, moved for a short period to Raidió Teilifís Éireann (RTÉ) in Dublin and spent the next twenty-five years as editor of the *Derry Journal*. Since retiring from that post, he is a regular contributor to both print and broadcast media and is currently a weekly columnist with the *Donegal Democrat*.

There was a man called Jack Harris who had a shop in Letterkenny, and one day he took me into Derry to collect his sister, who was living in England. I must have been about seven or eight at the time. When we got to the border there was this big fuss; he had to 'bond the car' – hand in some document – and if he wasn't back within a certain time, his car could be impounded. I remember at the time thinking, 'This is strange.'

We then went over to the Waterside train station to meet his sister. There was a guy who walked past and he had on a Union Jack–type T-shirt. I was even more puzzled: 'This is Ireland. Why is he wearing something that's so plainly English?'

My family lived in Letterkenny, about twenty miles from the border. And the border was like a kind of Atlantic Ocean between North and South. The North was seen as somewhere that Catholics got a hard deal, that was run by hard-line unionists. Someone explained to me that it was like blacks living in Alabama at the time. That would have been in the early 1960s, before the Troubles.

The first time I went into Derry on my own I was about fourteen or fifteen. I remember going up Shipquay Street, not feeling totally comfortable for some reason. The cops looked different, it had a British feel to it, with its Guildhall and that sort of thing.

Smuggling was always a feature of things. The story is told of a guy from Moville in Co. Donegal. He would go up Lough Foyle in a boat in the morning and he would wave to the customs people, making sure they saw him. They'd see this black boat going up and they'd say, 'We'll keep an eye on him on the way down – he must be smuggling something.' A couple of hours later, a white boat would go down. What they didn't cop on to was that he had the boat painted a different colour on either side. So simple but pure genius. Smuggling was considered a legitimate way of making a living, even if it was illegal.

Five, six miles from where we are now [in Co. Donegal], there's an artificial border. You invite someone from any-where – Canada, Australia, wherever – and ask them, 'Go up there and tell me where the border is.' The same language, the same people, and yet there's a border. I think that most people come to the conclusion, 'This is ridiculous.'

One of the reasons we moved South of the border during the Troubles was that when Shane, our eldest boy, was a young teenager, soldiers at the border would point and say, 'Who's he?' Next thing would be they'd be asking him to show his identification. We didn't want that.

The border during the Troubles made Derry one of the biggest open-air prisons in Europe. It was encircled on virtually all sides. I remember myself and John Hume [SDLP founder and former MEP] got into a big row one time. He had got some big report looking into Northern Ireland. He had sent me all this information on it on a Friday, to make a headline in the *Derry Journal*. But come Tuesday, the headline we printed was about a massive border delay. That Sunday had been fine and sunny, and the British army had decided to act the bollocks. The sun was shining so they stopped every car – it was deliberate harassment. Hume went bananas that we hadn't led with his important report. I said to him, 'John – there were queues of cars from Coshquin border checkpoint right up to the Strand Road in Derry. That affected more people in Derry last weekend than your report.' The sun was shining, it was Sunday, half of Derry wanted to go out to the beach on the other side of the border, so the army just acted the bollocks.

That kind of thing – I wouldn't go so far as to call it ghettoisation, but it did certainly make it feel like a prison for a lot of people. You'd see soldiers pointing guns at you. Particularly at night, there'd be a red light and a green light and soldiers in Sangers pointing their guns out at you.

Joe Frazier, the heavyweight boxing champion, came over to Ireland on a tour one time. He was crossing the border about two or three in the morning and he said it was one of the most frightening things he had come across. And this was the world boxing champion, who'd been from a family of twelve in South Carolina, where black people got a hard time.

When I went to work at the *Derry Journal* in the early 1980s, every person on the staff had a Donegal connection on the other side of the border. Either their mother was from Donegal or their grandfather was from Donegal or they had an aunt in Donegal. To call Donegal Derry's natural hinterland doesn't even describe it – they're more like brother and sister.

In the 1980s, *Derry Journal*'s three big markets were readers in Derry city, Co. Derry and Inishowen in Donegal. At one stage the newspaper sold around 6,500 copies in Inishowen every Friday, yet there were only 4,000–5,000 households in Donegal. We were selling more copies than there were houses. The reason was a lot of them were being sent away because there was so much emigration. The mothers were buying a copy for the house and posting the second one to the son or daughter.

I seriously worry about a return to violence if there's a hard border. There are these people who say there will be no problem. The fact is the anger hasn't gone away, it's just bubbling under the surface. There are Tories who claim this is a scare story. I don't buy that for a second. If they put up a hard infrastructure, it won't last – it'll be torn down by the people. And if the EU or the Irish government or the British government insist on a hard border in the event of a crash-out, somebody's going to have to protect it. So we'll have infrastructure and men in uniform and all that we left behind twenty-five years ago. We'll be back into that again.

If Britain crashes out, Ireland is going to be the back door into Europe for chlorinated chicken, Brazilian beef and

Chinese telephones. There was a Tory guy on Sky TV this morning, and he said at the Swiss border with the EU there was no difficulty. The presenter pointed out that if he were a lorry driver, he wouldn't be saying that. It depends on what deal they finally make, of course. But if there's any hard border, that's very much a slippery slope back to the bad old days.

A couple of years ago a meeting was convened in Derry and 600 dissident republicans turned up. If they can get 600 people who are still alienated, what will happen if a hard border is put in place?

People had the comfort blanket of the EU. You could be Irish or British or both and be in the EU.

Another form of alienation lies in the fact that 56% of people in the North voted for Remain. So there could be several sparks, not just one. I'm not saying conflagration is inevitable, but I am saying the situation's far from healthy.

Look at Northern Ireland after almost 100 years. Each year it needs an alleged £10 billion subvention from Britain, so that's not exactly a great economic success. We've had a thirty-year campaign of violence, so politically it hasn't been a success. We can't get an administration up and running. It's been over two years since the Executive collapsed, and we now hold the world record in non-government. So the border hasn't exactly been sprinkled with gold dust, economically or politically. And the border contributed massively to the outbreak of violence in the last Troubles.

Ireland is one land mass. If there's one place in Europe where you shouldn't have a border, it's on an island. There are brothers and sisters, one's in the South and one's in the North.

This border divide created problems, it created massive resentment. In the Waterfront Hall in Belfast quite recently, up to 2,000 people turned up to a discussion of the border.

The DUP says there's no need for concern, they can use technology to control the border. As far as I know, a camera can see a lorry approaching but it can't see what's inside it. The reality is, the technology does not exist. Between different jurisdictions everywhere, there are checks. And once you start introducing those kinds of checks here, you're going backwards.

In the 1980s, there was a survey done of the poorest wards in the UK. If I remember rightly, three of the top ten were here: Derry, Strabane and Newry, I think. And note that the poorest areas in Northern Ireland were all along the border. The border had destroyed those places economically, because it cut them off from their hinterland. The border was a disaster. It divided people politically, economically and socially.

With a seamless border, things have improved. Look at Letterkenny. Good God, twenty years ago you could have had your dinner in the middle of the main street, it was that quiet. Now it's thriving. At Bridgend there was nothing when the border was there. Now there are a couple of businesses, there's a warehouse. It's coming back to life.

The UFU and the CBI, I think, have already said a hard border would be a disaster. I think anybody with half a brain would know that. For example, with the transport of fresh food, a lot of stuff is perishable. I think creating a border is just going to introduce all sorts of difficulties. And all the businesses are saying that a hard border is going to be a disaster in Ireland. So the Farmers' Union, the CBI, the Irish government, the

EU – everyone is saying this is a disaster. But the DUP seems to think it knows better than everybody else.

In recent times we've had Arlene Foster referring to people as crocodiles. That's the attitude of the DUP towards the Irish language, part of their total lack of respect for Irishness. I think the middle-management types, the shirt-and-tie brigade who were insulated during the Troubles, are now beginning to resent all this too. The 2,000 people who turned up at the Waterfront Hall weren't your hard-line republicans. These were people saying, 'We've had enough.'

The attitude of the DUP has really pissed off nationalism big time – the fact that 56% voted for Remain, yet that counts for nothing. The so-called biggest party here, the DUP, doesn't represent the biggest number of people. Plus there was the deal the DUP had done with Sinn Féin [in February 2018] and then walked away from.

I have no doubt whatsoever that if there's economic damage done, there'll be a groundswell for a border poll. A lot of people are going to say, 'What are we doing here?' The fact is, the South's economy has gone way ahead of the North, and the South has gone socially way ahead of the North in terms of human rights. The old line about Home Rule being Rome rule – that's no longer sustainable. Then there's the matter of demographics: four out of six counties already have a nationalist majority. And as for this £10 billion subvention: if there's a hard border and times are hard, there'll be a lot of guys sitting in England saying, 'Why are we handing over all that money? Let's cut the hell out of that.' I doubt if a lot of guys in England are going to be well-disposed towards Northern Ireland. There are parts of England every bit as bad as Northern Ireland: Sunderland, Newcastle, the old mining communities where there's unemployment. The Treasury in London will be under serious pressure to have a second look at money going to Northern Ireland.

Then there are the farmers dependent on the CAP. What happens if that gets seriously cut?

It seems all right for unionists to talk about 'our precious union', but the minute a nationalist talks about a border poll, which was agreed under the GFA, that's threatening, that's inciting violence. Are nationalists to live without parity of esteem for their rights? Their rights must come second to not offending unionists?

If Catholics/nationalists are in a majority in the North, and they feel that this is not a fair society, that their rights and identity are being denied, are they not entitled to talk about Irish unity? The principle of consent works both ways.

I disagree with Sinn Féin about a border poll now. I think that's ridiculous. First of all we need to get Brexit out of the way and see what happens or doesn't happen. Then if we're serious about unity, a plan needs to be put in place. Not like Brexit, which is a complete mess. People should know what they're voting for and what they're voting against. This emotional run for a united Ireland without thinking it through could be the biggest disaster of all. But if structures were in place, if people knew what they were getting and not getting, that would be doable.

Should Ireland rejoin the Commonwealth? Should the national anthem be changed? And a bill of rights – what about that? Or education. What's going to happen there? A lot of people from Derry used to study in Dublin, some people from the South used to go to Queen's University in Belfast. What happens to all the health services, the education services? Unionists could look at what is finally on offer and say, 'Right, we can live with this. We mightn't vote for it but we can live with it.'

One way and another, Brexit has changed the situation totally. We were a Europe of the regions, and the North of Ireland was a region and the South of Ireland was a region; we could get on a Ryanair flight and go anywhere. All the things that people took for granted are now in question.

9

EDDIE MAHON

25 FEBRUARY 2019

Eddie Mahon is a native of Gleneely, Co. Donegal. He played as goalkeeper for Derry City in the 1960s and early 1970s. In 1972 he captained Derry City when they played their final game in the Irish Football Association (IFA). In 1985 he was central to Derry City's switch to the Football Association of Ireland (FAI), making it the only major soccer team in the world to play its football outside its political jurisdiction.

Gleneely in Donegal, where I grew up, is about ten miles from the border. When I was very young, one of the things you could get in Derry and couldn't get across the border in Donegal was a white loaf. There was a customs man called Eamonn Leahy who used to drink in our pub in Gleneely, and we were very friendly with him. So when I was maybe two or three – the family remembers this, but I don't – my mother was smuggling on this particular occasion a white loaf, and she put it in the back of the car and put a coat over it. Then she said, 'Now, Edward. No matter what anybody says to you, do not speak to anybody as we're passing the border.' So we got to the border, out comes Eamonn Leahy. He looks in the car and he says to me, 'Hello there. How are you doing, son?' Not a word. 'Are you all right today, son?' Not a peep. So he just looked at my mother and went back in – he knew there was something going on.

In those days there was a thing called pass books, which you got stamped in and out at the border. And as I progressed in life I got to the stage where my father would let me take the car and go to the Borderland dance hall. If you hit it lucky at the dance you might find yourself driving a girl home to Derry, on the Northern side of the border. But you had to put in a request, and that cost you two shillings and sixpence – half-a-crown. Say you had a request for 3 a.m., a customs man would come and let you through. But if you missed your request time, you sat there all night. In later times, I got to know all the customs men very well, and I was allowed to leave my book on the step. They would stamp it the next morning and I would get it the next time I was coming through.

The border was a big red-and-white pole – STOP – across the road, and you just got used to it and accepted it. There was no great fuss about it in those days. In the mid-1950s the IRA campaign included blowing up customs posts. I remember a cartoon in the *Derry Journal* by a friend of mine, actually, one of the McGonigles. And it showed a customs post smouldering and the caption was 'Ancient Irish customs'!

In 1972 the Ballymena team bus was burned – not actually at the Brandywell [Stadium], where Derry City played, but a crowd of young fellows pushed it down the Letterkenny Road and set it on fire – it wasn't even associated with the Troubles. At that stage, a lot of the teams in the east side of the province decided they wouldn't play in Derry. The guy writing a column in *The Belfast News Letter* [read mainly by unionists] said, 'I wouldn't go within fifty miles of the place,' which didn't help things.

We played home games at Coleraine for a while, but it wasn't working out, and Derry City FC was out of football for thirteen years. Towards the end of the thirteen years, me, Terry Harkin, Tony O'Doherty and Eamon McLaughlin – we were all ex-Derry City players – decided we'd make an effort to go to play on the other side of the border in the FAI. This was in the mid-1980s, and it was something that had never been done before anywhere in the world – playing in a league outside your own jurisdiction.

When we first started playing in the FAI it was like a carnival. There were 12,000 people every week at the Brandywell. When we were playing away, there was a big placard at the end of the bridge: 'Last man out put out the lights!' There'd been thirteen years without football in a football town and it was like a massive sigh of relief to be playing again. There was also a sense that we were giving two fingers up at the North who had shunned us. Derry never got a proper crack of the whip from Belfast on anything. So there was a sense of pride in the city and having done something that hadn't been done anywhere in the world – a team playing in a different jurisdiction.

Nobody now would favour Derry City going back into the North's IFA. You'd be going to places like Larne, with people shouting sectarian stuff at you. If we go down to Dublin and get slagged, at least they're ordinary decent criminals slagging us. I remember when we were playing in the North, we couldn't at one point go to Linfield's ground at Windsor Park because one of our players had been threatened that he'd be shot. I actually played at Windsor Park many times, and I recall once I was in goal at the Kop end and felt something hit me in the back. I was trying to ignore all that stuff, but a photographer for the *Belfast Telegraph* kept pointing at me. Eventually I put my hand round and discovered there was a dart sticking out of my back. I remember getting into a panic in case there was some kind of poison on it. But you got that kind of sectarian stuff all the time.

People always had a fair bit of interaction across the border, but now you can zip up and down, do your shopping – it has normalised things. At one time you'd have been aware you were going into the North, but now you wouldn't be conscious of it. The only thing it affects is the value of the currency in terms of petrol prices – we go out to Muff at the Donegal border to get our petrol. In fact, a lot of the Northern filling stations, especially the ones close to the border, closed over the years. And it wasn't just nationalists – you'd have seen the odd unionist politician filling up on the Southern side too!

As to the Brexit thing, I can't understand why all the politicians, North and South, say, 'No, there's going to be no border check.' There have to be border checks – there'd be chaos if there weren't. Say, if thirty Romanians arrive in the South, entitled to be there as part of the EU: what's to stop them going up into the North? You're not going to stop them with technology or a camera up in the sky with 300 border crossings. There will *have* to be customs checks – there's no question about it. Suppose Britain imports American beef, which is treated with all sorts of stuff that means it doesn't qualify to enter the EU – if you don't have checks, they could just flood the South if it's cheap. There are *hundreds* of different things that aren't going to be equalised.

Everybody seems to be in favour of an invisible border – except the DUP. I have this feeling that the backstop would be so good for Northern Ireland – we'd have the best of both worlds. But I think the DUP believe that if the backstop is established and Protestant/unionist farmers and business-men see how much of an advantage this will be in trading, with the free flow of goods, there'd be no turning back. That's why I'd have no problem with a seven- or eight-year limit to the backstop. Once the free flow of goods gets established, farmers and businessmen would never want the backstop's removal.

The DUP sees the backstop as a weakening of the link with Britain. I'm told there's a lot of the 'soft' unionists now who have no huge objection to joining the South, if things are look-ing better that way. If the backstop is seen to be a success, and the DUP sees it's weakening the link with Britain and its people wouldn't want to go back again, that's not terribly good for it, the DUP.

The business community in Northern Ireland, the big farmers – they're all coming out now and saying, 'Hold on a minute. This Brexit thing – it's not on. We're going to suffer hugely.' I think the DUP could suffer politically as a result. But I think they'll suffer even more if the government in Britain gets to a point where they don't need the DUP – the DUP will suffer a fate worse than death then – there'd be a huge British reaction against the DUP.

In the event of a border poll: would 100% of Catholics/nationalists vote for unity? No. And as for the people in the South: we in the North – Catholics, Protestants, dissenters, unionists, nationalists – we're all the Black North, we're all the same. Gerry Fitt [former SDLP leader] once said he had more in common with someone from the Shankill than with someone from Kerry – which puts it in a nutshell. I listen to a radio station in the South called *Newstalk,* and Ivan Yates – a true-blue Fine Gael – he just calls us all Nordies. That's his term of derision.

Let me relate it to football. We were picking a manager for Derry City this year, and since I'm pretty close to the club, they sought my views. So there was this possible candidate who is a great analyser of the game, talks a great game, was a great player, talks sense – but he's a Dublin guy. And his name appeared on the roster for Derry manager. I said, 'Look – he's terrific, he's fabulous, I have great respect for him, I've never heard anyone analyse a game as well as he does – but he's from Dublin. And I don't think the Dublin people understand our culture at all. Two different outlooks – chalk and cheese.' We've had three Dublin managers over the last ten to fifteen years. We had Pat Fenlon, who lasted two weeks and came very honestly to the board and said, 'Look, I don't understand anything here.' We had Dermot Keely, who lasted a month, and we had Roddy Collins, who lasted about four months. All because none of them understood our culture, our way of thinking. And that's a huge factor when you're trying to dispense views and talk to people.

I do a column in the *Derry Journal* every Friday. And a couple of months ago a guy wrote in and said, 'You're on the fence. You're a Donegal man, and now you're in Derry.' The next week I said, 'I am not a Donegal man. I deny completely that

I am a Donegal man. I am an Inishowen man.' There is a huge difference.

The fact is, Inishowen is half Derry, and Derry is half Inishowen. Up in Creggan [an area of Derry], every single street is named after somewhere in Inishowen, because of intermarriage and other links. The rest of Donegal – not at all. We in Inishowen always looked to Derry as our town; the rest of Donegal looks to Letterkenny.

If there were a border poll, I think people would say, more on financial grounds, 'Keep the border.' The people in the South see us as a load of trouble, as people who are fighting, who have sectarian problems – even twenty years after the GFA. That'll take one or two, maybe more, generations to weed out. I think the people in the South are happy enough with the way things are. They don't want bother, they don't want our problems coming down there. And we are two different cultures, there's no doubt about that.

Like St Augustine and chastity, the people of the South love the idea of a united Ireland – but not just yet. A united Ireland, yes, but do you want it tomorrow? Absolutely not. No way. We are a troublesome clan, and they see us as one tribe. 'You're all the bloody same.' Probably because of Sinn Féin's way of working. I mean, the Shinners are getting as bad as anyone now. See in this town? You'll not get a job in any public works unless you're Sinn Féin-happy.

We were down in the Point Inn, just across the border, one night during the Troubles. And a group of us stayed on after the band had gone, a few friends. Suddenly the doors bang open – the Provos are robbing the place! They lined us all up against the wall. They'd these short ropes with them. There was about eleven or twelve of us, and they told us all to sit down. And they were tying our legs to the chairs so that we couldn't move. They were coming down the line and Tony Dobbins's wife was screaming, and Tony was telling her, 'Shut up, nobody's going to do anything to you, you'll be all right!' So they went down the line tying the ropes. And the guy came to me with the mask on and he says, 'I know you're all right, big man – I'll not bother tying you ... But you were shite at the Brandywell yesterday.'

I don't think there's a majority for a united Ireland in the North yet. You vote with your pocket. With the backstop in place, things would probably look OK. But you'd still have a large section of the nationalist community who'd want their national health and all that sort of stuff that you don't have down South. And there's the dole. If there was going to be a big drop in financial earnings, a lot would stick with their pocket. The unionists would be more resistant.

I was in Singapore last week, and I brought a book with me – *Our Very Precious Heritage* I think it's called. It's about the Ulster-Scots in America. I have huge interest in America during the nineteenth century: the Civil War, the way west, moving out to California. In the move west, in the early part of the nineteenth century, the Ulster-Scots were just phenomenal. They did most of the donkey work. They fought pestilence, they fought floods, they fought famine, they fought heat, they fought Native Americans. They were that fucking dogged, they just stuck in – 'no surrender', really.

But translate that to the negotiating stable at Stormont? Those things that made the Ulster-Scots so successful in

America are not much good when you're negotiating at Stormont. That no-surrender, not-an-inch thing is still there. And I often say to some of my Protestant/unionist friends, 'Are you boys not sorry you didn't give a wee bit at the start? Because it would have saved us from so much.'

But the South still sees us in the North as that bloody lot, nothing satisfies them, they're always fighting. In fact the fighting stopped years ago, but there are a lot of scars still, including this whole legacy thing. I've never lost anyone in the Troubles, thank God, so maybe I'm the wrong guy to ask about it. But I think it would help if you could just forego that almost-revenge thing that exists and offer it up as part of the loss of the Troubles.

10

JOHN BRUTON

7 MARCH 2019

John Bruton was Taoiseach of Ireland from 1994 to 1997. He was first elected to Dáil Éireann (the lower house of Parliament) in 1969 and served continuously as a member until 2004. From 2004 to 2009, he was EU ambassador to the US. From 2010 to 2015, he was president of International Financial Services Centre (IFSC) Ireland. He was also a member of the board of Montpelier RE, a leading property catastrophe re-insurance company, from 2010 to 2015. He is married to Finola (née Gill), and they have four adult children.

I was at boarding school and one of my friends was from Warrenpoint, just across the border, and I visited him there once or twice. I felt I was going into a place that was quite different. I remember seeing an Orange parade in Newry, which I thought quite funny, but my friend explained that was not quite the way one might look at it. This was 1960–65, before the Troubles, and remember, I was quite young. One's critical powers are not fully developed at that age! My friend had a boat, and we went across from Warrenpoint to Carlingford on one occasion. It was very nice, that part of South Down – it gave you a benign view of the world.

When I was elected to the Dáil in 1969, at the age of twenty-two, I initially represented part of Co. Meath. Later in my career – in the 1970s – I represented North Meath, which is quite close to the border. In 1969 I visited Belfast with Sheelagh Murnaghan – a well-known Ulster Liberal Party member of Stormont. She showed the late John Kelly [Fine Gael politician] and me around Belfast – some of the areas that had been burned and so on. It was a chilling experience.

Also around that time, 1969 or 1970, a very large number of refugees came from Belfast, and they were accommodated in Gormanston Camp, which is in my constituency. I suggested to the then-leader of Fine Gael and subsequent Taoiseach, Liam Cosgrave, that he might visit the Gormanston Camp and talk to the people. I was pleased that he did – it was one of the first times I felt I had some influence on events. His visit was televised and it gave reassurance to the people. He was a man of very high integrity, Liam Cosgrave. People mightn't always have agreed with him but they respected him.

He talked with the refugees and I accompanied him. A lot of them were people who would have led pretty tough lives in Belfast. I represented a rural constituency, and it was an eye-opener to see some of the different conditions people came from, as well as the conditions they were in. They were of course apprehensive about their situation. And I remember there was a certain amount of apprehension in the locality as well, among the local people, with refugees coming from a very different life and area. It must have been similar to when people were relocated due to the blitz in England. Very different lifestyles coming in contact with each other.

My political career spanned the entire campaign of violence by the IRA and the response from loyalists. I found the violence horrifying; I thought it was completely stupid and pointless. I can understand fully the initial reaction of defending one's own area, where you have people coming in to burn your house; but when the campaign spilled over to become a more offensive type of activity – shooting and bombing and all of that – I never thought at any time that it made the slightest sense.

My perspective at all times was on the importance of preserving the integrity of our own state and not letting organisations that didn't recognise the validity of our state manipulate the suffering of the people of Northern Ireland. That was something which Liam Cosgrave and I shared. We had to maintain the integrity of the state.

I think partition is something that grew very gradually. Under the original Home Rule Act, there was a provision for some counties to opt out temporarily, but there was nothing permanent envisaged. However, in 1918 people in what became the twenty-six counties voted for MPs who refused to take seats in Westminster. Then in 1920 the actual legislation was introduced that established partition on a permanent basis – two parliaments, two separate jurisdictions. The legislation was introduced and passed with most of the MPs who represented Irish nationalism sitting at home. Sinn Féin of the day weren't taking their seats. If Irish nationalists had still been there, it probably would not have happened.

There are differences North and South, but if the GFA had worked as it should, those differences would have been mitigated more than they have been.

I don't think the border created different people. The fact that we have sporting organisations that operate on an all-Ireland basis is important. The GAA has kept Northern nationalists in touch with the rest of Ireland, and rugby has kept Northern unionists and nationalists in touch in ways that wouldn't have been possible without sport. I was minister for sport in the 1970s, at the height of the Troubles. I met my counterpart in the North, the late Ivan Cooper, to discuss how we could enhance sporting cooperation and involvement across the border. But in any case the sporting organisations continued themselves without that much government intervention.

However, I think it's important that when we have all-Ireland teams, we recognise that some of the people on those teams have a British identity. You could start recognition and respect by looking at the anthem. If there are people on the team who respect the British sovereign, her anthem might be played from time to time too. And the flags we use – it should be a neutral flag that doesn't present a particular concept of Ireland. The tricolour was originally a Sinn Féin flag. It is a party emblem as well as a national flag. We should try to find ways of respecting those who regard the Union Jack as their flag even though they're on an Irish team. And the Union Jack does have the cross of St Patrick on it. You can respect something without being part of it, respect the two identities that are on this island. Whether those identities take the form of different states or different administration, identity is much bigger and wider than institutions.

Cross-border bodies didn't realise their potential for reconciliation. To get the DUP on board, the original vision had to be attenuated quite a bit. The St Andrews Agreement, which put an emphasis on the first minister coming from the party with the biggest support – that entrenched the sectarian divide and thereby minimised willingness to enter into cross-border cooperation. That was a great pity. The more cross-border co-operation, the more secure the union would have been. The unwillingness to engage in cross-border cooperation, because of justified fears, only made the union more vulnerable. It's important to realise that the GFA recognises the two states. That was recognised in a joint referendum. That is the best form of security one can get. That's why I think it's so counter-intuitive for the DUP to be flirting with a no-deal Brexit. That would appear to be weakening the union.

There's a contrariness in the two big parties in Northern Ireland. If the nationalists want something, the DUP will be against it, and vice versa. There's no sign yet of the DUP losing support. I think, unfortunately, the way the system works in Northern Ireland, the people may disagree thoroughly with the positions taken by the party on their side of the divide, but they'll vote for them to add weight on their end. They balance each other off like people on a see-saw. I would hope financial pain might make inroads.

Looking at it from outside, in a second-hand way, I look at the results of elections. There was a by-election in West Tyrone recently, won by Sinn Féin. I'm afraid the same thing would apply now if there was an election. They unfortunately vote on sectarian lines. To my mind, the people on both sides have responsibility for the situation that divides them through their voting behaviour. They get the politicians they vote for.

Have they looked into the ability of the Irish Exchequer to replace the British subvention? If there's a united Ireland it'll be Irish soldiers and Irish police and Irish taxpayers' money that'll be paying for Northerners. And even though this is a very successful country, it's a very small country. Britain is a very big country with a bigger exchequer.

It's all right talking about a united Ireland in theoretical terms, and money will come from somewhere and it'll all be grand. But the more likely scenario is it might come with a 52–48% like Brexit – and with 30% among that 48% so opposed to uniting with Dublin they'll do anything to stop it. Yes, they signed up to it, but people sign up to a lot of things. We signed up to the GFA to get the violence ended and start the process of working together that would allow the significance of the border to diminish. A vote for the GFA was not a vote for a united Ireland but for a new Ireland, keeping Northern Ireland in the UK until such time as there was a clear majority in Northern Ireland for a united Ireland.

I look at the Framework Agreement I negotiated with John Major and compare that with the GFA – the framework has far more areas of cooperation than the GFA. Saying that, I'm not criticising the GFA, which involved all the parties.

Brexit has increased attention to the border, but I think the consideration of the border and unity is not yet deeply realistic. I don't think we've faced up to all the implications of this. I think it's still at the level of sentiment. There are financial implications, implications regarding security.

I think we have to be realistic that there is a significant section of the population in Northern Ireland who don't want a united Ireland. Talking about it in the wrong terms only gets their sensitivities increased. If you can talk about closer cooperation and leave the issue of ultimate sovereignty – which is a theoretical concept anyway – leave it out of the conversation or positioned more towards the back of the conversation, you'll get much further.

As to Brexit, I have no doubt that Brexit will inflict damage on Ireland. This is a cloud without a silver lining. It'll be less bad in some circumstances than others, but it's all degrees of bad.

I think it's inevitable, if there's a no-deal Brexit, there will have to be a border. We have to be realistic. To comply with EU requirements, a border will have to be created. A lot of people talk about Brexit as if it will require a border with heavy security, as during the Troubles. No versions of Brexit will require that. Customs posts, yes, but not watchtowers, etc. Two issues are being mixed up – a security border against terrorist activity and a border for dealing with trade.

We will have to put up the border. If there were any attacks on customs posts, this would be Irish people attacking other Irish, and Irish people who were trying to protect their livelihood by protecting their market. This is not comparable to the Royal Kent Regiment or whatever being on the border at Aughnacloy during the Troubles. I'm confident in the security forces' ability to deal with things.

We should not make our policy with regard to the EU on the basis of a threat of violence. The threat of violence is illegitimate. It should not influence. That's what guided me in politics, inspired by Liam Cosgrave: we will not let gunmen dictate our policy. Whatever we have to do, we will not let that happen.

11

ROGER McCOLLUM

11 MARCH 2019

Roger McCollum is a retired police superintendent who served in both the RUC and the Police Service of Northern Ireland (PSNI). Since his retirement, he has worked on several international policing projects in Europe, Africa and Asia and has been involved locally in peace-building initiatives, through organisations such as Healing Through Remembering and The Junction. He is a strong advocate of integrated education as a way towards building a more peaceful society in Northern Ireland.

I was born in Portrush in 1953. Then we moved up to East Belfast, where I lived my post-formative years until I joined the police in 1976. I had a couple of great-uncles who lived in the Inishowen peninsula in Donegal, and we'd have regularly crossed the border to visit them. At one time there was foot-and-mouth disease in the area and we had to get out [of the vehicle] – the tyres of the car were decontaminated and we walked through a wee trough of water.

The last two weeks in August we would have gone on holiday to the Dunfanaghy area in Donegal, and one year we went to Achill Island. And at Whitsun we'd have gone down to Bray. So we were a family that was very comfortable crossing the border.

Parts of Donegal were like the 1920s or 1930s. There were very few people living there, the houses were quite basic, and there was a lot of poverty and emigration. So yes, I was aware of a difference between the North and the South. Bray in Co. Dublin had probably more in common with Belfast than the rural areas of Donegal.

At the border the customs man would have stuck his head through the window and asked who we were, where we were going. But that was about it – all very friendly, no hard border. There was the IRA's border campaign of 1956–62, but I don't remember it affecting our passage across the border.

I went to a state/Protestant school, and we would have been taught about the English Civil War, the six wives of Henry VIII and nothing really on Irish history whatsoever. We didn't know about [former Taoiseach Éamon] de Valera, we didn't know about Michael Collins – we were isolated from what was going on in the South. All of these things contributed to us having a different view, a different way of thinking about things from our friends in the South.

With the Troubles, among the Protestant community in Northern Ireland, there would have been a memory that went back a long way: Home Rule is Rome rule, that the Catholic Church had great strength South of the border. That sort of thing would have been talked about a bit. Nowadays the South is in many ways a more relaxed and liberal place than the North is. But then there was a sense that we here in the North were embattled. We had quite a relaxed atmosphere here up until 1969–70, when attitudes became hardened.

As I saw it, the border was a dividing line. I never thought much about it as protecting us from them or them from us. There was just these 300 miles of border – so weird, the way it goes in and out of so many places. I'm sure there were many reasons it was drawn like that in years gone by.

I joined the police in 1976, but I was never posted to the border. Most of my time was spent in Co. Derry/Londonderry, and also in Co. Antrim and Co. Armagh. But of course I had friends who served along the border.

People in Northern Ireland like to be moved not too far away from where we are. So if someone was from Omagh, say, and got posted to the border in Fermanagh, it'd be no big deal. There was probably a bigger issue if you were from the Belfast area and got posted to the border.

Where I'm from, up in Portrush, there were two police officers murdered there in the 1970s. In Belfast, where we're sitting at the moment, there were police officers killed as well. So while there was danger along the border, there was danger anywhere, regardless of where a police officer was living.

Of the Belfast police officers who were posted to the border, very few of them took up permanent residence there. They'd serve for four or five years and then be sent back to where they were from originally.

The police officers in, for example, Omagh slept in the actual police barracks. Likewise Castlederg. In the smaller police stations like Castlerock, you'd have had the sergeant living there with his family. Before the Troubles kicked in, you'd probably have got that in most police stations in Northern Ireland. As the situation deteriorated, families would have been less likely to live in police stations. So it was more often single men who were posted to such stations. The police lived in the Strand Road station in Derry/Londonderry, the same in Enniskillen.

My first fourteen weeks were spent in the training centre in Enniskillen.

One of my colleagues I went through the training centre with was killed in Lisnaskea in 1977 – he was only eighteen years of age. The news of his death left me devastated. Several other officers I was in the training centre with were killed. When you lose someone you know – shot or blown up – it makes you think what life is all about. And how sad the loss of all those young people is. And for what? When you look at where we are today, was there any need for the whole thing?

The eighteen-year-old I mentioned who lost his life near Lisnaskea was shot in an ambush. Thinking back forty-two years, that guy would now be fifty-nine or sixty years of age, with a family, loved ones – but he never got the chance to go there. I'm not saying it's just our community that suffered – every community suffered – but it's an example of the loss of human life for … whatever.

The army initially came in here to protect the Catholic folk. But that turned around quite quickly. Our community felt that the army were there to help the state or the folk who wanted to be part of the union. Hence the need for the watchtowers, hence the need for the militarisation, for the armoured cars and tanks and guns. The civilian police weren't able to cope with the situation.

In the 1950s, the Catholic/nationalist folk and the unionist folk got on pretty well together. Clearly there were issues related to employment, discrimination – things like that. Then the Troubles started and people began to go back into their trenches. But back in the 1950s, it was almost an invisible border. You had the customs people there, but that was about it – it was a soft border.

Ever since Northern Ireland was created in 1921, there's been conflict of some description. You could say that the reason we're in the situation we are in is because things weren't addressed properly 100 years ago. The conflict made people look to their own communities for strength and made them see the others – 'them uns' – as the enemy.

The invisible border has been absolutely great. Since the GFA, we can have 'parallel constitutional beliefs'. In other words, some can believe they're Irish, some believe they're British, some can have both passports. It's an ideal situation. Nowadays we're talking more about a visible border if we have a hard Brexit. I can't see it happening, but it's a possibility that we're going to have checks, and the checks are going to have infrastructures, and the infrastructures are going to have to be protected, and the people protecting the infrastructures are going to have to be protected. And the whole thing has the danger of going back to where we were in 1969 or 1970.

But while that is something that is talked about, I don't think we're going to go there. I think we're all far more mature than we were. I think Brexit may make an attempt to destroy the ambiguity that was created, where we all got on with our lives extremely well. The danger is if we talk Brexit up, we could have that problem.

Any checks at the border are going to be difficult. I've been there, done that, worn the T-shirt with my colleagues. You have to be there to protect the customs men, or the cameras, or the wall, or the cratered roads.

I have quite a few friends within the Catholic/nationalist tradition and I've noticed a hardening of attitudes there, for a number of reasons. Things like poking 'the crocodiles' don't help. And on the other side, [talking about] a Trojan horse doesn't help. That's the language of war, the language of getting people annoyed.

People like being part of Europe – particularly people from a nationalist background, but also some people from a unionist background. They like Europeanisation, they like being Europeans. Brexit could threaten that by taking the UK out of Europe, particularly if it's a hard exit.

Traditional thoughts are being more and more eroded. For example, people from a nationalist background who were pretty happy to be part of the UK could call themselves Northern Irish without annoying anybody. But now they're thinking, 'If we need to be in a thirty-two-county Ireland to be part of Europe, we'd consider that.' Even a small number of folk from the unionist tradition are saying to themselves, 'Let's think about our finances here, let's think about quality of life – there might be something to be said for joining into Europe. And if that takes us to be part of the new Ireland that's talked about, let's at least listen to what the arguments are.' So it's an interesting shift in the dynamics out there.

We don't want a border such as was pre-Troubles – we don't want anything. I just feel it's an annoyance and it's a nuisance. We have more in common than divides us. But once you start putting up any sort of frontier at all, then the danger is the situation can escalate.

The fact is, 56% of folk in Northern Ireland voted to stay in

Europe. In the way that politics works here at the moment, the DUP is the biggest party and you have to respect the mandate, and it is very influential in Westminster – although how long that will last you'd never know. Is every single member of the DUP a Leaver? I think there are a few Remainers.

You could have the whole of the UK staying in a customs union or something like that, except that it wouldn't appeal to those who want to come out of Europe. They say, 'If we're going to come out of Europe, why do we want to stay in a customs union?'

The whole of the security and criminal situation is more complicated by the thought of any sort of border coming in. If you look at chief constables and senior police officers in Northern Ireland and in Great Britain, it isn't an ideal situation to be coming out of Europe. You have at the moment a policing tool called the European Arrest Warrant (EAW), which is a relatively easy way of issuing an arrest warrant for a person who has committed crimes and is residing in part of the EU. The process can be done pretty quickly. But before EAW's were introduced in 2004, the UK only extradited about 60 EU citizens a year – at the moment this ranges between 1,800 and 2,000. A no-deal Brexit could mean we would have to return to the 1957 European Convention on Extradition, resulting in it possibly taking years to return a suspect to the UK, rather than the current six weeks with the EAW process. Before the introduction of the EAW, it was difficult to extradite a suspect from the South, with some cases taking years. With the EAW, this can now be achieved in a few weeks. So there are all sorts of difficulties there. Plus there are databases which are common to Europol, which is the European police organisation, as distinct from Interpol, and we could possibly lose access to those as well. There are all sorts of scientific developments within policing that we could have more difficulty with. To have a border on the island of Ireland – it just makes things so much more difficult for policing.

I think there would be a belief among many unionists that anything which is seen to undermine the union in any way threatens the union. I don't think it does. As far as I'm aware, according to the GFA, the constitutional situation in Northern Ireland can only be changed with a referendum. To me, Brexit doesn't threaten the union, but others think it does.

I was recently speaking to a member of the Alliance Party who voted to leave Europe. His thinking was that it gave us back our constitutional sovereignty. He was thinking of the UK as a whole. But it's generally agreed, no matter what happens, for the next five to ten years, coming out of Europe, we're going to take a hit in the economy. Now you could say that's worth it if you want to keep your constitutional independence. Others would say it's all about quality-of-life issues, and they'd rather stay in because the quality of life is better. So it's getting that balance right that is the big thing. But this is Northern Ireland, and anything that is seen to undermine anything is sometimes seen as a ploy for a longer-term agenda to take the North out of the UK.

A hard Brexit would push some people into thinking, 'We'll go and take a chance with Europe.'

Maybe the DUP sees itself as standing up for the union and [believes] the best way to do that is to be very strident in its views on Europe.

The unionists who voted Remain are happy enough that it was a UK-wide vote – the union with Britain is number one to them. But in my opinion, you can be part of the union in many different ways. You could be part of the union and also part of Europe, which I think is where we want to be. We have the opportunity to have the best of both worlds, but we don't seem to be grasping that opportunity.

Even though we could have access to the UK market and to the EU market, to the unionist psyche that is a weakening of the Union. I don't say I agree with that, but I understand that that's their thinking. I think it's almost agreed that something which could be good for you economically could be bad for you politically. Even within the context of the UK, the greatest Brexiteers are saying, 'Yeah, we're going to lose some money over the next ten to fifteen years, but we've got our constitution back, we've got our independence back, we get rid of the human rights legislation, we can stop immigration at Dover' – that's the thinking.

In many ways I would like to have a second referendum and see how it goes, but I do understand that we've already had one. You could argue that we didn't know what we were voting for the last time. But I would imagine people believe they knew rightly what they were voting for: to come out of Europe. So I think we have to concentrate on Ireland, rather than what the UK wants to do. We need to be thinking about what's best for the people living on this island, rather than thinking what's best for somebody living in Dover or Devon or Hertfordshire.

What mark would I give our politicians out of ten? Nothing. Because we don't know where we are. They're going backwards, forwards, backwards, forwards.

A border poll will be triggered when the secretary of state thinks the time is right. Now, how long is a bit of string? I know it's in the GFA, but the GFA was a way of kicking the can further down the road. When I compare [the present] to my colleague who lost his life in 1977, and the 302 police officers who were murdered, and the many other people from all the communities who were killed and murdered during the Troubles, we are in a better place in the last twenty years than we were up until then. The GFA was, to some extent, all things to all people. You took out of it whatever you wanted to. But the fact that we have these parallel constitutional narratives was a very useful thing, so people could be Irish or British or the new term, Northern Irish.

So we are in a better place. But we need to make sure, as with all these things, that it's maintained and we stick with it.

A border poll will create great division. It will be like Brexit: people will be entrenched but to an even greater extent. I don't believe there's going to be a huge difference in the vote. I would say it could be 10% either way, so it's probably something better not to have at the moment. But having said that, if it goes ahead, let it go ahead and let's hear the various arguments.

It's a bit like elections here. You talk about what we loosely could call the extremes who get elected. You elect somebody so that the other – them uns – don't get in, and you get this every election. People here will still probably tend to vote the way they've done for a long time.

Are we helpless? We are individuals, we have a vote. Do we start street protests? Some people will. There would be a fear also, no matter what way this goes, that you could have civil disorder on the streets. That if people in the UK voted to come out and they don't come out, then they could become very upset – the extremes could be marginalised there. You could also see people very upset about coming out with a hard Brexit.

It'll not in fact happen, I would say, but if it did, you're going to put extra strain on police officers. The chief constable has recently been given an increased budget of £16.5 million to recruit an additional 307 police officers by April 2020 for contingencies in relation to Brexit. So already you're talking about adding some 5% to the PSNI. Who pays for that? The taxpayer. What better things could we be doing with health, education and all those important things? But contingency plans are in place.

So all those things have to be taken into consideration. And I know that the police throughout the UK are looking at the various possibilities: having another vote, or not coming out, or whatever the scenario is.

12

RAY BASSETT

12 MARCH 2019

Dr Ray Bassett was involved in the GFA negotiations as part of the Irish government talks team and participated throughout the discussions, including in the final session at Castle Buildings in Stormont. He has been a senior diplomat at Ireland's Department of Foreign Affairs in Dublin and served as the country's ambassador to Canada, Jamaica and the Bahamas 2010–16. Other diplomatic postings include Copenhagen, Canberra, Belfast (twice), London and Ottawa.

I was reared in Dublin, but I had first cousins in Derry. They explained to us that they had great neighbours eleven months of the year, but the twelfth month of the year they all went a bit mad. So our cousins tended to decamp to Dublin for the period. When we went to Derry on our holidays, we were going to visit our cousins – it wasn't exactly a political declaration or anything. Nobody liked the border, but we just went up and accepted these things as normal.

I went to O'Connell School, which in the old days was a very republican school. It provided about a third of all those who took part in the 1916 Rising, including people like Seán Lemass [former Taoiseach] and Seán T. O'Kelly [second president of Ireland]. Three of the former students were executed in one day – [Con] Colbert, [Seán] Heuston and

Éamonn Ceannt. And one of my early teachers was Mícheál Ó Muircheartaigh [the veteran GAA commentator] – so yes, you would have been conscious there was a border.

When I joined Foreign Affairs, I worked on the Northern side, the Anglo-Irish, for I think longer than anyone else – about seven years. A lot of that time would have been spent traipsing around the border – Glassdrummond and over in Newtownbutler, places like that, picking up information and talking to people.

I think the invisible border of the last twenty years has made a huge psychological difference. Yet in the Department of Foreign Affairs and with the EU, we did a survey and we found that less than 10% of people in Munster had ever been across the border. It was a geographical thing. If you drew a line from Dublin to Galway, people above that line were more likely to have been across the border.

But after the GFA there was a transformation. The nervousness people from the South felt about going North was largely psychological, and the Northern Ireland Tourist Board was very keen on getting rid of the military forts at the border. They saw them as a huge psychological barrier.

Only 1% of exports from the Republic goes North, and about 15% of stuff from the North comes South. That's largely the difference in scale between the two. Traditionally, the South used to have a big trade surplus with the North. Now it's the other way round.

The six borders on the Southern side were a bit of a fiddle in terms of border counties. When they were setting up all the peace programmes, particularly the International Fund for

Ireland (IFI), it was thought they'd apply it to six counties in the South and six in the North. Sligo, which doesn't actually touch the border, was included because the minister for finance said Sligo was really a border county.

The border regions – at least in the Republic – have probably been the least developed. Donegal in socio-economic terms is the poorest county in the twenty-six. That was in part because you had this type of cul-de-sac element to it. Derry city is really the city of Donegal. So putting a border there and dividing communities, particularly dividing places like Donegal from Derry or North Monaghan from Armagh city, had a very detrimental effect. And that's why those areas tend to be the most difficult to administer.

Since the GFA there has been economic development cross-border, but I think we need a much greater drive at it.

I opposed Brexit on the basis that it was bad for Ireland. But Brexit isn't an economic issue – it's a political issue. Like 1916 wasn't an economic issue. It's deeper than that, and that's why the anti-Brexit people haven't been successful.

I didn't want Brexit to occur because I thought it was bad for Ireland. In fact my son campaigned here in Belfast against it. But once [the referendum] occurred – I felt the history of the EU has been shameful in terms of democracy, where they got rid of Papandreou in Greece or where they've tried to overcome referenda.

Then there's the whole structure of the EU, where you've got a kind of window-dressing parliament but you've got a commission which is non-elected and which has huge powers to make legislation. So I could see the point of the Brexiteers.

But once they voted for it, I think the role of Ireland was to say, 'OK, you've made your decision, we're going to assist you to do this in a reasonable way.' I think we should have been a bridge, not kicking [the UK]. If you're going to bring about unity in Ireland, you're going to have 800,000–900,000 people who regard themselves as pro-British. So you're making no progress if you're going around kicking the political entity that they identify with. It's like unionists kicking the Republic and then trying to win Northern nationalists – counter-productive.

The British establishment are totally against Brexit – the House of Lords, all the great and good. Unfortunately you've got a few toffs on the Brexit side who give a different impression. But Brexit is very much a working-class thing. We shouldn't be getting involved in – and used in – subverting a democratic decision in a neighbouring island. They've done enough of that to us, so we shouldn't have done it.

I think we missed a huge opportunity to be helpful, because under the GFA – and I believe in the GFA, unlike the people who misquote it all the time – the two countries agreed to be good neighbours and partners. Now with Britain, whether they made a mistake or not, we had an onus under the GFA to assist them. We also had an onus under the GFA to discuss issues bilaterally. But when the British asked for that, we said, 'No – you'll have to talk to Brussels.' I believe that was a breach of the GFA. We signed an agreement to say we're going to meet, we're going to discuss all matters about mutual boundaries, and then when they asked us we said no.

The GFA is an agreement between London and Dublin. I was there. The only people who signed the GFA were Bertie

Ahern and Tony Blair. It is a bilateral agreement between Britain and Ireland. You have a section of it under the multi-party talks, which are the parties in Northern Ireland plus the two governments, but the central core of the GFA is a Dublin–London agreement. We're going to have a new start, a whole new beginning, we're going to be friends, we're going to work together.

We did the complete opposite to what we had promised to do. We showed little or no give with the British. We refused to talk to them, and the rhetoric we used, I believe, was completely counter-productive – coming out with 'the backstop – this is copper-fastened, bulletproof' and all this sort of stuff. And [Taoiseach] Leo Varadkar saying something like, 'The time when a British prime minister can tell an Irish Taoiseach what to do is long gone.' That's crap. A smart Taoiseach would not do that sort of thing. They say you should never insult a crocodile's mother until you've crossed the stream. You've got to get away from groupthink where everybody thinks the same. You have to examine the question: is it in our interest that Britain gets a reasonably good Brexit? The answer is yes. Then what are we doing making things difficult?

Leo was talking about trying to avoid a border, but what he was really talking about was protecting the integrity of the single market. The GFA hardly talks about the border. It does talk about parity of esteem. So if you think a land border is against the Agreement, and I think it would be, you also have to say that a sea border is against the GFA. We're supposed to be operating as people who accept the legitimacy of both traditions. But if you start saying, 'You cannot divide the nationalist people from the rest of the nation,' you cannot propose and push as hard as you can – which they did – for a sea border.

The British link is very precious to the unionists. I'm not a unionist, I'm an Irish republican in my background, but I believe that in the end we're going to have to accommodate these people. But you don't accommodate them by appearing to take no interest in basic identity issues for them.

We in Ireland are listening to our own propaganda too much. The Northern Ireland backstop is not deliverable – it was never deliverable. The backstop said, in its crudest form, that since the UK was leaving the customs union, you were going to economically detach Northern Ireland from the rest of the United Kingdom.

Why did Ireland accept from day one the red line of Barnier that the border in Ireland must maintain the EU's legal order? That put the kibosh on negotiations from the start.

There's a Europhilia among Irish politicians, who love the EU far more than the general population do. The Irish population have rejected it in referenda on two occasions. They rejected further integration into Europe. They're very much for it now because they see it as an arm-wrestle between orange and green.

There are lots of polls done – by the European movement – in Ireland asking, 'Do you think the EU is good for Ireland?' I'd say yes, of course. But do I believe in the way the EU is going, in terms of militarisation? The answer is no. But that's where we're heading. We've got stuck in Brexit, but just look at the rest of Europe. The German opposition is now calling for the abolition of the European Parliament. The Swedish government is on tenterhooks because it can't get a majority. The people of Europe do not want this union that's evolving. Brexit is probably the most extreme example, but it's not the last example. The UK will not be the last country to leave the EU.

The European Parliament can't initiate a law themselves, even if everybody in the European Parliament wanted to. It was designed by Jean Monnet so that elections cannot be allowed to change economic policy. And that's the philosophy. Why is Europe going this way? Because the EU is not delivering at the moment. Ireland is unusual because it's doing very well. But right across the eurozone, things are very poor. Germany is almost in recession – partly because they're so heavily dependent on the car industry and the car industry is now in collapse all over the world. Everywhere you look, the attraction of the EU is going down. I cannot think of a new policy Europe is bringing out that is good for Ireland.

You've got [President of France, Emmanuel] Macron calling for a European army, you've somebody else calling for standardised tax rates, you've somebody else calling for the ending of fiscal independence in countries. None of this I agree with. So I can see what the Brexiteers are going at. The EU has brought misery to Greece, Spain and Portugal. Why are we so attracted to the EU, why are we not more critical? The reason is we're in a dogfight. And when it comes down to a question of Dublin vs London, or the green vs the orange, we have to support our own people. Once the UK leaves the EU, watch how the EU becomes much less popular in Ireland. [Portuguese politician José Manuel] Barroso said,

'The European Union is a new empire.'[1] Our experience of empire is pretty bad.

We're going to be on the periphery of Europe, on the other side of an island and well away from the centre. Our ability to operate economically has been very heavily dependent on American foreign direct investment. That's coming under attack both from the US and from Europe. It may not continue as it is. So the attraction of Europe is going to lessen. The balance of advantage and disadvantage is changing, but because we're in this dogfight – the Brits are getting on our nerves – we're not paying any attention to that. We're focused on this localised fight with Britain. I think Leo has introduced the border as a diversionary tactic, because the only one who will ever introduce a border is the EU. We should say, 'No, we are not going to cooperate with that.' Introducing a border would be so destabilising to this country that we're going to have to stand up to Brussels. Because the Brits aren't going to introduce a border. They don't want one – they took the bulk of the hits during the Troubles. There are republicans in Ireland who think the Brits want to put up a border: it's just a fantasy world.

I believe the EU has had a corrupting effect on public life in Ireland. Why do they pay all these guys who go over there massive salaries? That's a corrupting influence. They want people who can benefit personally from it to be supportive of it. Most people will work because they have an identification with things. When I was asked if I'd go over and work in Brussels I said no, because I've no identification with it. I've a huge identification with my own country. I'd do anything I can to help it. But I don't have an identification with Europe. I don't want to help create a United States of Europe, it's as simple as that.

We have in Ireland an elitist group who are trying to graft European mainland identity on top of us – something which doesn't exist. I feel more at home in Boston than I do in Brussels. I mean, I love the diaspora. The Irish in the Ottawa Valley – they are much closer to me than a group in Flanders. When a bomb goes off in Bali, who do we ring? We ring the Australian foreign ministry, would they check [if any Irish citizens were injured], because the Irish and Australians go together. But in Europe there are language issues, there are cultural issues. I think we've got to be a bit more subtle than: 'The Brits are on that side, we're on the other side, so we're going to get them!'

I think Brexit for Britain will not be good initially. The EU has been doing very poorly internationally – around the world. French unemployment is two-and-a-half times that of Britain. In the last few years Britain has greatly outperformed France. I was on a radio debate recently with Bertie Ahern, and I said, 'In 1993, the countries in the eurozone had an economy almost exactly the same size as the United States. Today the United States is one-third bigger.' There are areas of Europe which have been decimated by the policy of austerity. The maintenance of a single currency is more important than the livelihoods of people in Spain, Greece and Romania – and that is wrong. There's no democratic control over it. The European Central Bank (ECB) is forbidden from working with governments.

I think the EU should never have got into the human rights issue because we already had the European Convention on

Human Rights (ECHR), which has nothing to do with the EU. The EU got involved because they were trying to create a state. They deliberately put together this Charter of Fundamental Rights, and it replicated what all these European countries had already. Certainly in the short term, the UK is not going to pull out of the ECHR.

Ireland's biggest export market is the United States. There's no trade agreement with the US. So this idea that we're going to crash is poppycock. Brexit is going to produce a negative factor, but in my view the British didn't vote for Brexit over the economy. They voted for Brexit because they don't like this idea of an ever-closer union. The EU grabs more and more power and you cannot get it back. That's the big problem – there's no mechanism to take back power. There was talk about subsidiarity, but subsidiarity didn't occur, because the EU commissioners' oath requires every minister going in there to swear allegiance and they cannot have allegiance to any country or government.

The European Parliament is a joke. It's a very expensive operation with 751 members. They don't even have to account for their expenses. You get in there and you're made for life. So it needs massive reform. Every UK prime minister has tried to reform it, ever since [Edward] Heath was thrown out.

And that's not Britain and its imperial past. The only person who talks about imperial past is Fintan O'Toole in *The Irish Times*. I have never read a book that is so verging on hysteria as his [*Heroic Failure: Brexit and the Politics of Pain*]. There are people in Ireland who will not accept the legitimacy of the British wanting Brexit. I think you have to accept the legitimacy. Why would people in Hull vote for it? Why would people in Grimsby? These are people who have no interest in imperial things.

When I go to speak at meetings, they are so well attended and people at them are so angry, but official Ireland has no room for them at all.

Fianna Fáil were originally Eurosceptic. De Valera certainly voted against it. We didn't join in the 1950s because Frank Aiken [Irish minister for foreign affairs] and others decided quite rightly they couldn't go into an organisation that had as its ultimate goal the abolition of the independence of Ireland. So Fianna Fáil made the decision in the 1950s not to get involved in the Treaty of Rome. Lemass came in and changed that in the early 1960s. Then the Labour Party and the trade unions were very Eurosceptic, but they went off and most of them got jobs in Europe at the Irish Institute of European Affairs. Then Sinn Féin craved respectability in the South. I don't for a second think Sinn Féin buy this European business at all. Any of them I speak to privately say, 'Ray, stop saying that. That's what we were saying ten years ago!' We have a suffocating uniformity and lack of examination of first principles. Where are we heading?

Varadkar runs through a motion to get Ireland to join the Permanent Structured Cooperation (PESCO), the European military thing, with a day's notice in the Dáil and they're whipped into line. We really need to start saying, 'Do we really want to go down this route?'

Last year, our net transfers were €1 billion. We gave the EU €1 billion more than we got. It took me a long time to get that information. Writing in *The Sunday Business Post*, I had to put in, I think, three Freedom of Information requests to get that information. They didn't want to say that Ireland is a big net contributor to the EU. Then, when the budget came up, the Dutch, the Finns and most of the countries who, like ourselves, are net contributors said, 'Look, hang on. The EU is getting smaller. You've got to stop doing all these things. You've got to stop paying your civil servants administration costs and these massive pensions.' But Varadkar seems quite willing to pay more for these European policies.

What is wrong with the country that people aren't up in arms? You've got people waiting on trolleys in hospitals in Limerick and this fellah is saying he'd pay more to Europe. The deficit went from €800 million to over €1 billion in one year. Next year it may be €1.3 billion.

There are farmers in the North wondering how they are going to survive. The British government has said it'll cover everything for two years, but it wants to change the CAP. It wants to make it much more environmentally friendly; it's not saying it's going to give less. The CAP has destroyed the uplands in Ireland. The whole place is overgrazed.

Ireland, as one of the richer European countries, is going to have to pay more. I don't mind paying more, but I don't want to pay more to boost the French armaments industry. Varadkar is saying he's signing up to 2% for military. At the same time, we have soldiers and their families relying on social welfare supplements. That's a disgrace. And part of the squeezing for PESCO is because the French economy is in dire order – in fact it's more worrying longer term than the Italian economy.

France can't maintain parity with Germany. It's been like that since the Second World War, and eventually the French will collapse.

They want to create this European preference and for us all to have standardised arms. Now the main arms industry, once the Brits leave, is the French. And they want us to pay money for the French arms industry. I don't want that. I think we should have a good, well-maintained military and treat our soldiers and their families well, and that's much more important than paying money for arms.

If there's a hard border, I'm going to be arrested. I've told Varadkar that. I think everybody should engage in civil disobedience. I think a border is just a no-no. That's what drove me from the start – I believed the way that the Irish government was going, we would end up with a hard border. By clinging to the EU as tightly as they were, they were creating no give for themselves whatsoever. If the EU wanted this to happen, then we were going to do it.

If you had a choice between a hard border on the one hand and customs regulations between Ireland and France on the other, I'll take customs regulations between Ireland and France any day. It's just too destabilising to have a border.

I wouldn't have a border between Northern Ireland and Britain because it's exactly the same as a border between the North and the South of Ireland: I think it breaches the GFA. I believe in the GFA. That's why I spent so much time there. I believe in parity of esteem. I'm quite prepared to hope, if not believe, that our government would have concern with the welfare of both communities. We're nationalists and our people are the nationalist people – my own flesh and blood are there. But I am not prepared to ignore the other side of the community, because I think there was too much of that in the past from London.

Business is not going to decide. I always used to say to staff that if you ran a poll now in Northern Ireland asking 'Would you be prepared to be detached from the UK market?' I think you'd lose. The anti-Brexit vote in North Down was enough to tell you that. They're not going to vote to put a barrier between themselves and Britain.

I think that if we had fought our case and been much more Eurosceptical, we would have got a much better deal. By being so obsequious to Brussels, we have no policy. They're exactly the same people who used to ingratiate themselves with Dublin Castle. It is the same fucking fawning. The only argument I hear is 'Ah, but sure the Irish can't govern themselves.' Sorry – my ancestors fought against that and I'm not going back to it. James Connolly [an executed leader of the Easter Rising 1916] said, 'We serve neither King nor Kaiser.' [Resisting the call to join in the Great War, Connolly had a large banner with these words draped across Liberty Hall, Dublin.] The problem at the moment is we're serving the Kaiser, and we shouldn't.

Remember, 60% of exports from Northern Ireland go to Britain; 15% go to Ireland – so Britain is much more important.

I think in the end we'll get a fudge. You know, we haven't even started talking about the future relationship. I really think Brexiteers and Remainers should have held their noses and accepted it. Because once Britain leaves the EU, the whole psychology changes. All the hangers-on, the whole EU industry that has such a vested interest … A former unionist politician once said, 'If you get two terms in the European Parliament you're made for life.' If there's no more incentive for politicians to do things like that, all the hangers-on will be gone. It's all being paid for by the Irish and British taxpayers. People sometimes think there's money coming from Europe. Europe only gets its money from the member states, and we, luckily enough, for a long period got more in. Now we're paying more out than we get in. There's no such thing as free EU money.

I think all this has a corrupting effect. For example, we don't have the Central Bank any more. It's called the Central Bank [of Ireland] but its primary role is to be a branch office for Frankfurt. Unlike the American Fed [Federal Bank], the only role of the ECB is to maintain price stability and defend the euro. The Americans give a second role to their central bank, and that is to promote sustainable employment. We don't give that. The head of the central bank in America can be called in front of Congress and asked questions. That can't be done in Ireland. Nobody can call in the head of the Central Bank. So who do they answer to? I have a huge problem with this. I believe there's no such thing as total independence. There's total responsibility, but there's no such thing as total independence. People have to be answerable to somebody.

The EU, when the UK joined it was 30% of the global economy. After the UK leaves it'll be under 15%, and in the future it'll be down to 10%. There's a world out there. Even the Republic trades more outside the EU than inside. Nearly 90% of our exports are now by multi-nationals, and the bulk of that is to America. In the Republic we are essentially an offshore economic unit, and that's why we in a sense escaped from the recession – unlike France and Germany, or Spain, or Portugal, which barely grew. We had a recession, but we got out of it because we had the United States, which was much more buoyant.

North America is a good example for Europe, because North America is booming compared to Europe. The EU has had a very bad run economically, and unless it changes, it's going down further and further. There are a lot of economists who say that in the long run the UK would be better off outside the EU. If you're building a small machine in Bolton and you're sending it over to Rotherham, you have to fulfil EU requirements. But if you're out of the EU, you don't have to. Many EU regulations are irrelevant and costly to local trade, but the EU demands uniformity right across the twenty-eight countries. The prediction is that Brexit will give these small firms a big boost.

Why was the Catholic Church adhered to by 95% of people when terrible things were going on? Why did we walk straight into a banking crisis? We have a very poor record of having a contrarian point of view on the most obvious things. *The Irish Times* interviewed me and the reporter said, 'You make perfect sense, but you know I can't print this.' I said, 'Why?' 'We have an editorial policy.' If you're giving an answer on the TV, it's very quickly, 'Oh, let's go over here.' There's a conformity in the Republic. I don't know why we have developed like this. I don't want to put it down to our old Catholic past, but we don't have anything like enough people questioning stuff all the time. I worked in the public service and a boss of mine said, 'Ray, I know your views, but keep quiet – they'll be career-threatening.'

All the politicians knew I was like this. They'd say, 'You can't say that!' And I'd say, 'You can and you should.' We don't seem to have this ability to disagree. One of my aims is to set up a think tank which would produce different views from the norm. And not paid for by the government. If you look at who is producing things now, they're all getting government grants. Or they have all the government departments or corporate bodies as members. So they're not going to say things that are against them.

The Department of the Taoiseach and the Department of Foreign Affairs are very alike – virtually everyone who's been in the Taoiseach's department has been in Foreign Affairs and vice versa. I meet them socially and I say, 'We're going to help the British get a decent Brexit.' The reaction was the classic EU one – We're going to try to reverse this. We're not really going to accept a negative result from the public.' So I was annoyed about it; I actually wrote an article, and it was a cathartic experience. And I said to a friend of mine who's a journalist, 'Would you read this?' Then I spoke to an editor, and he said, 'I think this is really important and that it should get out.' So I contacted my department and I said, 'Listen guys, nothing personal on this.' And I got a text back saying, 'In future, do not use the term "former ambassador".' And I said, 'I never used that term in my life!' But from then on I was a pariah. I was amazed. I said, 'Why are you so afraid of contrary views?'

I remember when we were dealing in the North, I used to go into the Felons Club [a republican club] and have these ding-dong battles about the efficacy of the armed struggle. I used to enjoy them, because you'd learn a bit from them. You don't learn from people who agree with you. I say, 'I don't agree with you, but do accept that that's a reasonable point.'

They also took a very strong objection when I said the problem with the Irish public service, both elected and professional, is that they suffer from huge groupthink; once the mantra is laid down, they do it. I think that has its strengths, but it has its weaknesses. A few people were very upset with my calling them groupthink. I used to call it the echo chamber.

The EU states unambiguously that the aim is full political union. I don't agree with that. I think it's very dangerous to sell our independence in this way. I believe we should have very good, close economic relations. Iceland has that. Iceland has full access to the European market. I don't have a problem with that. I just don't like this idea that if we're going to have an argument about how we pay for our water, the EU says you can't do this. Or that Frances Black [Seanad member] puts a bill through the Seanad that she wants not to import materials from Israeli settlements in the occupied territories, and the EU says no. I also don't want the EU to say that if we have a recession, we can't spend money on social welfare.

I just can't understand why we're not more critical. Big business loves the EU – absolutely loves it. As for workers' rights, there are workers' rights all over the world. We don't depend on the EU for workers' rights. Even on the social side –

the EU, apart from equal pay for equal work, doesn't really get into that area. In fact it is very heavily into liberal economics. They press Macron to 'reform' the labour market. 'Reform the labour market' really means 'impoverish workers more'. But it doesn't have any effect on France's economy, which continues to sink. The fact that France is tied into the euro is much more damaging to France than the fact that they take off an extra day a year.

I was talking to Michael Noonan [former Irish finance minister], and he was talking about the International Monetary Fund (IMF) and all these people who had done business administration or whatever in Harvard. You've got to deregulate the taxi market in Athlone because these people have a particular fetish for it. It's got nothing to do with the macroeconomics. They have some idiotic things they get into and none of them has ever run a country.

I can see a massive growth in resistance to the EU, and my worry in Ireland is, because we've had all this almost snow job about the EU, about how good it is, that we'll do like we did with the Church – we'll have a massive turnaround. Wouldn't we be much better off being critical and being in it?

We're probably now the most pro-Brussels government – apart from Macron, who at this point is a seriously diminished figure.

I don't think we'll have a hard border. I don't believe it's politically possible – the eruptions are so great. And I'm not talking about the dissidents, I'm talking about the average person. The dissidents can always be contained. I think we should be looking for exemptions. They should go back to

Brussels and say, 'It's not physically possible to put a border there.' And I'd call on everyone, short of violence – and probably staying within the law – to resist that. It's just not acceptable. Not having a border is more important than ingratiating yourself with Brussels.

13

JIM SHARKEY

14 MARCH 2019

Jim Sharkey was born in Derry in 1945 and educated at St
Columb's College and University College Dublin. He met his
wife, Sattie, who is originally from India, while studying Russian
history at Birmingham University. After teaching in Derry and
Dublin, Jim joined the Irish Department of Foreign Affairs. He
served as political counsellor in the Irish Embassy in Washington at the end of the Carter administration and during President Reagan's first term (1980–85). He was appointed Irish
ambassador to Australia in 1987 and subsequently served as
ambassador in Japan, Scandinavia, Russia, Switzerland and
the Council of Europe.

There were customs posts at the border when I was a kid, but
I was never really aware of the border as a frontier. Fifty per
cent of people in Derry had relatives in Donegal, and I always
thought that Derry and Donegal, and particularly Derry and
Inishowen, were umbilically connected. Like love and marriage, you can't have one without the other. If you biked, if you
walked, if you went on the bus – there weren't many had cars in
those days – you weren't really aware of the border at all.

In the days when you eventually could afford a car, you
had to go through a ritual of having an export licence stamped
somewhere down along the quay in Derry, and then you had

to have the book stamped every time you crossed through the Southern customs post. There was a certain inconvenience but nobody ever took it very seriously. (The customs officers with their peaked caps and their uniforms and their braid: that in itself was an incentive to outwit the system.)

In my own time fags and alcohol were cheaper in the South. But during the Second World War, tobacco and tea were scarce there. Which is why my mother's name will always be sung with praise in her part of the world – North Inishowen – because there would be plenty of tobacco (War Horse Plug) for the pipes and there'd be good strong cups of tay when she was visiting her home place.

When I was a kid at St Columb's College, we used to give Christmas presents to the teachers – twenty fags or so. The cigarettes were cheaper over the border in what we used to call the Free State. So you would head on the bike to the shop in Bridgend beside the border and get the loot there. The trick was to get a free class from the teacher once you presented the packet of fags.

A very important agreement was the 1965 Anglo-Irish Free Trade Agreement. At the time of that agreement, the Northern customs men went effectively off the radar screen. But the Southern customs remained open because there were certain items, above all agricultural products – not least, butter – which had resonance in the South and kept the customs officers busy. So they would sometimes stop you and occasionally even ask you to open your boot. But again, although it caused me a certain trepidation, my mother relished the thought of getting the odd pound of butter across undetected. Old habits die hard.

What was most important in those days was that the border did not present itself as a barrier to the intimacy we shared and the deep connections we had with Donegal. Before the Troubles, the unapproved roads were not staffed at all. By and large, you could find a hundred ways of travelling from North to South, and it just never had the feeling of a political frontier.

Of course, during the summer months, thousands of Derry people escaped to the real capital city, which was Buncrana – that was their summer spa. And there would be queues 'miles long' at the bottom of Great James' Street to get on the bus for Buncrana.

The militarisation of the border was progressive from 1969 onwards. One of my recurring nightmares – and the thought of a return to this fills me with dread – was travelling through the Aughnacloy checkpoint at night. My kids remember it well: the tension as we approached the checkpoint, the shrill loud-speaker orders, the blinding searchlights, the blackened faces of the soldiers and the big heavy guns pointed at both parents and kids. And if it was the wrong night, and the UDR were on a high, there was the odd sectarian taunt and so on. The return to that is really unthinkable.

For ordinary, decent citizens from North and South alike, the humiliation and sense of intimidation which were part and parcel of the experience were something we learned to endure and even assimilate. But young fellas, for example, from GAA communities, travelling on Sundays to matches across the bor-der, could find these checkpoints a point of provocation and even harassment, depending on who was in charge on the day.

That could help to reinforce the sense of division and alienation on which the IRA fed.

For nationalists the border post was often a humiliation. But for unionists there was naturally an embrace of the whole security apparatus – the RUC, the B-Specials, the British army, the UDR – because they were defending 'Ulster'. They were the guardians of the system. That dichotomy in perspective was part of the fundamental division within Northern Ireland. So we must be very careful in moving towards Brexit – that that sort of dichotomous dilemma should never arise again.

There was undoubtedly a direct relationship between the intensity of surveillance at the border, the level of IRA activity and the level of perceived IRA cross-border engagement. The militarisation of the border was certainly not without cause. However, that doesn't quite explain the alienation of decent, everyday nationalists from the security system, or the sense of separateness they felt going through one of these highly militarised checkpoints.

It was often part of the unionist analysis of the Troubles that in some way the South was a place of refuge and shelter for Provisional IRA men. I noticed while I was in Washington that senior political figures from Britain would sometimes make the same argument. There is no question that successive Irish governments were affronted by this argument and anxious to rebut it. They reminded observers that the IRA also presented a threat to the Republic, to its constitutionality and its stability; that the bulk of IRA activity was generated from within Northern Ireland; and that the border was a huge, rambling, porous border – as we now see from the Brexit debate – which was nearly impossible to police completely. Insofar as it could be policed, the Irish government was finding every possible opportunity to do so and to cooperate with the Northern authorities on a police-to-police basis.

I was ambassador to Australia and had a senior position in the Irish embassy in the United States. Because of the diaspora component of those two relationships, their approach to the Troubles was obviously different from that which I encountered in Asia and Europe. I would have to say that, by and large, there was a poor understanding internationally of the Northern problem and that it was frequently perceived in largely sectarian terms. Indeed, one of the frustrating and even annoying things for me was that the British commonly presented the problem as one between two warring tribes, with their good offices imposed in between, doing their best as neutral arbiters to keep the two sides apart. On our side, of course, we would have seen the British role in Northern Ireland, historically and contemporaneously, as part of the complex of problems which had to be addressed in the search for peace. And, importantly, that recognition underlay the tripartite approach to a solution which John Hume emphasised and which found effect in the GFA.

I would have to add that, internationally, even where there was misunderstanding or simplification in relation to Northern Ireland, I often encountered a sympathetic approach to the perspective of Dublin and to the nationalist position more generally. Unfortunately, throughout the Troubles, unionists lacked a major figure who could properly express their concerns, priorities and historical viewpoint – with the exception of the Rev. Dr Paisley [unionist politician and Protestant religious leader], albeit in his less persuasive, pre-reconciliation days. Northern nationalists had government figures from the South who could defend their position, and above all there was the compelling presence of John Hume, who was an influential figure in the US and within the EU.

One of the highlights in my diplomatic career was when I was based in the Irish Embassy in Washington, at the end of the Carter period and during the first Reagan term. It was in this period that a bipartisan congressional group called the Friends of Ireland was established, which emphasised the politics of peace and reconciliation as essential for creating a new Ireland. They made every effort – not always understood – to reach out to unionism. They naturally took an interest in the human rights abuses of the security forces and made comparisons based on their experience of the civil rights campaign in the Southern states. That domestic US perspective was arguably to the disadvantage of the British and the unionist case. But they did make a point of reaching out and showing goodwill. They received unionist delegations in Washington, and when they went to Belfast they engaged in a very broad-based round of discussions involving all sides, with the exception of Sinn Féin and the IRA, who they wouldn't talk to in those days because of their espousal of violence.

One of the reasons why – despite all of that openness, which carried into the Clinton administration, including the use of the White House as a point of contact for dialogue and new thinking – the unionists remained suspicious of the Friends of Ireland is that the British press, the tabloids in particular, on and around St Patrick's Day, would launch ferocious attacks against the Irish-American leadership. Simply put, they could not tolerate any interference by Irish-Americans in Northern Irish affairs. There was always a nervousness on the British side – and this arose with the foundation of the Friends of Ireland and during the early Clinton period – that an American engagement on behalf of peace in Ireland would tilt dramatically towards the nationalist side. The Americans went out of their way to try to soothe that concern, and were light-fingered and sensitive, but frequently, because of the countervailing sensitivity of the British establishment in rejecting any outside interference in their management of Northern Ireland, the message got obfuscated, and unionists may have been inclined to believe what the tabloids said rather than what the actual story was.

One of the great joys of the peace process for me, and I'm sure for others who travel across the border frequently, was of just driving across, never worrying or knowing where you were apart from the signs for the speed limit – the sense of free-dom, openness and interconnection between North and South. There was an exhilaration, certainly at the beginning, at the absence of any obvious border.

The GFA maintained the constitutional link and the gua-rantees which were so important for unionists. An important reinforcing concession given on the Irish side was the aban-donment by referendum of Articles 2 and 3 of the Irish con-stitution, which, in terms of the historic sense of isolation and of alienation of the Northern minority, had been a point of reassurance. That was a major concession made possible by the GFA – the expectation of power-sharing, the promise of a border that would be demilitarised and open, and the supposition within the new arrangements that there would be room for a full and free expression of Irish identity.

There's another point as well. At the beginning of the Brexit debate, some Brexiteers and unionists made the case that there's nothing concrete written in the GFA about soft borders and EU membership. This is naive and misleading. The truth is that the consensus underlying the GFA was achieved to a large extent because of the benevolent enriching oxygen of common membership of the EU – including the notion that there would be greater North–South cooperation with the support of Brussels, as well as permanent freedom of movement across the border. A future outside of the EU was more or less unthinkable at that time.

For Northern Ireland, I cannot see any advantage whatsoever in Brexit. For the Republic, there are potential minor advantages in relation to investment, but these minor advantages are far and away overwhelmed by the massive disadvantages, politically and economically, which would arise, above all with a hard Brexit.

Within the EU, Northern Ireland has the advantage of being free to trade in the UK and free to trade right across Europe. A number of studies carried out by the CBI, a British group called Oxford Research, the Economic and Social Research Institute in the Republic of Ireland and senior civil servants within the Stormont system have analysed the economic effects within Northern Ireland of Brexit, and all have come to the same conclusion: that it would be a very, very heavy burden to bear. Despite the intricate economic interconnection between Northern Ireland and Britain, there is a continuing interdependence in certain key sectors with Europe and the Republic: in agriculture, for example, in beef, in pork, dairy and chicken. Between North and South in recent years, there has been a huge interdependence in the area of infrastructure – in transport, in tourism, in the retail and wholesale sectors – all of which would be upset by a hard Brexit. In the area of investment, Bombardier has reminded us of the deep unease in certain manufacturing areas about the consequences of a sharp breach with the EU and the risk of disinvestment. And that would weigh heavily in areas like East Belfast, which are probably pro-Brexit.

Just as you cannot disassociate the referendum outcome in Northern Ireland from the political preference of the individual who voted, you cannot disassociate it from the historic background of inter-community division and the constant need to build consensus and reconciliation. In my opinion, in the light of the collapse of Stormont and the need to restructure consensus, the DUP lost a major opportunity to reach out to the nationalist community, who by and large are pro-European, and to reach out to other Europhile components of society in Northern Ireland, and to try to reflect their concerns more wholeheartedly and consistently in Westminster. The choice was there to act as a bridge on behalf of this middle position, given the special political and economic requirements of Northern Ireland, and ensure that moderate policies would prevail in Westminster. Instead, for reasons which we can debate endlessly, they chose to follow a hard Brexit line and to give comfort to the extreme elements within the British Conservative Party who are seeking the hardest possible Brexit and the most damaging for both North and South.

I am afraid that in the absence of institutional consensus in Northern Ireland, political unionism as a whole seems to have rowed in behind something like the absolutist DUP position on Europe, at least in arguing that Brexit must go ahead because the UK as a whole has so decided, irrespective of the Northern Irish interest. In the context of the heightened division and uncertainty which now exists, in a general election in Northern Ireland there is always the danger of people voting along sectarian lines, notwithstanding the more subtle voting patterns of the referendum in the North.

I believe that a consequence of DUP absolutism in the Brexit debate is a further alienation of the nationalist community. The more the nationalist community feel discommoded within Northern Ireland and believe that the GFA has been undermined and that their Irish identity and connections with the South are constrained, the more the question of another alternative – of Irish unity – arises. At the same time, we should be very careful not to confuse support for membership of the EU within the unionist community as support for Irish unity. The more you push and squeeze on the question of Irish unity, the more the tendency is for the traditional unionist community to circle their wagons.

There is no question in my mind that if the GFA breaks down in a more or less permanent way, middle-class nationalists, who are well-disposed but cautious on the question of Irish unity, will begin to shift position and opt for an all-Ireland solution. Whether a new focus on some form of unity can attract a significant unionist component remains to be seen. Personally, I would love to see new structures in Ireland within which unionists and nationalists could cooperate and express their identity and values, but my main point is that any such debate must begin carefully. It would be good if someone with the experience of Bertie Ahern on the nationalist side and, were it ever possible, somebody of the stature of Peter Robinson [former first minister and former leader of the DUP] on the unionist side, free of any preconceptions, were to begin a debate as to what a new Ireland would look like.

Even if unionists at election time operate as a largely singular community, with the union as the centrepiece of all their concerns, there is no doubt that in parallel there has been a more subtle evolution of society in Northern Ireland due to the GFA. This is reflected in the new complexities of the Brexit referendum vote and the cross-community nature of the pro-European lobby. Young people are certainly an intriguing factor in the mix and are under-represented in Northern Irish politics. There seems to be no party that has succeeded in mobilising the post-GFA enthusiasm of young Northern Irish people for change and modernisation. There is a challenge there for someone. It is also the case that certain larger interests in Northern Ireland – non-political, historically unionist but above all business-centred lobbies – are very nervous of Brexit and its long-term consequences.

So in that context, sensitively but very comprehensively, the question of what a new Ireland might look like should begin to be debated. Arguably the South is not ready for this question either, and there is a persistent partitionist residue in some Southern voices. The Republic will clearly have to make major accommodations if it is to attract traditional unionists into a united Ireland.

The principle of consent is quite clear – it is a majority of people in Northern Ireland who will decide. But common sense must also prevail. Above all, that would be the dominant reflex in Southern Ireland. There is no one in the South that I can think of who wants to coerce a reluctant minority in Northern Ireland – in East Belfast and Larne and Ballymena – into a united Ireland, kicking and screaming.

So, ultimately, we are talking about beginning a period of reflection and looking ahead over an extended period to a time when a new Ireland is not seen as a hostile threat. How long? A decade or so.

I believe that, for the border counties, partition was a disaster. The city of Derry has never properly recovered from partition. Donegal has suffered from the breach of its economic link with its Derry hinterland and Derry as its natural capital. The same is true in areas like Strabane/Lifford, Newry/Dundalk and Enniskillen/Cavan. It is undoubtedly the case that Northern industry initially prospered by its wholehearted connection with Britain. However, no one could have foreseen in 1921 the post-war pressures facing Northern industry, including the shirt industry in Derry and the shipbuilding and engineering industries in Belfast, through first the cheap labour pressures of the Commonwealth connection and later the globalisation of international trade. If anything, sensitive industries like these have got additional safeguards from membership of the EU which, for example, in the steel and manufacturing areas, has protected European producers against excessive dumping.

I am certainly concerned about the next five years. I wouldn't define it in terms of optimism or pessimism. I would prefer to think of it in terms of a challenge which exists – and it's a mighty challenge. It requires a sustained and unrelenting effort by the Irish and British governments, paradoxically together with the institutions of the EU, to counter all of the negative effects of the Brexit process. And I think they will have to do this also with the goodwill, encouragement and, at times, necessary intervention of the US.

More generally, of course, Euro-scepticism has become much more respectable in Italy and in Central and Eastern Europe. Unlike the UK, the balance of advantage for these countries, at least in the medium term, will remain with membership of the EU. However, it will make for more awkward and fractious decision-making in Brussels.

We can expect the integrationist interests in Brussels and elsewhere to respond to all of this by proposing greater centralisation and deeper integration. A sign of this can be seen in a recent speech by France's President Macron. Hopefully, common sense and a longer view of history will prevail – there is already some evidence of this from Germany, where the impossibility of strait-jacketing reluctant Eastern Europeans appears to be recognised. What we need is the emergence of an EU which is more accommodating of national differences, sensitivities and priorities, while retaining its core commitment to democracy, human rights and economic progress.

In the absence of the UK, I believe the EU must be seen more and more to distinguish its external priorities from those of NATO, which is increasingly obsessed with the Russian threat, far beyond Moscow's political and conventional military capabilities. The real danger is of an unexpected, accidental nuclear confrontation, something we thought we had left well behind us. So, more than ever, it is essential that the EU begins to act – as it often did during the Cold War – as a bridge between Russia and the US, and to try to moderate and reduce their competition.

It's important to keep this global backdrop in mind as we try to come to terms with Brexit's effect on the UK and Ireland.

14

DIARMAID FERRITER

22 MARCH 2019

Diarmaid Ferriter is Professor of Modern History at University College Dublin (UCD), a position to which he was appointed at the age of thirty-four. He is the author of many books, including the acclaimed biography of Éamon de Valera, *Judging Dev. The Transformation of Ireland 1900–2000,* and *Occasions of Sin: Sex and Society in Modern Ireland* (2009). He is a regular contributor to radio and television, hosting the RTÉ radio programme *What If* from 2003 to 2009 and the RTÉ programme *History Show* from 2009 to 2011. He is a weekly columnist with *The Irish Times.*

I was born just after Bloody Sunday. My father was on the march in Dublin that ended with the burning of the British Embassy, and he wouldn't let my mother go – something she was very annoyed about at the time – because she was eight months pregnant, with me. And I was born on the day of the Aldershot bomb – that's the Ireland I was born into. My mother remembers the atmosphere of the time and, as she said herself, it was a terrible time to be bringing a child into the world. If that was the feeling there was in Dublin, you can just imagine what it was like in Belfast.

There was in the South what I would now term a transient empathy, and sometimes it could be vehement. At times of heightened tensions, like Bloody Sunday or the hunger strikes, there was a strong sense of solidarity with the nationalist community in the North. But as I discovered later on, there was also a determination that those Troubles should not be allowed to spill beyond the border.

We tended to see people from north of the border as a strange species. Even when I got to university, there was a handful of Northern students and they did seem different. They would have come to university in Dublin for a variety of different reasons: some of them because they wanted to go somewhere different, some of them because they wanted to get away. And yes, they would have been different from, say, Kerry students, because they were from Northern Ireland, they were from the troubled land. We had a very partitionist mindset.

Partition originally comes from the seventeenth-century plantation of Ireland, when you had social engineering on a massive scale. Coming closer: the pressures that are still present today, in terms of a British government that is looking at its Irish problem and seeking to come up with a temporary solution, were there 100 years ago. Then, the issue was how the British government would respond to Sinn Féin's mandate arising out of the 1918 general election, when it won nearly three-quarters of the seats. Britain wasn't going to recognise a mandate to leave the Empire and establish an Irish Republic. They decided to deal with the Ulster issue first, and that was the real crunch point 100 years ago: can we devise a solution that's based on excluding part of Ireland from any solution? Irish unionism became Ulster unionism – the question was Ulsterised.

Irish unionists never embraced the notion of a new state of Northern Ireland because they didn't trust either side. There's a siege mentality there that's not just relevant to Southern nationalists, it's also relevant to London. Unionists don't trust solutions that are devised in London because they're worried they won't quite be a fully integrated part of the United Kingdom. And they're right to be worried, because what the cabinet was told 100 years ago, when they were proposing these two parliaments for Ireland and the partition of Ireland, was that citizens of Northern Ireland would not be on the same footing as citizens in the rest of the UK, they would be subject to a different regime. But that wasn't made clear to Irish unionists – it was made clear to cabinet.

This is the skulduggery that went on. People like British prime minister David Lloyd George were speaking out of several sides of their mouths. They would tell unionists one thing and nationalists another. There's also a feeling on the part of unionists that they were being dispensed with. Edward Carson articulated that feeling. He said in the House of Commons in December 1919, 'You still want to kick them out as if they were of no use.'[1]

But Carson and the unionists were still prepared to accept this because by choosing the six counties and not the nine counties of Ulster that were on the table at one stage, they guaranteed themselves an in-built two-thirds majority. So they were going to accept that, but that didn't mean they were trusting London. James Craig was still deeply distrustful of Lloyd George during the Treaty negotiations, when Lloyd George was trying to bring him into an all-Ireland solution and he was having none of it. What he was saying was, 'What we have, we hold.' In fact it was Craig who told Éamon de Valera, 'Never trust what David Lloyd George says.'[2] Isn't it interesting, that advice from the first prime minister of Northern Ireland to the president of Sinn Féin is 'Don't trust the Brits'?

Today, in terms of health, a border does not make sense. If you have a heart attack in Donegal, where do you want to end up? Obviously you don't want to end up in Sligo, you need to end up in Derry. In practical terms, it doesn't make any sense to have a border. We all accept the need for urgent medical care at the nearest spot. That makes sense whether you're a unionist or a nationalist. There was always a recognition from the earliest stages that the border was inconvenient for both sides when it came to practicalities.

There have been ongoing, fairly low-key cooperations in economic terms. Again, this was something that was flagged 100 years ago. Lloyd George wrote to Craig in November 1921, 'You're cutting off the natural circuits of commercial activity.' That phrase 'the natural circuits of commercial activity' is also made for today. Because when we talk about a frictionless border, a soft border, with 30,000 people going over it every day, or 110 million car journeys in any year – we're talking about the natural circuits of commercial activity. What we have had in recent years is that all-island economy. It works for everyone.

The DUP's position is riddled with contradictions – as is Theresa May's. Before the referendum May said that she couldn't conceive of an invisible border if the referendum was passed. Straight after the referendum she was talking about the need for a frictionless border. The DUP says it doesn't want a hard border, but it doesn't want to be treated any differently from the rest of the UK. These are all contradictions.

There's a lot of talk about the constitutional integrity of the United Kingdom, its constitutional purity. Which is an absolute nonsense, because Northern Ireland has always been treated differently within the UK because of its particular circumstances. For example, with the partition of Ireland, with what happened 100 years ago, they were looking on Northern Ireland as a different entity. The GFA was formed to cater for a part of the United Kingdom that was different from the rest of the United Kingdom. Even the whole idea of self-determination for Northern Ireland that was agreed during the peace negotiations – that is about Northern Ireland being different. Even when there was the foot-and-mouth crisis, when Ian Paisley was first minister, he started emphasising the clear blue sea between Ireland and Britain. It suited him at that point to make that claim: 'We're different.'

But as to whether that has a knock-on political effect, or whether people can use the economic argument to make a political point: obviously those in favour of a united Ireland were going to try to extend the economic argument into politics – in the sense that if we're going to be talking about the Northern Ireland border and seamless economy, do we not also need to think what this would mean politically? Rather than having a complicated exit and different regimes on the island, should we not be looking at the politics of it?

That's also about recognising demographic change. Because about 100 years ago, where you had a two-thirds unionist majority, we're now all aware that that has been whittled away. So there's a vulnerability there on the part of unionists, which is one of the reasons why the DUP has been bleating so loudly about not being treated differently from the rest of the UK. It feels vulnerable.

But talk of a united Ireland is shallow. I have yet to see anyone who can elaborate, in concrete, convincing terms, on what a united Ireland might look like. At the same time, I said the day after the referendum that it made a united Ireland more likely. Because ultimately the economic logic might develop such a momentum that it could carry over into politics. But it's not something that is going to happen anytime soon.

In relation to traditional fears, I'd be very interested in what a younger generation in Ireland would think of that. Because the old rallying cry was that Home Rule would mean Rome rule – which looks like a joke in the twenty-first century. When you consider the secularisation of the Republic of Ireland and the numerous changes we've had, many of us look on Northern Ireland as a complete backwater when it comes to social issues and attitudes to sexuality and abortion and so on. So it's interesting to look at some of those historic fears and how the ground has shifted considerably.

But I also think there's still a substantial minority in the Republic who don't want Northern Ireland. I think a lot of people have an emotional aspiration to a united Ireland. But if you put it to them in concrete terms, what it might involve, would they be prepared to take the substantial cut in living standards that would be required to replace the British subvention to Northern Ireland? I know the amount of the subvention is contested, but would they be prepared to come up with the shared Ireland that would be needed to cater for the needs of those they regard as completely alien? Some would have great reservations about that.

That brings me back to some of the archival material I've found over the years. At one stage in the early 1970s, Jack Lynch [former Taoiseach] was asked by John Peck, the British ambassador in Dublin, 'What would you do if you were handed Northern Ireland on a plate in the morning?' and Jack Lynch replied, 'I would faint.'

Peck had another conversation with Lynch, again in the early 1970s, and Lynch said that the majority of people in the South couldn't care less about a united Ireland; what they wanted was peace and friendship. I think that sentiment is still there. But there will be those more formally involved in devising political strategies who will see that there's a great opportunity here to pursue a united Ireland. Whether it's through a border poll or whether it's just continuing to build momentum, as is the case with Sinn Féin – building Sinn Féin North and South – they will see this as an opportunity. But again you have to ask yourselves, how do you deal with the very substantial minority who would not want to be in that united Ireland?

We can understand the circumstances of 100 years ago and say that the alternative to partition was civil war. Indeed I believe there would have been civil war, so we have to factor that in. But the real tragedy is that the border is still in existence, when so much has changed in attitudes to borders and to trade and when we've had constant talk of the need for a shared island and recognising our shared history. But we still can't share the island without a border. Even though it's been a soft border for so long.

I think the DUP has backed itself into a corner and is clearly out of step with its own constituency. You can hold the balance of power in Westminster but your time in the sun is going to be fleeting, as the DUP is going to discover. Irish nationalists held the balance of power at a much earlier stage in British politics and managed to get commitments to Home Rule which never became a reality. And there is a sense that the Irish question can be used as a pawn in English politics, and the DUP would be aware of this. But because of the stance it has taken, by insisting Northern Ireland cannot be treated any differently, it has flown in the face of North–South history and Anglo-Irish history, and it's flying in the face of those it's supposed to be representing – as some of its constituents have made clear.

But this still leaves you with a substantial number of union-ists who would be implacably opposed to a united Ireland. We know there's been a spike in applications for Irish passports, and some of those are coming from unionists. Does that mean they want to be part of a united Ireland? No. They're being pragmatic. But it does suggest that they're not averse to holding Irish passports. And if they're not thinking with the passion of their parents' generation, they may well see that being part of a unified Ireland does not have to be threatening to them.

What the GFA does not allow for is for unionists to have a permanent veto over a united Ireland. But if there was a pro-posal for a new Ireland, for a shared Ireland, even allowing for the fact that it would have to involve strongly federal elements, a continued Northern parliament and so on, that would matter. If there were a plan there or a structure that people could vote on, in the knowledge that this is what a proposed new Ireland would look like, then we could say OK, there is a majority in favour of this on both sides of the border, and unionists would have to accept that.

Are they going to remain opposed, as their forefathers did in 1912 and 1913? I don't think so. No matter what solution you come up with, there's always going to be implacable opposition and there's also possibly going to be violence as a result of it. That said, I think the likelihood of that is lessened as a result of the weight of history and the passage of time, and of course the recognition that the violence can only exacerbate all of those divisions.

One of the things I always do with first-year students [at UCD] is ask them how many have been over the border, because they're peace-process babies – they were born after the GFA. It's still striking how few of them have actually gone over the border. If I had, say, a small seminar group of eighteen or twenty, I would say three or four of them would have been. That may be partly because of what they inherited from their parents' generation – a sense that it was a dangerous place or just wasn't part of their travels. Or maybe it's just not a place they have an interest in – it wouldn't have a reputation as a hot destination that they need to travel to. But there's also the lingering sense of it being different, even though it's only ninety miles up the road – that they see it as an alien country. I don't think that's as strong as when I was a child, but it's certainly still there.

However, I'm much more aware of people who'll say, 'Here, we'll go to Belfast, take the kids and go to the Titanic Quarter.' Belfast has some very good restaurants! And then the beauty of the landscape in Northern Ireland – as is the case with the rest of Ireland – people are beginning to see that this is a beautiful island, and that you can be a tourist in Northern Ireland, and that you can get value in Northern Ireland.

Brexit has damaged Anglo-Irish relations hugely – you could even say it has poisoned relations. Now we need perspective. When you consider the really, really low points that were reached in the 1970s in particular, when there was almost a fervid atmosphere and a deep, deep hatred – we're not there. But there has been a return to the lack of trust, the coarseness, the watchfulness and the sense that people cannot be taken at their word – that's very damaging. It takes a long time to build up that sense of trust. I mean, we saw all of the milestones – the peace process, with the visit of the queen the icing on the peace-process cake. But it doesn't take a lot to unravel that, and we have seen an unravelling.

It's also a difficult political challenge for the Republic, in the sense that they're trying to strike a particular tone that's not too aggressive, while trying at the same time to make common cause with Northern nationalists. Wasn't it interesting that Leo Varadkar said, in 2017, 'We will never abandon you Northern nationalists again'? It was a very rare public acknowledgement and an indication that there's an opportunity here to try to think about a different Ireland and a different North–South relationship post-Brexit.

In relation to the damage that Brexit has done to Anglo-

Irish relations, there's also the fact that there are 650 MPs in Westminster. Of those MPs, 108 were there at the time of the GFA. Now that's inevitable with the passage of time, but it is a reminder that those politicians who were at the coalface during that period in the late 1990s are passing on, and there isn't the same sense of urgency on the part of others about protecting that hard-won peace.

The language in the GFA is crystal clear: the British government is required to be rigorously impartial when it comes to Northern Ireland. Obviously that's not the case now, and the way Theresa May has been 'leading' in recent times and the deals that she has been doing with the DUP have completely undermined that idea of impartiality.

No matter what happens in Brexit, that flower of Anglo-Irish relations is a fragile flower that has to be tended to, looked after. Regardless of what happens after Brexit, it's still a hugely important relationship. We have had EU membership and we talk about EU solidarity; but for all of that, that Anglo-Irish nexus, that Anglo-Irish relationship, is still hugely important. We're still going to have the North–South issue to be dealt with as well, which is still going to involve input from London.

In the South there is a lingering partitionist mentality. You can see that manifested in politics as well. More recent presidential elections were very interesting. For example, I interviewed Martin McGuinness [Sinn Féin, former deputy first minister] not long before he died, for a BBC programme on the Anglo-Irish century – it was on the back of the 2016 centenaries – and I was very interested in asking him about his run for president, because obviously Sinn Féin had an all-island political project. I was very interested in remarks he had made about 'down there' and 'up here'. Even the use of those descriptions was very revealing about an irritation he felt that 'You don't understand.' That presidential campaign had not gone as well as Sinn Féin had hoped. Later on, Mary Lou McDonald put her own revisionist gloss on it – that it was about the mean streets of Derry meeting the affluent Dublin 4 brigade. There's the semblance of something in that, but it's a complete simplification. The most contentious moment during McGuinness' campaign was when he was confronted in Athlone by the son of a victim of the IRA. That wasn't about Dublin 4, it was about something else.

But going back further to the Mary McAleese election in 1997 [in which she was elected Taoiseach] – that was fervid and quite vicious. There was resentment of someone who was seen as an upwardly mobile Northern Gael, but perhaps the salving of guilty consciences in the South about what was regarded as their historic failure to engage more.

So in relation to education, to culture, to dialogue, I think the irony is that we've become so preoccupied with emphasising the need for dialogue between both sides in Northern Ireland that we often forget about the need for dialogue between South and North, as if it's their problem and not our problem. Which is why I find amusing some of the newfound empathy that's been articulated – even when Mark Durkan, who had been in the SDLP, recently declared that he was going to stand for Fine Gael in the European elections in Dublin to represent Derry. He was criticised by some in the Labour Party and responded by saying that they were 'borderist' in their attitudes. Of course Durkan could just as easily have ended up standing for Fianna Fáil if that had been arranged first, but those tensions are still there.

Looking at the cross-border bodies, there's an element of tokenism: they're there on paper, but in practice they're really not going to be attended to. We have attempted to do more with Universities Ireland, an all-island entity that was established originally under the impetus of Andy Pollak with the Centre for Cross-border Studies. We got involved as academics in committing ourselves to organising an annual conference to mark the particular year in the Decade of Commemorations [the years 1912–22 contained many major events in twentieth-century Irish history, including the Ulster Covenant, Easter 1916, the Civil War and the partition of Ireland]. It's done North and South – we've done it in Belfast, we've done it in Dublin. That's just an example of a framework that can work, because you're recognising that this is an all-island conversation about our collective past, and that's very constructive. But you have to make it happen. And you have to organise those conferences, you have to bring all of these people together and you have to move it around. It's quite a small thing in overall terms, but I think there's a framework and a model there that could be used in a wider sense within education.

We have to remind ourselves that there are very compelling reasons for the UK leaving the EU. One of the things I wanted to do in the run-up to the referendum, and after, was to try to explain why the UK, emotionally as well as politically, could no longer, it seemed, be a member of the EU. One of the first university courses I did with the late, great Albert

Lovett was a history of European integration, and he often emphasised the degree to which the UK had always been an awkward partner of the EEC (as it was then) and it only came in in the 1970s because it had to – it had no other option. Its alternatives had failed. So we need to be conscious of that history, and of the long decline of Britain's status, the long decline of Britain's empire and its struggle to find a place for itself. There's no point in us completely dismissing Britain for being ignorant Little Englanders who in a nationalist fit decided to cut off their nose – it's much more complicated than that. So we should start by recognising the complexity of British history as well as recognising our own complex history and those historical legacies to be attended to.

But you can see a growing irritation in Ireland with the way that this has been handled, and it has been an appalling failure of leadership and politics. You can also see that we are becoming very snobbish and contemptuous in how we regard the Brexiteers. That's understandable when some of the most public faces of the Brexiteers are the likes of Jacob Rees-Mogg, Boris Johnson and others, but we have to get beyond that. To go back to the point about the fragile flower: there's still going to be a need for attention to that.

So what does history tell us? Not to catastrophise. We have to know from history that what appears to be solidarity doesn't always last. We've constantly heard about EU solidarity around the backstop. But will that last? Isn't it interesting that Angela Merkel [chancellor of Germany] has called for creative solutions to the backstop dilemma? That suggests that there still could be some alteration to what is being proposed.

And people do adapt to changed circumstances. Things can change and pressures can build. It's not that long since we were very angry with Europe for holding a gun to our head when it came to the economic crash – you cannot allow a European bank to fold or contagion to spread. We were very harshly treated then and were reminded that we were small fry within the EU.

Now solidarity from the EU has lasted to a degree. But the lesson from history is that that solidarity won't necessarily continue to last and we have to be conscious of that.

The other lesson from history is that Northern Ireland has to be treated differently. And that, of course, flies in the face of what the DUP has been asserting, but then the DUP's position has been flying in the face of the realities of history – including a history that it has benefited from, you could argue, because it got itself into a position where it was able to lead a devolved administration. Because Northern Ireland came to this particular solution through the peace process that it benefited from. So the lesson of history is that Northern Ireland is treated differently and there are numerous examples you could give of that. Even when the Anglo-Irish free trade agreement in the mid-1960s was being negotiated, it was accepted that free trade could begin first between the North and the South of Ireland before it applied to the rest of the UK. The British government didn't have any problem with that. And the British government had frequently maintained, in private at least, that that made sense for those arrangements between North and South, even though it didn't necessarily fit with the rest of the UK.

Another lesson from history is, be careful about how you frame your aspirations. I think there's a consciousness of this, at different political levels. You can see in my book *The Border* the ease with which the Southern political establishment could articulate its desire for partition to be ended. De Valera often insisted that Britain had imposed partition and therefore Britain had to undo partition. History tells us, of course, that it's never as simple as that. Partition was born with plenty of assistance from Irish midwives, so we need to be careful about how that's approached. Going back to the point I made about the need to come up with some template for a shared Ireland: we should begin that discussion. Don't keep using the phrase 'a united Ireland' without anything behind it.

Again, to go back to 100 years ago, I think the real lesson is, don't create new boundaries that are going to be contested, don't resurrect hard borders that are going to attract violence – and that's not scaremongering. The border always attracted violence when it was hard. Smuggling was always an issue, and smugglers are always one step ahead of technology.

So you can highlight all sorts of lessons from history. But unfortunately what we also know is that lessons from history are rarely learned.

In the long run you may well look back at Brexit as a turning point that facilitated a united Ireland – I do believe that. But we shouldn't assume either that all nationalists in Northern Ireland want a united Ireland. There have been a plethora of opinion polls, sometimes with very conflicting results depending on where they're coming from, about attitudes. Some nationalists may well have very valid reasons for wanting to have very little to do with the South. So it may well be that Brexit will advance the cause of a united Ireland, but it may in turn create new complications around how that united Ireland is managed, how it's shared and how it's structured. What you would hope is that 100 years on from the creation of partition and the state of Northern Ireland, there is enough recognition of history and enough maturity within the political system, and enough social and demographic change, to ensure that we can actually handle this as a mature democracy – and certainly handle it much better than Britain has handled Brexit.

15

MARK DALY

27 MARCH 2019

Senator Mark Daly was appointed by the Joint Oireachtas Committee on the Implementation of the Good Friday Agreement to compile the first ever report by a Dáil or Seanad committee on the issue of Irish unity, entitled *Brexit and the Future of Ireland: Uniting Ireland and Its People in Peace and Prosperity* (2017). In 2019 he released a report addressing the prevention of a return to violence in advance of a referendum on a united Ireland.

I was brought up in Kerry, but all you had to do was watch the news every night and you knew the border was the issue. I watched everything from the hunger strikes up to the GFA. The general feeling among people was a sense that the ongoing violence should come to an end and a peace process that would work should be established.

The demilitarised border has transformed things, from where there were only twenty border crossings actually open to 308 or 310 or 200 now open, depending on who's doing the counting. Openness and accessibility transform borders. We've seen that across Europe.

There has been progress in Ireland since 1998. The more people meet, the more interaction they have, the better it is. When you boil it down, all issues relate to people. A small number of individuals can cause a huge amount of trouble, and that's what we're trying to avoid.

I presented my report – *Brexit and the Future of Ireland: Uniting Ireland and Its People in Peace and Prosperity* – to a group of unionist politicians, Church leaders and paramilitary leaders. It was a tough crowd to talk to about the economic benefits. One Church leader said, 'It's not about economics, it's about identity.' I said, 'I understand that, because in the 1950s, as thousands of Irish men and women were getting on boats to go to England, if they had been asked when they were getting on the boat, never to return to live in Ireland other than to visit on holidays, if they were told, "Look, you're going to England, you're working there for the rest of your life, we're having a referendum to rejoin the UK," they would have all voted for Ireland staying independent, even though economically Ireland would have been better off in the UK at that time.' Seán Lemass [then-Taoiseach] and T. K. Whitaker [secretary of the Department of Finance] spoke about that and wrote about that in the 1950s, saying we should actually be looking at rejoining the UK because if we didn't change our economic trajectory we were finished. So when we reverse the situation, economics is secondary to identity in both jurisdictions.

Today you have Catholics in the North in favour of staying in the UK because the perception is that economically they're better off. But there's a cohort in the middle ground for whom economics trumps identity. And it is that middle ground – of the overall population, about 25–30% – who will decide the future of Northern Ireland and where it's going to be, and that's where the economic argument is made. For some in both communities, economics plays no part in their decision-making.

Brexit has changed the entire debate, and it has changed it in a way that raises the question: 'Is Northern Ireland's best future in the UK, or is its best future in the EU?' Quite clearly economically it is better off in the EU, and the UK's future would be better off in the EU. But the only crowd who has the opportunity to stay in the EU is Northern Ireland.

Attorney-General [Rory] Brady says that achieving a united Ireland is not a constitutional aim or objective, it's an imperative. It's an objective which the government must work to achieve. But the government isn't doing that. There is a court case being taken against them as to where their policy is, because they don't have a policy. Attorney-General Brady said that Articles 2 and 3 [of the Irish constitution – these articles originally said that all of the island of Ireland was a single national territory] make the achievement of a united Ireland a constitutional imperative. Articles 2 and 3 were not removed with the signing of the GFA – they were changed. They were amended to make it clear that a united Ireland could only come by consent.

But there are still no signs of this being acted on. The government has a long way to go between statements and reality. It hasn't produced a policy on it. Nor has Fianna Fáil.

The cross-border bodies established by the GFA have made little headway. Peace isn't an event, it's a process. Those particular bodies need to have somebody on the other side. There is the absence of Stormont and the absence of political will by the British government as well as the Irish government. That political will should be there and the governments should be working continuously.

Things like the Language Act were part of the St Andrew's Agreement but haven't been implemented. I was on the Implementation of the Good Friday Agreement committee. I asked for a report by the Department of Foreign Affairs on what is left to be implemented. The fact is they won't do it. They won't do the report.

My report's core recommendations? The need for government engagement. A 'new Ireland' forum would have to be established to set the pathway forward. Because if you have a constitutional imperative of achieving a united Ireland, you need to have more than just the imperative, you need to be doing it. And the government isn't doing it.

Any referendum on the border shouldn't happen until all the issues are debated: white papers and green papers and citizens' assemblies; you engage with everyone, you appear on committees. The groundwork is considerable and it needs to be done well in advance.

Every stakeholder should be represented: from farmers to tourism, from the army to the police, there's no government department that wouldn't be affected by this. The issue of Brexit has tipped things away from the belief that Northern Ireland is better off economically in the UK. Brexit has reversed that, so that people in the unionist community are thinking, 'Well, maybe we're not better off in the UK.' That's the middle ground who are weighing things up, which is about 25–30%. And that is made up of 15% from one side and 15% from the other.

There's a range of unionism that has forty shades of orange, just as we have forty shades of green. Within the DUP there are people like Peter Robinson, who said, 'I don't believe they'll vote for Irish unity but I think we should prepare for it.' Lady Sylvia Hermon has said there'll be a referendum in her lifetime because of Brexit. And I've met unionists who, off the record, will say there's going to be a united Ireland and we need to negotiate our place in it. I'm speaking of members of political parties, party voters, party activists, members of the public. I've met them in Belfast, Ballymena, all over. They're there, but there is no one view.

In the last 100 years, Northern Ireland has gone into reverse. At one point Belfast and the three counties around it were producing 80% of the whole island's GDP. Now the South is producing fifteen times as much and has two-and-a-half times the population. Nobody in unionism has been able to articulate how Northern Ireland is going to be better off in five, ten, fifteen, fifty years' time.

They point out that the UK is the sixth largest economy in the world. Britain is; Northern Ireland is not; it just happens to be a part of the UK. It's like saying the Shetland Islands are the sixth biggest economy in the world. But they're not; they're part of it.

I asked the library here [in Leinster House] to try to figure out where Northern Ireland stands as its own entity, in terms of the UN Human Development index, in terms of health, education and income. So the Republic is sixth in the world; Northern Ireland in health, education and income is ranked forty-fourth in the world. The UK is sixteenth.

There's no doubt that we would like the North's health service, but we wouldn't like the education attainment in the unionist community. The unionist community and parts of the nationalist community: of the ten poorest regions in Northern Europe, nine are in the UK, and Northern Ireland is one of them. Then how in the world can anyone say, 'We're the sixth largest economy'? Yes, you are, but you're not benefiting.

It's about identity – 'the deep heart's core' as Yeats put it. Some unionists are not going to vote for a united Ireland, in the same way as some nationalists would never vote to stay in the UK. It's the people in the middle. They are the ones who decide the future, not the people at the extremes. They've their minds made up no matter what.

The people who are doing most for a united Ireland are Arlene Foster and the DUP. If they had respected language and culture, then people in the Malone Road, Catholics, would have voted for the status quo. But the DUP is not playing a very intelligent game. If it wants to sustain Northern Ireland into the future, it needs to win over the middle ground. But it's doing the opposite. It's alienating the middle ground. If you were to do a business analogy, you would say that unionism as a business is going out of business, because it's losing customers, and the next census will show that. So what do you do? You have to win new customers. How do you do that? You must ask yourself what they want. Identity issues are very important, so if you respect identity and language and culture, then you've some chance of winning over customers.

I've carried out polling here in the South, and it has been consistent that between 60 and 80%, depending on how you frame the question and how you allocate the undecided, will vote in favour of a united Ireland. That's constant.

The lesson of the Brexit referendum and any other referendum is that it's a contest of ideas. Who has the best ideas, the best vision for the future? In High Court Justice Richard Humphreys' book *Countdown to Unity*, which was published long before Brexit, he talks about a 'political status quo-ism' in the South, an inertia in the system here where everyone says, 'Don't talk about it.' That's pervasive and it still exists. But the general public, they are the ones in favour of a united Ireland. You just ask them the question and they go 'Yeah!' If you're given a choice between ending partition, the main aim of the state, and continuing it, and you're faced with a ballot paper, you could assume that they would probably vote for ending it. But before that all the steps need to be taken, and there are a lot of steps required.

On a smaller scale, there is a problem within the political system here. The government and the civil service are just petrified of upsetting Britain, of upsetting unionists. I was on the government's Decade of Commemorations committee. On the committee at one stage they were suggesting (this was floated to me by one of the civil servants) that they were going to bring over regiments from the EU army to participate in the Easter parade. And I said, 'All right. Would that be every EU army?' 'All of them, yes.' 'Including the British one?' 'Yes.' 'Well,' I said, 'that's not the worst idea I've ever heard but it's very close. If you wanted a live re-enactment [of the Easter Rising] that would be the way to go about it. That's a really bad idea. Because bear in mind,' I said, 'Britain doesn't care about us commemorating Easter 1916, it's our day.' Then they were for bringing over the queen, and that eventually got stopped as well. But they were more concerned about not offending Britain than they were about commemorating the aims and objectives of 1916.

The same mentality is now here. Bear in mind, at one point there was no clarity as to whether there was going to be an Easter parade commemorating 100 years since 1916, but for that parade 1 million people turned up. So while the civil servants and the entire government were paralysed with fear, there was no plan twelve months ahead. It was a kind of post-colonial stress disorder, not wanting to offend anybody – we don't want to be seen commemorating our independence or the establishment of our republic.

You transfer that attitude into the debate about a united Ireland and you have this inertia, this fear, inside the political system – but in the general public it's different. Are you in favour of a united Ireland? Yeah.

The reason for the inaction on achieving the constitutional imperative of a united Ireland, as High Court Justice Humphreys says, is the fear of kicking the sleeping dog of loyalist paramilitary violence.

But I did a report [*Northern Ireland Returning to Violence Due to a Hard Border as a Result of Brexit or a Rushed Border Poll: Risk to Youth*] with two UNESCO chairs (Professor Pat Dolan and Professor Mark Brennan, along with US diplomat Michael Ortiz). These are experts on the subject of preventing extremist violence. The report makes clear that you need to engage early with the unionists and the loyalists – those most disadvantaged loyalist areas. Make sure those kids aren't radicalised and mobilised by paramilitary leaders and drug dealers for their own ends. But that requires action now. In the run-up to a referendum, it's too late.

With Irish unity, unionism basically would have a permanent say in government. If you ask most of them in the establishment when they think there's going to be a referendum, most of them think it won't be for twenty years or more. If ever. If it's beyond the next election, most people wouldn't look further.

Do you know who runs the government? It's the civil servants who run the government. This is five, ten years of work that's required, and they're not doing it.

First of all you have to understand that there's a referendum coming. They haven't got that far. At some stage there is going to be a referendum. If Lady Sylvia Hermon says there's going to be a referendum on a united Ireland, then there is going to be a referendum on a united Ireland. The problem is, the political system in the South hasn't figured out there's going to be a referendum. The only issue is when. But the lesson of Brexit is that you don't hold a referendum and then try to figure out what the future looks like.

I saw an article recently saying to a politician, 'You do realise if there's a united Ireland, unionists will have a big say in government all the time.' They hadn't figured it out. That includes all parties here. The fact is, unionism would be in power more than Sinn Féin. In order to be in government, you'll have a situation where you're going to have a bloc vote of unionists who, more often than not, currently and in the future, in the way elections are decided, are going to be deciding who's the Taoiseach.

As to the annual £10 billion subvention to Northern Ireland – that's not true. That's why I got in contact with Gunther Thumann, the senior economist at the German desk for the IMF during German reunification. He calculated the true cost to Northern Ireland in a reunification scenario.

He and I looked at the figures for how Britain attributes the expenditure for Northern Ireland. Included in that figure of income and expenditure is Northern Ireland's share in global military spending, Northern Ireland's share of EU contributions, Northern Ireland's share of the UK national debt, Northern Ireland's share of expenditure on the British royal family (about £2.8 billion). The civil service, when rationalised to the same level as the South, is a saving of about £1.7 billion. Then there's £1.1 billion, an accounting adjustment figure which includes Northern Ireland's share of Royal Mail pensions, student loan scheme and quantitative easing. Gunther's analysis concludes that the pension payments for Northern Ireland, which account for £2.9 billion per annum, would remain a liability of the UK state and not a liability to the Irish state. That's RUC pensions, British army pensions, old-age pensions. What you're left with is £700 million.

When Sinn Féin did their analysis, I think they had the figure at £3–4 billion. That's why you get the guy who is the senior economist at the German desk.

The UNESCO report showed that in the event of a hard border there would be a return to violence. The only question is the scale of the violence. And likewise in the event of a rushed border poll without planning and engagement, you'd have a return to violence again, with the only issue being the scale. That is why we need the whole of government engagement: not just the Irish government but the EU, the US and the UK governments. Bear in mind that there has been only one reunification within the last 100 years – we are the longest-partitioned country in the world. Longer than Cyprus, Korea, Germany, longer than Taiwan and China, Pakistan and India and all the rest.

There's also the changing demographics in the North, which coupled with the economic case will make an overall argument that people will support. So it's not just one issue, it's not just Brexit. It's Brexit plus changing views in Northern Ireland, changing demographics, which are quite clear. So it's a huge project in itself.

There is going to be a referendum. The only question is when. I was talking to a demographic expert, and I asked him when census figures converted into a Catholic majority, and he said in August 2016, but that a voting majority won't happen until about 2024 or 2026. That depends on whether your voting age is sixteen and up or eighteen and up.

There was never a majority of nationalists who were asked if they were happy in the UK. Democracy must have its way. The GFA says it quite clearly, and this is a very important point which High Court Justice Humphreys makes time and time again: if there was a referendum held in Northern Ireland and 50% of the people plus one voted to stay in the UK, would anyone question the result? So why is the reverse not true? It's because there might be a violent backlash. Democracy must have its way, and people who want to use violence to achieve their own ends or maintain the status quo must be faced down. Otherwise democracy fails. When you don't stand up to bullies and people who threaten violence, well, then you have failed and democracy has failed, the government has failed. No government can allow that to happen and say, 'Oh well, we must have more than 50% plus one – we must have a different standard because of the threat of violence.'

As to the threat of violence: when asked what would be their response to a referendum won by nationalists, the majority of unionists say they would accept the outcome, albeit with huge reservations. But the majority would accept it. It's only a small minority that wouldn't accept it. Bullies who threaten violence should have their way? The entire Troubles were fought on the premise that in Northern Ireland, with all its inconsistencies and how it was set up, democracy would have its way. Well, you can't have it one way for one group and a different way for another group.

You're stuck with the situation where you have no choice but to wait until the British secretary of state makes the decision, and there is no policy around that. It's the next phase of the GFA, and clarification is needed. When does that happen? Nobody knows.

16

PEADAR TÓIBÍN

4 APRIL 2019

Peadar Tóibín was first elected Teachta Dála (TD) for Meath West in 2011. He was re-elected in 2016 with the highest Sinn Féin vote in the state. He is a graduate in economics and politics from UCD and a postgraduate in enterprise from the Michael Smurfit Graduate Business School, UCD. He was the Oireachtas Enterprise Committee rapporteur into the development of the all-Ireland economy. He left Sinn Féin in 2018 and in January 2019 founded Aontú, a party dedicated to Irish unity, economic justice and pro-life legislation.

We lived about fifty miles from the border. As I was growing up it was a feature on television and in family discussions. My father was a businessman with three small petrol stations/garages, and anybody who made life easier for him, he would have considered voting for them. My mother was from a farming background so she would have been Fine Gael at the time.

I was born in 1974, and one of the strongest memories I have of being a kid is watching the hunger strikes on TV and asking my parents what was going on there. My mother replied – this was an example of the black propaganda that was there at the time – she said that if the men didn't go through with the hunger strikes, their families were going to be targeted by the IRA. So in other words, these were really victims of the republican movement rather than leading the republican movement to a certain extent. That had a big impact on me, so from an early age I started to read books – Tim Pat Coogan's *The IRA* I read at twelve or thirteen. I remember Loughgall happening [when eight IRA men were ambushed and killed by the Special Air Service] when I was fourteen. I brought a copy of *An Phoblacht* back to the house after signing the book of condolences for Loughgall, and I got clipped across the ear with the *An Phoblacht* and told not to bring it into the house again.

I got a job in my early twenties with a firm in Armagh. I remember driving through the border and being stopped by soldiers with guns, and noticing when I passed the checkpoint there were other soldiers I hadn't seen in the ditch – they'd been completely invisible to me.

I spent a total of three years working in Armagh. One of my jobs was to work with a lot of small businesses in the area, and I remember going to places like Bessbrook, Beragh, Cappagh and Crossmaglen. These were all names that had played out in my political interest as a youngster, and now I sat in rooms with people from both sides of the community. I remember hearing of people from the nationalist community who had lost materially because of things the IRA had done, and sitting with unionists who were involved with businesses, hearing about the material and human cost they had paid. I remember sitting with republicans in places like Pomeroy and Cappagh, republicans who had become detached from the republican movement and who had been immersed in tragedy, and the sense of hopelessness they had. In many ways I thought theirs were the most sorrowful cases because they had lost loved ones, brothers and sisters killed while standing on the street, killed by people driving by and shooting them because they were nationalists, and they had no sense of support any more from the nationalist/republican community.

Since 1998, it's a radically different border for sure. The towers perched on the hilltops, with sound equipment that could be focused on cars – that invasive, oppressive feeling has disappeared from the border. But there is still a sense that the border is a line which is imposed and which prevents the natural expression of self-determination, of economic development. At the time of partition, 80% of industry in Ireland was in three counties around Belfast. The income of the individual in the North was far higher than in the South. The South was known for making beer and biscuits. It was an agricultural backwater.

That has now completely flipped, and the reason it has flipped is that London cares about the Home Counties when it comes to economic development. Even the North of England and Wales and Scotland are afterthoughts with regard to economic development. There's no doubt the North of Ireland is an afterthought economically as far as London is concerned. The border in Ireland is what prevents the self-determination which could change that.

When people are in charge of their own social and economic destinies, they make better choices. So Aontú would be very strong on the point that self-determination is key. You can make decisions, you can hold the decision-makers to account. When you can't do that, you are on the back foot all the time with regard to those decisions.

I think in the South there has been a massive awakening. A lot of people I know who would have been cautious during the Troubles now are tipping up to the Titanic Quarter in Belfast, they're tipping up to the Glens of Antrim, they're doing the *Game of Thrones* stuff – they're far more likely to do that now. But I think it's still a voyage of discovery for many people, that they have this part of Ireland on their doorstep. It's happening, but it could happen a lot more. I still think there's a detachment that is lingering because of the political dysfunction.

For example, I worked with the North of Ireland retail association [Retail NI] and the Southern one, and they would say that there's about €700 million-worth could be done in the retail sector North and South if they were integrated more. And that's just on tourists coming to Ireland. So that's not even indigenous people living on the island spending more, this is just people who come to the South on holidays but maybe never venture North, or go to the North on holiday and never venture South.

I listened to the radio this morning and everyone's talking about how we live in this all-island economy. We have an all-Ireland economy that's still stultified in its growth. It's probably 30–40% along the way, but a real all-Ireland economy would be people planning to get their funding together and delivering together, it would be ironing out the differences North and South, it would be reaching convergence on a whole swathe of issues North and South.

The cross-border bodies set up with the GFA worked, but I think the DUP did a good job of clamping its development. So take InterTradeIreland [an all-Ireland trade and business development body set up as part of the GFA], which was one of those great opportunities. InterTradeIreland has a cap on the number of people it can employ. For every euro that you put into InterTradeIreland, you probably get about two or three euros back, because of its success in helping people trade. And yet that logic is completely deleted because of this border mentality. So I would ask the question: the GFA in 1998 – what has actually happened since then? And the answer is, very little – and I'm tempted to use stronger language than that. This should have been an evolutionary process, and yet it's frozen in time, frozen in 1998.

Take Stormont. Everybody wants to talk about how great the GFA is, and Aontú thinks that the GFA was wonderful. But the GFA created a Stormont which, if you ask anybody if it's working, they'd have to say it's not. Stormont is built to fail and that's the truth of it. At best it was a carve-up between the two large parties; at worst it was the two parties in a non-stop stalemate on issues. So when I was still in Sinn Féin, I would ring up people in the North and ask, 'Is there any chance we could get X, Y and Z?' 'Oh, we can't even ask that – bejakers, the DUP would go nuts if you said that at all!' The way the system works, is that both parties spend most of the time blocking the progress of each other.

As to cross-border trade, there's no doubt you have radical divergence in many different areas. Excise duties are a divergence, there's taxation divergence, divergence in currency. Say, if I was CEO of Monaghan County Council and if I was delivering training for people, and Fermanagh or Tyrone were doing the same training. Logic would demand that the two of them come together and deliver training in a joined-up fashion, with less cost to both and higher impact where you want to achieve it. Fine Gael pay lip-service to cross-border infrastructure – yet they pulled €27 million for the A5 about three weeks ago, at a time of this Brexit crisis. So when cross-border funding should be accelerating, they were actually pulling money from it, saying that there were no ministers there.

If it's a hard Brexit – and the government in the South of Ireland have been skipping around this issue for a long time – there will be checks on the border. The reason why Britain was forced in a way to call for a Brexit referendum is that, for the EU, the sanctity of the single market is paramount. They're not going to mess with the single market because it is central to the European project.

Now if there are no checks on the border, there's a hole in the single market. And if the Southern government doesn't implement a border, it will occur at the Irish ports. If you're not going to check for regulation, if you're not going to check for quality – for all of these things – between Cullaville [in the North] and Castleblayney [in the South], you're going to have to check for it somewhere else. There's no doubt in my mind there will be checks at a border if there is a hard Brexit.

I would say a hard border will trash so much cross-border activity. There will be at best a time constraint, there will be queues at the border, there will be the extra costs of paperwork, preparation for all of those issues. And if there is regulatory divergence, then there are materials which will not be able to be sold North and South in the same manner. So that has to have a massive impact.

There are supply chains North and South, where the border no longer matters, and those supply chains will crash. If there is a product that has a European stamp of quality in the milk sector, and now it has 10 or 20% of its inputs that are not achieving that quality: it won't be recognised as being of European quality, so it won't be possible to sell it and the people will have to stop. If they want to achieve the European recognition for quality and standards, they'll have to stop purchasing that milk. And that doesn't go anywhere near the £250 million in CAP funding that Northern farmers are actually going to lose as a result of not being in the EU.

It's bizarre. Every time the question is asked of Simon Coveney and the Irish government, they say they're not preparing for a hard border. But there have been a couple of slips. Shane Ross [minister for transport, tourism and sport] was asked and he said of course there's going to be – and I'm sure that they are putting in contingency plans. If there's a hard Brexit, there will have to be massive investment from London for the North of Ireland to protect it; in Dublin they'll have to invest massively to make sure that businesses that suffer as a result are helped. And the EU is going to have to help in this regard. People almost forget the EU's role in this.

The EU is the biggest threat to the EU. The inflexibility, the way it hasn't tailored its systems to the needs of people around the EU is causing massive anti-EU sentiment right across Europe. In Hungary, in Greece, in Italy, in the Netherlands and in Ireland and Britain, people are questioning why this rigidity can't be fixed, why we can't create some level of flexibility.

The EU is a one-size-fits-all project. If you take it back to the crash that we experienced in 2008, a big chunk of that was the idea that there was an interest rate for Germany and an interest rate for Ireland. Both countries were at different points of the economic cycle at the time: Ireland was burning up, Germany was very quiet. So they had a really low interest rate to motivate the German economy, which poured petrol on the Southern Irish economy, which helped it explode and crash. Right now a lot of people around Europe feel that they should have some level of managed, sustainable immigration policy – and that's really affecting a lot of countries. But they can't do that under the single market. There's an inflexibility in the EU. And that was one of the reasons the UK voted to leave. If Cameron had got some concession for the UK on sustained and manageable immigration, the UK would still be in the EU.

I always ask the question of people: would they be happy if another individual – say their best friend – were making all the decisions for them for the rest of their life? Most people say no. Now as human beings we make mistakes, but we know that we are still the best person to make our decisions. It's the same with nation-states. France, Germany, Brussels, Berlin are never going to make the decisions best for us. They're always going to determine their decisions on what's best for them. That's human nature. But different countries have different needs, they're at different points on the economic cycle, different points on cultural cycles, on immigration cycles, environment cycles. We need a Europe that is a community of nation-states, democratically working together for trade and the environment and the big issues that we can't as small nation-states deal with. But if they don't add a little bit of flexibility into it, like the bough of a tree in a storm, they're going to have these breakages along the way.

Economic cooperation is brilliant and it should be at the heart of all our relationships across Europe. Aontú wants to see that. The difficulty comes when you cede monetary and fiscal powers over to the EU. When you do that you can't address the specific economic challenges your country has.

The major benefits of the EU are that it is a free market and people can get their products and services into other countries without difficulties, that there is standard regulation within environment, within quality of product, within workers' rights – all of these are good things. But when the EU tells you that you can't set up an organisation to build 100,000 houses over a period of five years to deal with your housing crisis, that's a problem. When the EU tells you you can't set up an organisation to fix your water infrastructure unless it's a private organisation, that's a problem. When the EU tells you, when you have spiralling house prices, that you can't change your interest rates, that's a big problem. When the EU wanted to tell us what taxation we should have – these are all big problems, problems that reduce our ability to fix our economic issues.

I would have thought the whole Irish unity project was in serious trouble up until Brexit. I would have seen that a lot of the energy had gone out of the unity project. For example, many people saw Stormont as a transitional parliament. I would have said the four main parties in Stormont, before

Brexit happened, had come to a view, without admitting so, that this was it. I made the argument at the time that we needed to be of the view that this wasn't it, that we can't be captured by Stormont in its existence for lots of reasons. So there's no doubt in my mind that Brexit has woken up the whole of Irish society to the necessity for unity.

Jacob Rees-Mogg, Boris Johnson and Theresa May determine what's happening in Ireland. They determine whether we can move products, services or people across the island. They're determining what's happening in normal people's lives. Now, they know nothing about Ireland. They'd probably admit that on a personal basis. And they care very little about Ireland. Nominating Karen Bradley to the position of Northern secretary shows the lack of interest there is within the Tories about the North.

A hundred years ago we had people who fought the biggest empire the world had ever seen. They challenged a flag that had flown for 500 years in some iteration over every town in Ireland. They were the weakest generation Ireland had ever produced – they came out of the famine, when 1 million people were killed and 1.5 million people were forced to emigrate. Yet they realised that self-determination was really an existential issue. They realised it wasn't a fluffy, pipe-dream romantic issue. If there had been a government in Dublin during the famine, there is no way there would have been the extremity of the famine.

So I think people have realised that in the North of Ireland, people voted to remain in the EU – they self-determined to remain. The Tories took this decision, crumpled it into a ball and threw it in the waste-paper basket. Right across Ireland there's an idea that having the whims and egos of Tories who don't know and don't care what's happening in Ireland making decisions about Ireland – it's just illogical. And that's why you see in a Claire Byrne [journalist and television presenter] poll recently, 87% of the people said that in the case of a hard Brexit, they would support a united Ireland.

Clinton's campaign strategist, James Carville, hung up a sign at the campaign headquarters: 'It's the economy, stupid.' I would say that 85% of the population of Ireland, North and South, vote with their wallets – probably more in the South than the North, because of the constitutional difficulties with regard to the North. Many people have come to Aontú from the Protestant population in the North of Ireland – they would have been small 'u' unionists, and they would not ever have looked at national unity. Now they are appalled at what's happening in London and they see the logic of some kind of further integration North and South, some way the North can stay in the EU. They see the fact that the market would increase in a united Ireland, a larger home market. They see the fact that we would have more influence in the EU; they see the fact that in the North GDP per person is around €20,000 whereas in the South it's about €39,000. There are of course difficulties in the Southern Irish economy, but there is definitely an economic logic to Irish unity and people are seeing that. And I think that's one of the driving forces towards Irish unity.

I've no doubt Fianna Fáil and Fine Gael projects would be damaged by unity. They would go from the dominant parties to smaller regional parties. The logic of that would be that they would start to stand in the North, that they would start to build in the North, and maybe now they're starting to cop on to that.

There's no doubt that the political sphere is becoming more all-Ireland. Fianna Fáil grass roots and membership want that for sure; SDLP grass roots and membership want that too. Fianna Fáil are paralysed at the moment. The problem is that traditional Fianna Fáil members – Éamon Ó Cuív, Mark Daly, Marc MacSharry and John McGuinness – have been pushed to the periphery of the party, and Micheál Martin has surrounded himself with people who probably are less representative of the grass roots of the party. So it's hard to see the next Fianna Fáil leader coming from that traditional space; they're more likely to come from a new space.

One of my major disagreements with Sinn Féin for the last three or four years is that Sinn Féin comes out looking for a border poll and then that's it. My instinct in all of this is we should have a poll for Irish unity, for sure. Aontú supports that fully. But we need to start properly selling it, properly explaining it and properly dealing with what it may look like.

Now I'm an incrementalist politically by instinct. And I've always been of the view that while you're standing around waiting for a border poll, let's get busy taking small steps to take you along that way as well. I've always been of the view, and I've sold this previously in Sinn Féin, that the border is a wall with a thousand blocks. Each one of those blocks is an individual issue which has an effect on people's lives. So a cross-border ambulance service, a cross-border air ambulance service, an all-Ireland soccer team, an all-Ireland excise duty, an all-Ireland police force, all-Ireland education and investment and infrastructure: all that stuff could actually be worked upon now. That would have material benefit individually for everybody on the island. It would reduce the height of the border; it would make transition less difficult and less scary for those who have a problem with it.

If Aontú was in government at the moment, what we would do is set up an all-Ireland convention on the future of Ireland. We would invite all of the political parties on the basis of their strength to have a debate and a discussion about how Ireland is going to look in the future, to start to be able to ameliorate the fears of some people within the unionist community around what exactly [Irish unity] means for them.

Change happens from crisis. So political parties need to put aside their own political ambition in the South of Ireland and start to reach out and create a structure – maybe even based on the New Ireland Forum produced by Fine Gael years ago, but creating a structure for political representatives to start talking about the future of Ireland now.

The GFA was a wonderful agreement. It created a peace that most of us thought wasn't going to happen. It's over twenty years old at this stage, and it was created at a time before Brexit and when there was a unionist majority. I think we have to have a discussion now among ourselves about how we push on from the GFA.

The GFA created institutions and the institutions are not working. We have food poverty, house poverty, health poverty in the North of Ireland due to the fact that the institutions are not up and running. Anybody who wants the resurrection of those institutions as they are, is only going to create trouble into the future. We need to be making decisions that are relevant to the current state of Ireland.

Part of the reforms we should be looking for would be that the timing of a border poll would no longer be the decision of a Tory minister. The idea that you give a person like Karen Bradley, with so little knowledge of the North of Ireland, a decision about the destiny of Ireland is just bonkers.

There's always this notion that the basis of the union between Great Britain and Northern Ireland was a democratic majority. And are we then saying any change would see the goalposts moved? It's one rule for the status quo, but oh bejakers, if you want to talk about anything else, you have to use a different set of rules – it would be democratically immoral to go down that route.

Don't get me wrong. I don't want a situation where we are pulling 1 million people of a unionist persuasion into a state that they'd radically oppose. That's why I'm saying let's get busy with the incremental changes, start to show people that there's no threat to them. We need to build a republic that fully recognises and respects people's cultural, religious and nationality backgrounds.

The establishment won't admit they fear change. They know change is popular among people so they find a heap of reasons: 'Oh, we support unity – but not right now,' or 'We support unity but it can't be 50% plus one.' My logic dictates that it should be a democratic process. If the majority want to achieve unity, that's what we should see.

Ten years ago – five years ago – the establishment down here would have dismissed talk of unity as a pipe dream, an impractical proposal. There's no doubt that now that's completely changed. Even your hardened Blueshirt would understand that there's a logic here.

I have no doubt that unity is now in the realm of the practical and logical, and not just for the Southern establishment, who still obviously find it a political threat, but also for an increasing number of people from the North of Ireland, from both traditions. I worked, as I said, in the North for three years with Catholics and Protestants. At the time, I think, people in the North from a Catholic perspective were kind of happy that their cultural Catholicism or their cultural nationalism was at least recognised and relatively respected in the Northern state. And while they loved the idea of all-Ireland institutions and all-Ireland sports and all-Ireland language, etc. they were not always pushed regarding actual change: they would have taken a second look at it, would have been cautious.

But that has changed, for sure. The status quo is an economic threat to people in the North from both sides, and that's recognised by more and more people. So I think we need a serious job of reaching out to people, inviting every party, every elected organisation on the basis of their electoral strength. We need to get them into a room and start working out what Ireland's going to look like in the future.

And I wouldn't be surprised if within the next three to four years, actual unity or some constitutional change occurs.

17

COLIN HARVEY

20 APRIL 2019

Colin Harvey is professor of human rights law in the School of Law, Queen's University Belfast, a fellow of the Senator George J. Mitchell Institute for Global Peace, Security and Justice and an associate fellow of the Institute of Irish Studies. He has held visiting positions at the University of Michigan, Fordham University and the London School of Economics and Political Science. He has written and taught extensively on human rights law and policy and recently led a project funded by the Economic and Social Research Council (ESRC) on the consequences of Brexit for Northern Ireland.

I grew up in Derry in the 1970s and 1980s. The border I remember as very heavily militarised, with stops and searches. In those days that was normal. Guys with guns stopping you on your way out to the beach – as a child you saw this happening to everyone, so it must be normal.

But you did sense a resentment among adults at the hassle of getting pulled over and all the rest of it. Plus, remember: I was brought up in Carnhill in Derry, where you had soldiers marching around the streets with guns.

With the arrival of demilitarisation along the border, there was a sense of relaxation, of breathing out. I wouldn't underestimate the importance of that for people in border areas. In

England there's an incomprehension of the anxiety people in border areas feel that all that might be coming back. We've done a research project here in Queen's University – Brexit Northern Ireland. We did town halls, we spoke to people, and the word that kept coming up was 'anxiety'.

I think growing up in Derry in that militarised environment, you always felt that you had done something wrong! You had this massively over-policed militarised society, so going through life, you felt that coming from where you did, you were intrinsically suspect as a community. When I was growing up, my community was fenced around, suspect, under constant surveillance. I think this is a post-conflict society, and the traumas and the memories are still there. For a lot of people, Brexit is re-traumatising them.

And whatever people's backgrounds and whatever their historical memories, I think a new border would be resisted. Not by armed groups but by Josephine and Joe Public living in a border area, who have got used to the absence of a border. The ease with which people move over the border, and the way the EU has facilitated that – people won't allow things to go backwards. The possibility of civil disobedience is real; it will happen. For people who remember the bad old days, any attempt to backtrack will be met with a reaction.

My sense is that there's something happening in this place. People are no longer apologising for who they are or what they are or what their aspirations are. Because of that self-confidence, particularly in communities that have suffered, there is a sense there will be no going back.

The difficulty is that those of us who raise this matter

often get criticised. You'll hear Brexiteers talk about scare-mongering. But what we're actually trying to do is to learn the lessons of history and as objectively as possible say that this is what might happen. Myself and others have been criticised for saying this but it still remains true.

Let's just name it for what it is. This region in the North of Ireland is being taken out of the EU against its will. Irish citizenship is still European citizenship. And there's a real anxiety for Irish citizens here that European citizenship will be a second-class citizenship on the island. Bear in mind that Irish citizens in the North already feel like second-class Irish citizens on the island, so if you add on to that the category of a second-class European citizen, it's really offensive.

For nationalists and republicans in the North, the idea that people here voted against Brexit but that is being so easily overridden is remarkable. It's a major matter of constitutional change and it has really rattled nationalism and republicanism here.

There's a joint EU–UK report from December 2017 which contains the famous Paragraph 52. Promises were made to Irish citizens in the North that special arrangements would be put in place to protect our rights. The voting rights issue is symbolic of a bigger problem. The EU has been very clear that the Irish government could have done something about the two extra seats in the European Parliament. The fact that the Irish government has decided to do nothing about addressing that is a big problem – especially when we remember all that rhetoric and those warm words from the Southern government: 'You'll not be abandoned,' 'You'll never be left behind.' People in the North have heard successive Irish governments use that language.

There are a lot of positives about the approach the Irish government has taken to the backstop, but they have retreated into a sort of 1970s/1980s community narrative about not upsetting the apple-cart, which ultimately will lead to the lowest common denominator approach. In order not to upset one community here, we're not going to give any rights at all to the other community.

Some of these rights and equality issues are very clear-cut, and they need to be named, as do the impediments to progress. Human rights are not orange and green issues – they are entitlement rights. If we secure equal rights protection for everyone in this society, everyone will gain – nationalist, unionist and others.

The current Conservative government, when it was in coalition and when it was in government on its own, has waged a war against rights, particularly socio-economic rights, for people throughout the UK, and that had an impact here well before Brexit. But once we get the small matter of Brexit out of the way, they're talking about repealing the Human Rights Act, to replace it with something called – guess what? – a British Bill of Rights. So how is that going to resonate here?

Brexit to me is part of a bigger agenda that has put the peace process in peril. There's been a rights and equality crisis in this society for a long time. The GFA has been chipped away at for years, and Brexit has brought all that to a head.

There was a promise in the Agreement around a bill of rights for this society that would protect everyone and would deal with broader socio-economic issues as well. There was supposed to be a charter of rights for the island of Ireland – that hasn't happened either. The Human Rights Commission that was set up has had its budget slashed over a number of years, and there's a sense that the whole promise of the human rights and equality agenda hasn't been delivered. Irish citizens in the North have had to experience sustained, systematic disrespect over many years. That's a failure to grapple with the Agreement's vision of what this society is supposed to be about.

Brexit has brought it all to a head with campaigns like Emma DeSouza's around the birthright provisions. [A Belfast court rejected the Home Office's attempt to appeal against a ruling that Emma DeSouza's American husband should be allowed to live in the UK without going through immigration procedures because she carried an Irish passport.]

We're discovering that a lot of the Agreement's language over parity of esteem, mutual respect for the main identities here, hasn't been legislated for effectively.

Talking about a border poll is absolutely not intended to deepen division, and I resent the way in which this whole debate has been framed. Some of the noises coming out of Dublin make it clear that at the moment everybody around Europe is talking about the GFA. Everybody loves the GFA. Well, this is central to the constitutional compromise at the heart of the GFA.

The constitutional status of this place is supposed to be based on consent and on a democratic principle, and everybody is supposed to have accepted that. So what is the problem with raising that as an issue? If that is a divisive point to make, then you pull away one of the central pillars of the constitutional compromise that is the Agreement.

What is the problem with testing consent? I have been really surprised by some of the reactions from people, who on the one hand will stand up and say 'We need to respect and implement the GFA' and on the other hand say 'Oh, you're being toxic, divisive and dangerous, you're pouring petrol on the flames by mentioning what is a core element of it.' We need to have the debate. I've even named the date for a border poll: I think it should be held on 22 May 2023, which is the twenty-fifth anniversary of the all-island vote on the GFA. And I am amazed by those who see that as a threat – particularly those who constantly talk about the principle of consent. Why not test it?

The mechanism in the Agreement gives the secretary of state – Karen Bradley at the moment – the discretion to call a border poll where it looks like a majority would vote for a united Ireland. As soon as the evidence begins to suggest that this place has gone over 50% in terms of wanting to get out of the UK, then in my view the sovereignty arrangements here are de facto illegitimate, and that's why they need to be tested through a border poll. Concurrent referendums, one in the North and one in the South.

A border poll needs to be preceded by a British–Irish intergovernmental body setting down a framework document, including who in the North gets to vote, what the question is going to be – things that are likely to be highly contested. It needs to be preceded by British–Irish intergovernmental discussion.

People are talking at the moment about a forum in the South that would bring people together to talk about that. I've said that you could have a two-year limited forum or assembly to do that. But it'll take the British and Irish governments to map out a framework around some of the harder questions on how it's to go forward.

The parameters need to be sketched by both governments in terms of the question, the date, issues around voting rights in the North, how all that's going to work. So the procedural stuff needs to be sketched. We need some idea as to what a new Ireland will look like, so we're not left in the Brexit mess, where people didn't know what they were voting for. The document produced for the Scottish referendum needs to be a model for the conversation we need to be having on this island.

I have a feeling people sometimes exaggerate the challenges of Irish unity. This is a small region; Ireland is a constitutional, well-developed system with its own institutions. And while it will be done in a way that respects the GFA, you're still talking about combining a region that is relatively small with a larger region. Some of the scare stories overemphasise the problems and don't acknowledge the opportunities.

I'm not suggesting it's a matter of absorbing the North into an existing arrangement. I would strongly advocate that the new Ireland should be a different Ireland. But I think there are people who throw out scare stories about the impossibility of Irish reunification, that it can't be done or that the challenges are insurmountable. This will be a new Ireland that will challenge the South as well as the North. 'Absorb' is possibly not the right word for that, but it's also possible to over-egg the challenges of Irish reunification. This can be done. This island can do this. It's logistically achievable.

It'll also happen in the context of us rejoining the EU and it's unimaginable that the EU will not be a big supportive partner in the process of Irish reunification. That adds a new dynamic to that conversation.

A new Ireland has to be based on parity of esteem and respect. The GFA principles will challenge this new Irish state to be respectful of British unionist identity. That is made more difficult by the experience nationalists and republicans have had in the North, which has been an experience where parity of esteem hasn't been delivered, where mutual respect hasn't been observed. But the vision for a new Ireland has to be a welcoming, inclusive one where unionism and British identity are respected, where people are made to feel welcome. And the GFA in part anticipates that move to a new Ireland where their identity is respected.

Relationships around these islands were easy to some extent in the period before Brexit, and there was a sense of more and more comfort with each other. Relationships were healing and getting better. So I think that's the vision you hold out for unionism: the new Ireland that will emerge will be welcoming and accommodating to everyone. But it'll have to match the words with deeds; it'll have to involve challenge and change for the new Irish state.

I think the possibility of violence from a small core of loyalists has to be considered and debated now. It has to be done in a way that you would in any democratic process.

This place emerged through the threat of force. Thanks to the GFA, we're supposed to live in a place where all that has melted away. What worries me in talk about a loyalist backlash is, are we still saying that what operates in this place is the punch in the face for raising a legitimate constitutional mechanism? If that's the case, where is the GFA? We're supposed to be in a new era, and people who lightly throw that into the mix need to reflect on the responsibilities we all have.

To me, this is the biggest test of the GFA. If we can hold concurrent referendums on this island, in a peaceful, democratic and consensual way, and the outcomes are respected, that's the test of whether the consent principle in the GFA holds up.

But talk of a loyalist backlash sounds to nationalists and republicans like an entity that was established by the barrel of a gun still persists by the barrel of the gun. And post-GFA, that shouldn't be the thinking. If there are law-and-order issues that need attention, it'll be a test for the institutions here – we need to be able to have this constitutional process without fear of the use of force, during it or at the far end of it. And that'll be a big test for the GFA.

The evidence of recent polling shows that over 60% of people in the South would vote for Irish reunification. I think that's very welcome: the South will vote for Irish unity.

I think there are many scare stories around. If this is done in a coherent and correct way, a proposition could emerge which could prove very attractive to a majority of people in the North and in the South. It's in the strategic interest of the Southern state to see the North as part of a unified Ireland.

And increasingly I think it will be in the strategic interest of the EU, too. One way of dealing with the sort of Wild West up here – non-aligned to the rest of the island – is to simply get rid of the border permanently.

It's in the strategic interests of Ireland and the EU to use the GFA mechanism and to see the border melt away permanently.

The job of the British–Irish government is to make sure there is a coherent framework put in place for all that, and it's not just the secretary of state waking up one day and deciding to do this. It needs to involve all civic society on the island, all political parties on the island. There are models recently in the South of constitutional conventions and citizens' assemblies. Discussion needs to be time-limited so it doesn't turn into a ten-year talking shop but maps out a set of propositions around health, education, social security and other elements that people are anxious or worried about. So that people go into the voting booth on this with a clear idea of what the outworking will be. That's the big lesson of Brexit.

The reason for naming a date is, I believe, that is the only way you will get unionist engagement in that process. The way to get civic unionist society and unionist parties engaged is to have a date. They'll know they're faced with heading into a vote, and that will help to encourage minds to focus on big propositions.

It goes slightly against the grain of big scare stories out there, but I see this as a massive opportunity for the island. I see this as an exciting, energising conversation that challenges nationalists and republicans to articulate their vision for the future. But most important at the moment, there's a big challenge to unionism to walk away from the fear stories and come up with a proposition. What is unionism's proposition for the future of this place if they want to stay in the UK? My view is, rather than scare people and make them anxious, let's become energised.

Once the date emerged in Scotland, there was a sense of energy around that debate. So let us have our debate. A positive, energetic discussion. It's a win-win, I think. Because whatever emerges, people will have to make a proposition about how we're going to share the island in the future.

What's been really intriguing in the last while is the sense that Irish citizens in this society are already feeling sufficiently confident to stand up and say, 'This is who we are, this is what we're about, these are the rights that we want to see respected and this is the future we want to see, and we have a right to say that out loud.' I spoke at that Waterfront event and I had people sidling up to me afterwards to talk. Something is happening here and it won't be put back in any box. This is a civic mobilisation of people who are proud to be Irish citizens, proud to be European citizens, who've been through a traumatic experience. A society told people, 'You have to live life on your knees,' and people have said, 'No. We've had enough.'

But of course there's also a backlash, and you do feel the force of that backlash. Speaking in my role as an academic, since being involved in that civic nationalism conference at the Waterfront Hall, there's been a reaction that's been quite strong at times. There's a mobilisation, some of which looks different and new and has a self-confidence about it, and I think that's unnerving unionists as to how they should handle this.

What's new is that people in civic society outside political parties are willing to speak out loud. That's not to say there haven't been political parties and others who have been saying this for a long time. The integrity of the argument doesn't spring from the person who says it. The argument has always had an integrity. But in the sort of world we're in now, if a certain sort of person mentions it, the media notice or they pick up on it, whereas in the past they didn't.

What's been really noticeable in some of the nationalist comments is that they've had enough of this place. They bought into something, tried to make it work, and had all that thrown back in their faces. In the context of Brexit, there's a very obvious solution to this. It's in the Agreement and we need to be able to talk about it out loud.

For many people, the South seems increasingly the more attractive bet, in the longer term, within the EU. Ireland is going in a direction that's appealing perhaps particularly to the younger generation, who maybe see themselves more in Leo Varadkar and Simon Coveney than they do in Theresa May or whoever.

So that is the debate at the moment around Stormont – is it past its sell-by date? One thing is clear: if it ever does go back, it needs to be acceptable for nationalists and republicans; it cannot go back to the way it was. I think many of these matters around parity of esteem, equal treatment – need to be copper-fastened, the rights and equality stuff needs to be completely addressed.

I'd flip round the traditional argument: the challenge now for unionists is to earn the respect of nationalists and republicans here in a way that will persuade nationalists and republicans to share power again. So the onus is on unionism to show what it can do to gain the respect of Irish citizens here who have felt utterly disrespected, who have other options and are increasingly confident in articulating what those options are.

I appreciate that I'm speaking entirely anecdotally, but I think there's a dynamic towards Irish unity now that I have never seen in my lifetime. And for many people that is the exciting agenda for the next five to ten years. That seems the more exciting conversation to be in. If you're a younger person, that seems the conversation that's more attractive to be part of. I think that's taken off. Even if you look at social media and the various initiatives there – it has captured people's imaginations.

Working as an academic here in Queen's, interaction with students is always in a very formal setting of teaching, but what I pick up is that there's a tremendous interest among them in issues of human rights, social justice, environmental justice, worry about the future of the planet. Contrary to the stereotype of young people, they are actively engaged, very concerned about their own future, which adds a new dynamic to the Brexit conversation too. People want the opportunities we had in a previous generation.

That presents a challenge for the island to be better on equality, to be better on matters of climate change, social justice, environmental justice. But we're talking about an engaged group of people, particularly the ones I work with in human rights and equality. Increasingly I get a sense that people around here are frankly embarrassed when they go elsewhere and have to explain that they're from a place that's been left way behind across a range of issues.

I think the momentum for change is unstoppable. In ten years' time we may be sitting in a very different constitutional setting on the island. But some of the challenges in that new context won't have gone away. I think it's very likely that in terms of these islands, Scotland may also have left the UK. But I believe there are opportunities around the new configurations that are going to emerge in these islands for more respectful conversations between people in a more equal and respectful way. And rather than seeing that in anxious and fearful terms, why not see that as a brilliant opportunity to reopen the conversation around these islands, in Scotland, Wales, England and this island, to speak to each other as equals in the future? That could be a great conversation, and hopefully that's the conversation we'll be having in ten years' time.

18

JOE BROLLY

26 APRIL 2019

Joe Brolly is an Irish barrister, Gaelic football analyst and former player from Dungiven, Co. Derry. He was part of Derry's
first-ever All-Ireland Senior Football Championship-winning
side in 1993 and was known for his goal celebration of blowing kisses to the crowd. Since retiring he has fashioned a niche
in television punditry, described by one critic as 'the most lippy
and articulate pundit on Irish television'.

Francie McCloskey, a sixty-seven-year-old bachelor farmer,
came into Dungiven. There was an Orange parade going on,
and he made his way up towards Jim McReynolds' bar to take
a pint and have a chat. He was batoned to death in the doorway
of Hasson's draper's shop and was widely seen as the first death
of the Troubles.

The people of the town saw it happening. It was covered
up, of course – no one was ever charged. And there wasn't
much point in calling the police when the police were doing
the killing. Then you had the civil rights movement, and everybody saw what happened to the civil rights protesters – baton
charges and assaults. And the fact that it could be done with
impunity.

There was no law and order – the Brits could do what they
liked, the cops could do what they liked. They could kill all

those people up in Ballymurphy, they could kill all those people in Derry city. My father was on the Bloody Sunday march. Everybody knew what happened – they opened fire and killed people, left so many people in the hospital – and that was it. Reginald Maudling [British politician] stands up in the House of Commons and says, 'Good job, well done!' You're living in that context, where they can do whatever they like – they could kill Francie McCloskey, they could baton-charge in Dungiven, they could shoot you, the Ulster Defence Regiment (UDR) could come and murder people as part of a murder gang, the [loyalist] Glenanne gang, could move about with impunity. Pat Finucane, a prominent solicitor, could be shot dead.

When I went to St Pat's [College], Armagh, I was no sooner there than the hunger strikes started. We had two hunger strikers from Dungiven. There was no room for sitting on the fence. You wouldn't have gone home to Dungiven and said, 'Should we not be trying to get the boys off hunger strike?' 'Fuck off!' This was a very sacred thing that was happening, and it was the same everywhere. In Dungiven we felt, rightly or wrongly, that it was them against us. On one side you had the forces of the state arrayed, the government at Stormont and the British army and the RUC and the B-Specials. And on the other side, us.

When I arrived at Trinity College in Dublin, I arrived with what I thought were very liberal views. But the Trinity students laughed at me when I talked about the Troubles and the Provos – they thought it was hilarious. It wasn't that they didn't believe me but that my ideology was very immature and very biased. I just assumed that everybody could see that the

Provos were in the right, that this was a great human rights struggle and all the rest of it. But they lampooned me until I had to say to myself, 'Christ, I'd better have a look at this again!' Because if you were a Dungiven person, nobody ever said, 'Should we be involved in this? Should we be blowing up soldiers? Should we be shooting a prison officer in the face in front of his family? Is this all right? Or does there come a point where we have to look at a different way of proceeding?' We never thought of that. We were in the middle of it, ding-dong, you were in it to the death. We were the good team and those guys were the bad team. So Trinity was a big experience for me. You had the intelligentsia there, they were relating it to other conflicts, and so I was able to look at the world in a more holistic way. I was very immature at the time. I arrived at Trinity with the maturity of an eleven-year-old. I came to see that there might be another way that observed the sanctity of human life.

There is a bias against Northerners by a section in the South. You look at the *Sunday Independent* and you see some of the writers – pathetic stuff. I see people getting angry and I think, 'Oh for God's sake, don't be getting upset with that.'

One of the things the open border has done is promote massive cross-border alliances between GAA clubs and counties. An example: you look at Cushendall hurlers who went to the all-Ireland semi-final this year. I met them in the Carrickdale Hotel [Co. Louth], where they were stopping for a bite of breakfast. They were on their way to Tipperary for a weekend of hurling. They were going to play the Tipperary hurlers on the Saturday and the Cork hurlers on the Sunday. They told me that was their fifth weekend in a row on the go, to the South, to get the right level of competition. And they're welcomed with open arms wherever they go. And they're not saying to themselves, 'Right, there's going to be a two-hour delay at the border.' There's no issue with the border, it's invisible.

All that makes a massive difference, and a difference in your mind. Because being Irish is a state of mind, as is being British in the North.

The hesitation of Southerners to come North doesn't exist any more – they come North all the time. Derry city, for example, is thriving. We had the Fleadh [music festival] in Derry city, which was a huge breakthrough. And you wouldn't have seen a police officer or an army man or anything like that. So the invisible border is crucial. If that were to change, you most definitely would see a hardening of attitudes.

There's a problem with the DUP and the deep-seated sectarianism that's there. The supremacist attitude, the contempt for all things Irish. The scorn of the Irish language, the homophobia, the creationism. It's all on record. You cannot underestimate the sectarianism in the North.

We had this big organ donation day. Peter Robinson and Martin McGuinness were very enthusiastic supporters, and I have a great regard for Peter. I saw him as a secular presence, really trying to modernise the party, but he was eventually destroyed by the bigots. Peter, no more than myself, would have started off with a very immature view of the world, because that was the world he lived in. I can understand that entirely.

Anyway, Jim Wells was invited; he was the minister for health in those days. We invited him because presumably he'd want to be informed about the latest developments in organ donation and transplant. I was sitting there with Tim Brown, the surgeon, and Aisling Courtney, who has presided over the most successful organ donation and kidney transplant programme in the UK and now possibly in Europe. These are serious people.

So Jim arrives and he says, 'Ah, Joe Brolly! I will always remember the day that you brought the Sam Maguire Cup to the United Kingdom on behalf of Londonderry!' This went on all day – it became excruciating. But I just kept smiling politely. You could see Tim Brown and the others looking at me – 'Jesus Christ, is this where we are?' And it is where we are. I told the story some time later, once Wells had left as the minister for health. When I told the story, he was interviewed by the *News Letter:* 'Well, I did say that, but I only said it in the spirit of fun!' But there's nothing funny about that – not when you've repeated it fifty times. I wouldn't poke jokes at his religion or sporting allegiances or anything like that. I mean, it's just basic human stuff.

So that's a massive problem, and one of the reasons why the cross-border bodies haven't worked out the way they ought to have.

But there still has been a massive coming together. You look at the way the Protestant middle classes are holidaying in the South of Ireland now, travelling to Dublin regularly, the way that Ulster rugby has been received in Dublin any time they go to play a game there. It's all been breaking down barriers. And Brexit has presented us with a massive opportunity because you've got this unresolved question in Ireland: what we want to be, what works best for the citizens of the North.

I think the DUP has realised that any sort of Brexit is the fast road to a united Ireland. It doesn't matter what kind of Brexit it is. Because slowly but surely the anchors are being pulled up. I mean, everyone knows that it's completely disingenuous what Theresa May and the ERG say. As if anybody thinks that Jacob Rees-Mogg would piss on the DUP if it were on fire, and you can quote me on that. He wouldn't. Rees-Mogg and these guys are playing their own game. It's about finance, it's about their own business.

At this point the Catholic middle class have turned their face from Stormont and are looking towards Dublin. Catholics in 1998 weren't used to politics at all. We had no experience of governance. It's all very new for us to have our representatives in there. But I think we're very quick to realise that they're powerless. They're fighting over things of no importance, like flags. Fucking *flags*!

I was at a thing up in Lagan [Integrated] College. Naomi Long of the Alliance Party was there, Gavin Robinson of the DUP, and Michael O'Neill, who had just been made the manager of Northern Ireland. Several different schools were there – A Level – Methody, St Malachy's, Knock – the intelligentsia. So Naomi Long started on about flags. Máirtín Ó Muilleoir [former lord mayor of Belfast] was also there. I said to the crowd, 'It's just unfortunate there's no baby here today for him to hug.' Máirtín's all winking and selfies and all the rest of it. Holding meetings out in America.

Anyway, Naomi started going on about flags and oh, the progress we're making, we've had meetings. I said, 'Hold on, hold on.' There were about 300 kids there. I said, 'Can any of you who has ever discussed flags during the school day, or thought about flags, or thinks that flags are important, raise your hand.' Not one hand went up. I said, 'Do any of you have any real issues you'd like Ms Long to deal with?' And this kid said, 'I would like to ask you about the decreasing budget for disability services. That's what I'm interested in.' And he had facts and figures.

It's easier to talk about flags because those are questions of no importance. Increasingly people are seeing the sectarianism in that and are saying, 'What's the point of this?'

We have three Irish schools in Dungiven; it's vibrant there. And the Irish Language Act is an indication of mutual respect. That's all it is. 'We respect you. You can be Irish if you wish.' That's the whole point in the GFA: 'It's fine to be Irish, it's fine to be British.'

There's increasing pressure coming on Sinn Féin about this because people are becoming more logical; we're coming away from the Troubles, and people are saying, 'Hold on. Why are Sinn Féin not taking their seats in Westminster but are sitting out there?' And Mary Lou is making these weighty pronouncements about Brexit, when Sinn Féin would negate the DUP were they to actually take their seats in the House of Commons. People are having debates like this.

We need more activism. You look at Sinn Féin, for example. They're not *doing* anything: in many constituencies it's enough just to be Sinn Féin. Get your face on the poster and you'll be elected. I'm delighted to see the community activism that's started now in London over climate change. The *gilets jaunes* are destroying Macron's austerity programme, which was only designed to create a closer bond with Germany in relation to Europe. We need more community activism – real community activism.

Do you think the Protestant working classes are being represented by the DUP? The DUP is supporting Brexit, which it's predicted by the government's own think tank will result in a 9% decrease in the Northern Ireland economy, which means a severe and prolonged recession. The DUP knows that no matter what sort of Brexit there is, it's going to weaken the union. That's the reality.

In a way this is the DUP's last stand. They're enjoying basking in power at the minute. I don't think they've got any particular regard for their constituents.

The DUP has gone from one scandal to another, and it instinctively knows that Brexit is the beginning of the end for the union. As soon as Catholics begin to see any sort of presence on the border – any presence – should it delay you ten minutes, should you be sitting in a queue – it'll be 'What the fuck is this? Is this what we fucking signed up to?'

It will create activism, it will create a new approach, a new dynamism around the idea of a united Ireland. There's going to be a united Ireland anyway: everybody knows that. It's just a question of time. All this will do is hasten it.

The people in the South will vote for a united Ireland. They will have no choice. You mustn't forget the vast influence of Irish America. You watch the reaction to Nancy Pelosi [US speaker of the House of Representatives]: Ireland is extremely reliant on America, on American business.

The Americans say, 'This is what we want. Hey, Fine Gael, Leo Varadkar. Here's where we are with this.' Which is how they speak to you – the Americans are in charge here. 'You want these billions every year? You want every American multi-national to be in Dublin, in Galway, in Cork? Well, this is where we are with it.' The Free Staters will vote for a united Ireland, and there is absolutely no doubt about that. Because Sinn Féin has a solid base there, Fianna Fáil will go for it 100% and Leo Varadkar will not stand against it.

Then what'll happen is – don't forget, don't forget – American money. What American president or American presidential candidate isn't going to say, 'Hold on. OK, so here's $100 billion as a starting point. This is what we're going to pledge to this new state. This is amazing, this is a day of celebration.' The American-Irish are unbelievably sentimental about this country and they're a very powerful lobby on Capitol Hill.

The other thing about the Americans is they hate the unionists. They fucking hate them! Yes, unionists may hate them back, but it doesn't matter. It's like the fucking flea hating the rhinoceros. It doesn't make any difference.

The fact is, the Northern state is illogical. What it required to operate as a standalone state was logical politics, which we haven't had and the DUP will not allow to happen – logical, mutual respect. There was a time when they could have made it, but now it's not going to happen.

The Americans know, and the Brits too: how do you really create the peace process? The real essential for the peace process is to bribe the loyalist paramilitaries and bribe the Provos. Give them all fucking jobs. Pour money into the community centres. Make sure they're all made community leaders, pay them salaries. Brilliant! That's how the peace process was cemented. Every Kalashnikov-holding loyalist or Provo in the country was given a job as a community representative. Money was fired at them. Simple.

The UVF and the Ulster Defence Association (UDA) exist because they're selling drugs and controlling the communities. I'll tell you something. In one way we're lucky that we have them, rather than the situation which prevails in Dublin and Limerick. There are frequent assassinations there – it's just par for the course.

Of course money will be used to solve this problem here. Let me give you an example: Casement Park and the residents. You had a £65 million project; you have an £80 million project now. We've now lost £9–10 million in the delays because the residents have employed a superb review lawyer who is putting maximum pressure on. If they had been approached by the GAA Ulster Council and it had said, 'For each of these families, here's £50,000' or 'Here's £100,000 for your inconvenience,' this wouldn't be a problem. Casement Park would have been built, we wouldn't be £10 million down. Weigh that against what it would have cost for the residents – a suitable sum so they'd say, 'Hi – we're happy enough for you to play there the odd Sunday. Most of us have double glazing anyway, we won't hear a thing.' But the GAA didn't do that and now look what's happened.

So one of the key things in the peace process was that buying off of the loyalists and republicans.

You cannot underestimate the level of sectarianism in this society. You put in a Freedom of Information request about the religious make-up of the police or the prison service and you'll find it's largely Protestant at every level. One of the reasons Catholics haven't bought into the PSNI or the prison service is that they're looking at the DUP.

Now, I do not vote for Sinn Féin, I've no time for them. But for me the real problem is the DUP: it keeps rubbing your nose in it. Fuck's sake, boys, back the fuck off! A bit of statesman-like behaviour wouldn't go amiss. And that's what Peter Robinson was trying to achieve, but it wasn't going to wash with them. The tub-thumpers and the creationists and all the rest, they put an end to him.

Look at the behaviour of the DUP in the House of Commons: why does it seem to disparage everybody? It always appears to be chortling at people, and seems to think jokes about women and homosexuals are funny. I think Bernard Manning would have gone down a storm at the DUP conference. And the difference was, Bernard Manning didn't mean it.

I don't actually think Brexit will happen. There are no agreements anywhere. The problem with Brexit was that it was an election stunt and it wasn't sold as a set of pre-ordained outcomes, telling people what's going to happen. For me, it provides an amazing opportunity to have democratic debate. It is already doing that. May's deal is doomed; she is doomed. There are only two possibilities: a second referendum or a general election.

The Leave campaign is utterly propagandistic. That said, I have serious problems with Europe. I think the ECB, the way the European community is so in thrall to the elites ... the entire country of Greece was destroyed, rather than saying, 'Here are very preferential long-term ways where we write down most of your debt' – that's what you would do with any private individual.

As Yanis Varoufakis [former Greek minister of finance] said, in the old days before companies were invented to protect individuals, people who didn't succeed in business went to debtors' prison. It was a disaster: there was no industry, there was no entrepreneurship. So what do you do in Europe, which is supposedly a modern multi-state organisation that's working in harmony with the Greek people? Close their banks down. Here's the package, accept it or else. They will not write down the debts, give them preferential treatment, not give them a boost. All those things could easily have been achieved.

So there's an opportunity here to look at Europe and see how it works and whether it's working at all. It's working in some respects. It's kept the peace. But look what happened to Ireland: the South of Ireland got absolutely fucked with austerity. Fucking take it, gun to the head. Greece tried to go it alone and look what happened. They shut down the ATMs, the country went into meltdown.

There is a different way for Europe, it could work out very well. You could have harmonisation of taxes, you could have the closing down of tax havens, all those sorts of things. You could look at the real issues: tax, big pharma, the real issues that beset a society.

We should only be in the EU if it's actually going to benefit the citizenry. The problem now is that the Irish did well for a while with roads, motorways, all of that. The Irish economy was going well. Which was of course a bubble economy and it was overheating. It was based on personal debt and property prices that were illusory. While everything was going well, that was fine. But once we needed the EU? Fuck off and die.

With Brexit, the EU has stood by the South of Ireland, but only for their own interests. Their leverage is being used in the South to prevent the UK from leaving because they know the DUP holds the balance of power. That's why they are saying at all times, 'There'll be absolutely no question of a hard border. It will not happen.'

What we need now is progressive leadership in the North. Sinn Féin is better than the DUP, but it needs to come away from the yah-boo stuff. We need progressive leadership, particularly progressive unionist leadership, to prepare unionist people for a different society.

The problem is that none of the real issues have been dealt with. You go up the Shankill or into East Belfast. You'll see the ghettoes, the terrible poverty. It's a fucking scandal what's happening. And what passes for politics is the propaganda machine that is the DUP. That's what passes for politics. And so the reality is that they're going to be dragged kicking and screaming into a different society.

Everybody knows it. It's going to be a painful enough process for some of them, but they need to start getting real. It's going to happen anyway. We need to set up a body now that has the political leaders, the business leaders, leaders from every walk of life. We need to set about a new constitution guaranteeing the rights of people who see themselves as British: passports, all that. Everything that is needed should be done.

And it should be in writing. A new constitution. We should be deciding, for example, in the first phases of a new all-Ireland parliament, whether a unionist should be jointly in power as the Taoiseach. You could have a joint role, the same sort of mechanism that they have used here, which has cemented the peace process even though it hasn't worked politically in the North. All those things need to be done in advance, and it needs to be started soon. We need an all-Ireland forum that will deal with that.

Who should set it up? The British and Irish governments, with the US. The Americans are always useful to bring in because there's a bit of star quality around the Yanks. Not Donald Trump, though.

I've written a column about this recently. How does the health service work, how do we fund everything, how much European money is needed, how much American money is needed?

Of course it can be done. It's inevitable. Northern Ireland is dead. And within fifteen years it will be buried – it's gone. Fifteen years from now isn't really long. People think as I do that the GFA was signed yesterday – because that's about as much progress as has been made. But time's up. Time's up! They had the chance. They had the chance.

19

NIALL O'DOWD

10 MAY 2019

Niall O'Dowd is an Irish-American journalist and author living in the United States. He was an important figure in the Irish-American drive to enlist the support of President Bill Clinton for the Irish peace process and was influential in the negotiations leading to the GFA. He is founder of *The Irish Voice* newspaper and *Irish America* magazine in New York City, and he oversees *Home and Away* newspaper. He is also the founder of IrishCentral, a website which he launched in March 2009.

I grew up in Co. Louth, twenty-two miles from the border. Across the border was a place everyone went for shopping – a different country, a far more advanced country. Any time we went up there, you knew when you had hit the North because the roads improved dramatically and there'd be a sense of wealth in the size of the houses and farms. And there were rumours that there were sexy magazines you could buy in the North that you couldn't buy in the South – which proved to be a big lie as far as I was concerned. But it was another place, a different place.

We were very keenly aware that once you crossed that border, the money changed, the police looked different, the cars were different, the highways were much better, the buildings were much more spic and span. Occasionally you'd find people in shops who were quite unfriendly to you – they didn't like somebody from 'down there'. And there were stories that Newry girls were very loose – much more loose than the girls in the South. Our dream was to meet one of these fabled girls. [*Laughs*]

The militarisation of the border meant it went from the back of your mind to the front of your mind, purely because of the intrusion of the media. My father was a real media hound. He would read everything – *The Irish Times, Irish Independent, The Irish Press – and* listen to the RTÉ news. And every day there was something new about the border. Every day was about people like Bernadette Devlin, John Hume and Austin Currie – that was the original group – and events like Burntollet [where People's Democracy marchers going from Belfast to Derry were attacked by loyalists]. Suddenly you went from being indifferent, frankly, to caring very much about what was happening. Because you could see that there was us and there was them, and you were part of us and you were getting the shit kicked out of you.

I remember a football tournament where I was with the Co. Louth team and there were four counties involved: Antrim, Armagh, Down and Louth. I remember talking to the other players, which was the first time I'd ever had a conversation with such people. When they went to training they all went together, for protection. They had been stopped on the way to the game; the police were very nasty and violent. I had never thought of the police as other than legitimate and fair-minded. So that was an eye-opener for me.

I had a pervasive sense of fear every time I came to one of those border spy-posts, particularly when I was working with

Sinn Féin. There was one right outside Dundalk: a green mon-
strous building on a hill with armed British soldiers. It was a
totally alien experience to me. I never ran into any aggressive-
ness from them, to be fair. But they would search the car and
they would look at my licence, and you had to wait before you
were allowed to drive on. It was very much a militarised zone.

Did people resent it? Very much so.

When the Troubles started, there were definitely a few more
Northern accents around Drogheda town centre. So it was
clearly some sort of staging post. It seemed to me that everybody was turning a blind eye, initially anyway. A lot of Northerners fled down South on 12 July. They'd go to Butlin's and
spend a weekend there. And you'd suddenly find hundreds of
Northern Irish people shopping in Drogheda, staying at Butlin's, and you'd slowly but surely put it together in your head
that, well, that's because they have to leave. On the other hand,
you'd see on TV the Paisleyites and others, banging their big
drums.

I began to get a deep sense of unfairness about the whole
thing, which was generally shared by people in the South.
Something very bad was starting to happen.

The absolutely critical moment was Bloody Sunday. After
Bloody Sunday, everybody was ready to go North. I think it
transformed the Irish. They went from almost indifference
to deep compassion and anger about what had happened on
Bloody Sunday. On your own island of Ireland, fourteen un-
armed people had been shot dead. I had a sudden realisation
that holy fuck, things are really bad up there. I would say that
was the reaction of most of my friends too.

Then over the years, with the IRA violence, it all got very re-petitive. The initial anger faded and you were encountering the attitude: 'Let them at it, it's got nothing to do with us.' Which was very regrettable, but probably understandable because of the fear of the violence. I remember my father believing it was only a matter of time before Southern intervention after Jack Lynch said, 'We won't stand by.'[1] I often think to this day that if the South had acted, it might have been an awful lot better in the long run. In retrospect, all they had to do was take Derry or someplace – the whole thing would have collapsed.

Over the years I was coming back to Ireland frequently and dealing a lot with Sinn Féin. Basically I was the intermediary between the White House and Sinn Féin, in terms of things like the Adams visa [a forty-eight-hour visa for Sinn Féin leader Gerry Adams to visit the US] and decommissioning. So I would have had my own fears when I was over there that I was being followed or observed. And I had enough evidence that I probably was.

Certainly when we went over with the American delega-tions, the drivers we got were clearly British intelligence. These guys would keep asking us probing questions. After about twenty minutes I said to the other people – Bruce Mor-rison, Bill Flynn and Chuck Feeney – 'Do not talk in the car.' The feeling of a confined, secretive, claustrophobic, xenopho-bic society was very strong. We would obviously have been targets, because they were quite upset about the American dimension. We were the people who had originally brought Clinton to the table on the issue, so we weren't the most popular people in Ireland.

I was particularly frightened on one occasion when I was being driven to a meeting with some senior Sinn Féin people in Belfast, and the driver literally drove at 100 miles per hour, and I thought maybe I'd been kidnapped or something. He picked me up at the Wellington Park Hotel and he brought me to West Belfast, and he was clearly a Formula One driver. [*Laughs*] He was just driving up and down streets, reversing, turning – making sure he wasn't being followed. So of course I was scared – absolutely scared.

The border doesn't feature in the GFA, but we were pretty much aware that it would be demilitarised, like everything else. In retrospect it was an incredibly important issue for everyone, psychologically. Certainly it was one of the great underpinnings of the Agreement, whether or not it was explicitly in it.

In the Brexit referendum, when they were voting for it, nobody talked about the border. I think it was the same with the GFA: I never remember being contacted and told, 'This is very important, we have to get American pressure,' whereas I was for decommissioning and a lot of other issues. But never on the border, no.

After the GFA I remember the day I drove up and suddenly it wasn't there. That was a profound moment. The idea of driving from Dublin to Belfast without being stopped by a land border was hugely, hugely important. I remember doing the trip by train as well, and nobody got on at Dundalk or Newry to investigate where you were going. Those were moments of great relief and happiness.

This is a small island. It's had some terrible times, but we have got something very right here. With the natural symmetry of the country there is no natural physical border, the highway should run all the way. I think there was a general welcome for that, even I think from unionists. There was a huge difference in mentality.

I think it altered nationalist mentality profoundly, as a huge benefit of the Agreement. There was the parity-of-esteem issue and the border was gone. Psychologically that was hugely important, especially to people on the border but also to people in the North generally – that they could move freely.

I think there is a sense among thinking unionism – and I don't think that's necessarily an oxymoron [*chuckles*] – people realise that you can be different things. You can be European, you can be Irish, you can be British. We don't have to obsess about this fact of Britishness. And there are definitions of Irishness. There are Irish-American, Irish-Australian, Irish-Canadian – all different experiences.

The thing I noticed the most was the emergence of the Celtic Tiger in the South, making better roads, better highways; suddenly you stopped thinking the North was the superior one. You'd cross the border and suddenly they had a much smaller highway. And you'd begin to think, 'This is very interesting!' [*Laughs*]

But I also remember going North of Belfast and seeing no development. Beautiful scenery, fantastic opportunities for tourism – yet nothing there, nothing at all. Then going into the town of Bushmills and seeing all this hatred and slogans, and thinking, 'Jesus, this really is the land that time forgot!' [*Laughs*]

I think what's fascinating is the mistake made on this occasion by the Brexit people and by the unionists, in terms of the importance of the border issue. I mean, the return of the border would be catastrophic. Absolutely – psychologically and in every way, it would be completely catastrophic. Because there's been a war and there's been a peace. And the border is an incredibly large part of the peace. You cannot return a border without a resumption of violence – that's my view.

If you can't get in your car and drive from Dublin to Belfast, that's not good news for peace in Ireland. It's a highway, a fantastic highway. There is no border and the game is over. That's it. You bring back a border, you bring back violence. And I can see why people on the border would justifiably say, 'Fuck this. This is not working for us.' That's not just dissident republicans. There are ordinary people who suddenly find their daily lives interrupted by this ridiculous and artificial entity known as the border, which has 381 unapproved roads or whatever. It's just a recipe for disaster.

I don't think our generation would be galvanised towards violence, but there are youngsters out there, as we saw in Derry, who can be very easily manipulated into the position where they'd start shooting again. You put up a border and a lot of people will support them, because it would be an imposition, a gross act of vandalism on the GFA. Which is what Brexit is anyway – a gross act of vandalism by the British government on an international agreement that has brought peace to the island of Ireland for twenty-one years now.

George Mitchell would be the first to say it – the GFA is not negotiable. It was negotiated and it's accepted within that Agreement that there will be no border, otherwise you lose a whole cornerstone. It's not explicit, but it's part of the overall reality that has been there since the GFA was signed. You can't take back a goal, you can't take back an ambition. The ambition was to create a frictionless border, which was created. It was a huge part of the mentality of people. Let's remember – people voted, what, 78% to pass the GFA. There are those who talk about Brexit as the will of the people: so was the GFA. A free vote. So to go back on that, as I say, would be an act of tremendous vandalism.

Talking with Niall Murphy [lawyer for the Loughinisland families, whose loved ones were killed by loyalist paramilitaries], he was adamant that people on the border would become extremely militant. Not necessarily IRA militant, but very militant. Would it be people lying down on the road? Would it be attacking the physical structures? It's so dangerous to even think in that direction. The sad part is, when Barack Obama was elected I thought my life would be a series of progressions. And then comes Donald Trump! [*Laughs*] You had great leaders like Mitchell, like Tony Blair, like Bertie Ahern – for all of the bad things he did. And now you've got these pygmies who can't make out what day of the week it is, making up the rules as they go along. It's tremendously damaging.

I can tell you that over the years since the GFA, there have been a number of attempts by Irish militants to energise Irish America again. All have failed due to the fact that the key people within Irish America are for the peace process. That's it, they've made their bet. But if the border came back, those same people could very well be open to re-energising and saying, 'Fuck this.' I absolutely could see it. And these are very serious people who, behind the scenes, played major roles in making sure that people toed the line. The American attitude was always very important for Sinn Féin. And that would absolutely turn in favour of militancy again if there was a border. I can absolutely guarantee that.

I'm sick of these arguments that economics rules: it doesn't rule. What rules is emotion and passion. That's how it started up in 1969, and it would start up again through emotion and passion. I would have very ambivalent views if a border came back as to whether it was worth it at all. Because I think it's that big a deal. I think there are certain fundamentals such as the vote on unification, the border, the three strands being fully negotiated. I think those are the things that are not negotiable. Otherwise you'd just tear apart the whole GFA. Brexit would do it.

Economically I can tell you that Northern Ireland would be in deep shit right away. Business leaders over here would say, 'Time has moved on – nobody wants to go anywhere violent.' The businessmen are already dubious enough, but new investment in Northern Ireland would be extremely hard to get. I don't think the South would be that impacted – it never was during the Troubles. They were pretty successful in cornering off that aspect.

Sinn Féin people say to me, 'Now the people of Britain know what we were dealing with in the DUP. They're incorrigible, they're unreasonable – you can't deal with them.' I think that would be true more and more. So the nationalist middle class would have a very blunt choice that they wouldn't have had ten years ago, because Peter Robinson and people like that were not unsympathetic figures. But the DUP's present leader is tragically short of any courage to deliver. Maybe Arlene Foster just can't deliver.

Losing McGuinness and Adams was a huge blow. No matter who came after them, it would be very hard to have the same level of control if violence started up again.

A border poll? I like it – 2022. And I am serious. I think it's part of the GFA, freely negotiated. I think anything that is part of that Agreement should be, as far as possible, introduced. The sentiment and the demographic is moving in that direction. I'm not afraid at all of the fact that there'd be a nationalist majority in Northern Ireland. That's reality. It was a headcount to begin with: the creation of the state was absolutely ring-fenced so that they would have a majority in perpetuity – which they don't have any more. I see some of the moderate unionists and even Peter Robinson saying that now is the time to talk about this. I don't think anyone is talking about an imperialistic view of a united Ireland, but something where the island of Ireland would be governed in a different way. A border poll doesn't necessarily mean unionists lose out, but that they accept a different role, which would be a leadership role still.

But there's an awful lot of work to be done before we get to that point. I have no qualms at all about a border poll that would show a united Ireland. I think the unionist middle class and the SDLP-type middle class are starting to look at it.

But there is a lot of work ahead. You would have to do what the Scots did. They released 670 pages about what would happen if Scotland became independent. Unlike what the Brits did, you'd have to have major preparations in place. You'd have to have discussions about every aspect of what would occur in the event of unification. And I think that would be in a major way down to preparation. If you look at the way the Irish government has handled issues like abortion, issues like gay marriage, where they went to 100 people picked at random, then they went through the Dáil, so approval was there the whole time. If you did the same on the basis of unity, I think it would be a very different animal from Brexit with its 'Brexit or bust'. What does Brexit mean? Oh, we forgot to ask. The border wasn't mentioned once in the Brexit campaign.

Human rights are a very big deal in terms of Brexit. You're talking about a discriminatory form of nationalism, where one person can be part of the EU if he's in the Republic, but the guy's brother living in the North can't. I think all of this comes down to a lack of forward planning, a lack of thought in the unionist community and in the Tory party. And in the Labour Party too, unfortunately. It's like people here [in the US] who elected Donald Trump and didn't think twice. But now they're going, 'Holy fuck, the guy's a nut-job!'

You can't have Brexit with a border. You should go back to the original one, which is a line in the Irish Sea. That was the only relatively mild way that had any prospect. The Labour Party in London should be saying that. They should run an election on the basis of it, and I think that would be the end of it.

If nationalists in the North find themselves back to being second-class citizens, back to being Rosa Parks, I think they'll say 'Fuck this' and put a very profound two fingers up to it – which I think would then generate a border poll, which could make things worse, depending on how it was managed.

From what I've been reading, the 2021 census will reveal pretty much a nationalist majority in the North, or very close. At that point, if you were looking at it as just a pure exercise in democracy, and there appears to be a nationalist majority, we should find out if there is or not. Then it's game on.

Allowing the British secretary of state to decide about the timing of a border poll was a mistake on the nationalist side. It should have been on the basis of agreement between the British and Irish governments. But I think the demographics will force a poll within five years in any event. Because if you don't hold it, you're just driving people further into the united Ireland camp. So it's a zero-sum game for the Brits. The day the British secretary of state, by calling a border poll, indicates that the British are packing their bags – that'll be a great day for Ireland. I'm not a bit afraid of that day and I hope I live to see it. [*Laughs*]

Right now, middle-class nationalism is there for the taking. I think they're not convinced yet about a united Ireland, but the more the British press Brexit, the more will go into the united Ireland camp. I think that's the key to this whole thing: what the middle-class Malone Road nationalist is going to do when he's actually faced with the reality. Is he going to stay with what has been a relatively good system for him, in terms of his advancement, his career? Or is he going to do the historical thing and say, 'This was unfair from the beginning. We belong as one island, one people.'?

I've never taken the economic argument seriously, or that a united Ireland would be disastrous for the Republic. You would have money pouring in from the EU, the US. There would be tremendous backing for any agreement like that.

There's no such thing as a soft Brexit. There's either Brexit or there's not. May has a fundamental incomprehension. She promised there'd be no border and she promised there'd be a border. There's no way to solve that. The only thing that can be done is to go back to the original idea, that there's a border in the Irish Sea. Which I thought was a very fair way of dealing with it. But any of the other solutions means there's a profound winner and a profound loser.

I don't think the UK Parliament will vote for a customs union because it's completely delegitimising Brexit if they do.

One of my biggest regrets is the failure of Jeremy Corbyn [Labour Party leader] to show leadership – which is very surprising, because years ago he was quite a smart guy ahead of the curve on the whole issue of Ireland. But this nonsense of sitting on the fence is destroying his party.

There's an article in *The Guardian* today that the Tories may finish sixth [in the local and European elections]. Just think about that for a minute. That's how crazy Brexit is. It's a completely insane proposition to begin with.

I think there'll have to be another referendum. The fundamental issue in the local election is Brexit. The only party that was legitimately saying 'We'll get rid of Brexit' was the Liberal Democrats, and they won 704 seats. It's pretty clear where the British are. They're re-thinking it and saying, 'This is a dumb idea.'

But that's OK. Ireland did it with the Nice Treaty. You can go back and say, 'Yeah, we fucked up.' Look at our president, for fuck's sake.

There was an original vote to go into the EU. That has now been set aside. If you can't enforce what the people voted for, you have to go back and renegotiate it. I mean, democracy isn't some fragile flower. It's quite pliant if you get the right people working on the solution.

You know, I blame [Rupert] Murdoch. I blame Murdoch here with Fox News and over in the UK with the tabloid newspapers. He is a malevolent force wherever he goes. He brings hate, suspicion, anti-immigration [sentiment]. And he gets away with it. That's what happened in Britain. Look at some of the stories in the Tory press – I mean, they're horrific about Brexit. Complete lies.

Some republicans got their birthday present early with the Brexit vote because they knew it would be destabilising. But that's the mad thing. In the name of expanding the Empire, the UK risks losing Northern Ireland and Scotland.

I think a border poll was a GFA creation – nothing to do with Brexit. So why wouldn't there be a border poll anyway? If there's a belief that there's now a nationalist majority, if the census shows that?

Sometime inside the next five, ten, fifteen years, there will be a decisive nationalist majority of people who will say, 'There has to be a poll.' I think the ignorance of the unionists in dealing with nationalists, more than anything – I think that's the profound mistake the DUP has made. Instead of reaching out and doing what Robinson was speaking of, talking about all this, it's actually put the boot on the neck one more time, 'croppie, lie down'. The idea of Sammy Wilson getting up in the House of Commons, when Brexit failed in Northern Ireland, speaking on behalf of the people of Northern Ireland. [*Laughs*] Claiming the right to speak even though the proposition had been lost.

If we were sitting here in 2030, there'd probably be 20% more nationalists in Northern Ireland than unionists. What do you do then? If in 2025 there isn't a nationalist majority, and they take a vote, well then, they can come back again and vote in seven years.

Demographics is destiny. There's no question what's going on in Northern Ireland, and even the unionists have to acknowledge that. There is a wave of nationalist upsurge in terms of the numbers, so it's not going to end well for the unionists, no matter what they do.

The Irish population in the South voted for gay marriage and other liberal measures. Ten years ago it would have been impossible to predict that. There's actually a depth of thought in Ireland about these issues that people have overlooked. Yes, it's a cheap headline to say it would cost us 10 billion – but I guarantee you it wouldn't cost 10 billion, with European money and American money and all that behind it. I think the South would vote for unification. No doubt. No doubt at all.

20

SEAN McMANUS

14 MAY 2019

Originally from Co. Fermanagh, Fr Sean McManus is founder and president of the Capitol Hill–based Irish National Caucus. In 1984, he launched the MacBride Principles, one of the caucus's signature initiatives, which called on US companies investing in Northern Ireland to operate a fair employment practice. He continues to lobby for justice and peace in Ireland. Since 2013, Fr McManus has been chief judge of the World Peace Prize, headquartered in Seoul, South Korea.

My local parish of Kinawley in Co. Fermanagh is divided by the border. So not only is my country divided but my parish is divided by – and you'll excuse me, I've never called it anything else – the damn border.

I was born in 1944. My parents, my uncles, my aunts – all the older people were born in a borderless Ireland. This was a farming community and suddenly, here was this border. It had a profound effect on them and their thinking.

Kinawley is a little village and also the parish. Across the border is Swanlinbar. In the IRA 1956–62 campaign, that customs post had been blown up a number of times, without any injury, by my brother Patrick and his colleagues in the IRA. Patrick was the IRA O/C [officer commanding] for South Fermanagh, and later on the Army Council of the IRA. He was a highly regarded guerrilla, according to everyone who knew him.

He was killed in a premature explosion. He was handing up quite a powerful bomb from behind a ditch and it went off. The other guys were shielded by the ditch and had only minor injuries. Patrick was totally blown to bits.

We were then a marked family, for years and years. When the Troubles started, my brother Frank was an MP, and he was harassed constantly by the soldiers and by the UDR. When I was travelling with him, they would insist on searching me. I remember at one point coming from a family wedding and Frank said to the fellow, 'I'm your MP, you know.' He said, 'No, you're not my MP.'

I remember coming back from America, crossing the Lisnaskea way, and I was stopped by the UDR on the bridge. The guy in charge asked for my ID. On my ID it said, 'District of Columbia'. Some ignorant lout asked, 'Hi, are there many mosquitoes in Colombia?' He thought I was coming from Colombia. And then when they read the name, another fellow ran up with a gun and pointed it right at my head. He said, 'Are you Father Sean McManus?' You could smell drink on him a mile away. His captain or whoever he was had to physically drag him away from the car. He might have been a neighbour. I didn't recognise him.

There wouldn't have been one person in that area who would have thought kindly of the border. I don't think even the farming Protestants did. The border totally inconvenienced everyone. Instead of just showing your identification and going through, there were lines of traffic. And there's nothing as aggravating for country people as having to wait in line. If you live in the country, you don't have traffic-jams – but here, right in the middle of nowhere, there's a mile-long queue of traffic and there are sandbags and there's incivility and the mood of: 'We're in charge. We're the boss, you do what we tell you.'

I came back to Ireland every year. The militarised border began to disappear only after the GFA. The barracks in Kinawley had been heavily fortified – and then it's gone! I couldn't believe that. I used to love, once the peace process started, to drive seamlessly from Dublin to home. Never seeing an Alsatian, or a sandbag, or barbed wire or British soldiers or UDR – nothing.

It grieves me that there hasn't been more unionist/loyalist outreach towards Catholics and the South. The *Belfast Telegraph* gave us a hard time because we produced a video on the Irish National Caucus website. On it I make the point that, despite the wonderful progress, in a significant section of the Protestant/loyalist/unionist community there is still a deep reluctance to accept Catholics as equals. The DUP has never actually accepted the GFA. That's quite astonishing. The DUP is led by Arlene Foster, my colleague from Fermanagh – the other side of the lough! – God bless her, I wish her nothing but well and every time I've met her here in DC she's been very friendly and gracious. There is that Fermanagh respect there. But I wish she would loosen up a bit and do more to reach out. I am aware that when she went to a Gaelic football game, she was criticised by her own DUP people, so I realise it's difficult. But when does the outreach begin? Twenty-one years after the GFA and things are still deeply entrenched.

In the early days after the GFA, people in general who were critical of David Trimble would say he moved too slowly. He should have embraced it, he should have brought his people with him. He should have said, 'Hey, I'm 100% behind this.' He didn't do that. Now, twenty-one years later, there's still no great movement. And I am still very conscious – even though I wish Arlene the very best – that she and Donaldson left the UUP because she thought Trimble had gone, in effect, soft on Catholics. That's a sad thought. I wish that was not the case.

Many people have stressed that there'd be violence if some kind of physical structure appears after Brexit. I don't mean the return of the IRA. It's bound to really offend people who are continually crossing the border. It's an unnecessary provocation.

But that's the nature of Brexit. There has to be some sort of distinction if the UK leaves the EU. You cannot maintain that the UK leaving the EU will have no effect – I'm afraid it's going to have an effect because there will be a border. This is where the EU ends, in the Swanlinbar–Kinawley area. There's no way we can avoid that. The ordinary folk will resent it, and they'll tear down signs and so on. Ordinary people. Furthermore, it's an open invitation to the dissident republicans, who are waiting for an excuse to have a go at something.

I think the return of a border will be worse for younger people – under thirty-five – because we are supposed to be past Empire days. In 1920, this is what the British Empire did. I find it extremely ironic that Britain, the one country on the planet that had a record over hundreds of years of disrespecting all borders – because that's the meaning of an empire, we do not respect borders, except the ones we create – now they're so insistent on having a border.

As [journalist] Fintan O'Toole has pointed out, what we are witnessing is an upsurge in English nationalism. It's certainly not Welsh, it's certainly not Scottish – it's England, and a very tiny part of England. I find that troubling, because I see it with Trump and Putin and all the strongmen who are actually weak men, frightened and scared, and who resort to this bravado. When I think that everybody had agreed, even the Brits – and by the Brits I mean the London government, I don't mean Protestants in Northern Ireland, I don't mean Wales or Scotland, I mean the London government – that the days of the Empire were allegedly gone, out of the blue we have this extraordinary high-handed development. And I don't know what the solution is.

From a British or Northern Irish point of view, Arlene Foster is perfectly right to stress that the vote was a UK-wide one and the North's 56% to remain in the EU is essentially irrelevant. But that brings us back to the fundamentally undemocratic nature of the border in Ireland.

It's also true that in the North of Ireland, the majority of people voted to remain in the EU. And so we're confronted with a dilemma. Which, as I say, brings us back to the damn border. It makes nonsense of everything, it's a contradiction of everything.

We try to forget it and to ignore it, but it comes back to the fact that this was undemocratic, unjust, never going to work. It complicates logic, it complicates everything. And I don't want to seem to be fundamentalist here, but I keep coming back to the question: why should the parishioners of Kinawley suffer –

the historic parish of Kinawley, which has in effect been in existence since the sixth century – because of some ferociously anti-Catholic bigots – Churchill, Lloyd George, Balfour – every one of them not only anti-Irish but anti-Catholic? All these intelligent statesmen, these great statesmen, fanatically anti-Catholic. I mean, what the heck?

A border poll is inevitable. People want to say, 'Ah, but it takes time.' Where does it say that? And they say, 'There's no point in having 50% plus one.' That's not in the Agreement. And why when it comes to the republican/nationalist common-sense position, do people say, 'Oh, wait now. It'll take time. We need to have a massive majority.'? Where is all this coming from?

I now increasingly see we're facing a reality of demographics. If, for example, there was a constituency in America that was gerrymandered in such a way as to exclude blacks from ever reaching power – if in such a constituency over the years, blacks become a majority, is it totally irrational and illogical that the blacks should say, 'Well, now we're going to have democracy'? Would we criticise them for that? But Catholics now have been blackmailed into a situation where they're told, 'You can't think in those terms, because that's sectarian.' The point came when the whites in Birmingham, Alabama, had to say, 'Well, we don't like this but there's no going back. We have to accept equality.'

I believe the bulk of unionism would accept democracy. I think we are past the notion that the IRA will drive the British into the sea, and we're past the notion of the dissidents becoming what the IRA were – that day is gone, I believe. I think we are also past the idea of the Protestant backlash, or some kind of independent Northern Ireland, and that if the vote goes against them unionists are prepared to take on not only Dublin but also London, and then they'll take on America and they'll go down fighting to the very last man. Mother of God, I hope we're past that.

There's no longer a Lloyd George who said there's going to be six counties whether they like it or not; there's no Churchill; there's no great general threatening mutiny on behalf of the loyalists of Northern Ireland. That day is surely gone.

The idea that the British secretary of state gets to decide if there'll be a border poll – is a ridiculous thing. That has to go. It is colonial thinking at its very worst.

I believe a border poll should be called. I don't mean tomorrow or next week. I know the unionists are opposed to it. But if there's a strong nationalist push for a poll, it would need a great deal of agreement for it to be effective. Because if the border poll isn't won by nationalists, it can't be called for another seven years.

I think what [lawyer] Niall Murphy is doing – helping civic nationalism find its voice – is important. It gets away from the partisan position where the SDLP will oppose anything Sinn Féin stands for and vice versa. That's an important development.

I have never met one Catholic/nationalist/republican in my life – and I'm seventy-five – who ever believed that when we get a majority, we'll persecute the Protestants. That is totally foreign to Catholic/nationalist/republican thinking. There has to be a constant reach-out to unionists, and in my own way I've done that consistently. No Protestant that I've ever met, in the

US or in Ireland, could ever say that I did not show them total respect and, indeed, understanding.

People have to engage. My Fermanagh colleague Arlene – I wish to God she'd reach out more. I don't mean this in any condescending way, but one of Martin Luther King's basic principles was that if you're on the side of injustice and oppression, you also need to be liberated. I think that's a profound insight. If the federal government in the US had not moved forward with civil rights aggressively and constitutionally, there would still be a number of whites in the deep South who would want to continue the old way of thinking.

The British and Irish governments should be involved in the preparation for a new Ireland. I'm impressed by Leo Varadkar. I met him around the St Patrick's Day celebrations at the White House. I was especially impressed by the fact that he said Catholics/nationalists in the North would never again be abandoned by the Dublin government. It's important that he follows up and implements that.

But the problem is that Mrs May is in hock to the DUP, so I do not see that she can convince, persuade or urge Arlene to move a bit.

I wish to God Tony Blair was still around. In saying that, I try not to think about Iraq. But I think that, even though I spent my life working in Congress about the situation in Northern Ireland, pushing it all the time – I do think that the people in Ireland should get over the idea of bringing in an American to solve things. I think that time has gone too. I'm not opposed to the idea of another envoy – that's fine. But Irish people need to get over the idea that there's going to be a new

George Mitchell who'll hold their hand for five years. I told Mitchell that he wouldn't have to do much time in Purgatory, given that he'd already done five years in the North. [*Laughs*] I told all the American envoys the same thing.

I can't see a border poll any earlier than in five years. I don't know how much preparation is being done on it. Varadkar said there'd be no point in a border poll that produced 50% plus one. I hope he's got over that, because that's rewriting the rules a bit. I know it's a delicate thing and that everybody would like a decisive referendum. Even the wonderful Speaker, Nancy Pelosi, who I've been honoured to meet many times, says that in the coming American election the majority has to be huge, otherwise Trump won't leave office. Well, that's a helluva way to approach an election. Is it 51%, is it 55%? It would be nice to think it would be a healthy, pretty-good vote, but we don't know.

It would have been much easier for me not to be involved in Irish affairs. But if you are to be your brother's keeper, if you are to be concerned about justice and human rights, and freedom and solidarity, you must be. And if one is to believe in the Gospel – not just in the Eucharistic presence or Trinity, but in the fundamental teaching of all religions, that the doing of justice is absolutely demanded of a follower of Jesus – you cannot be Catholic, or a genuine Protestant, or a genuine Jewish person, or a Muslim, if you say, 'The hell with other people, Number One is all I care about.' That is the antithesis of faith and religion. The older I get, the more clearly I see that. My favourite quotation is from a Protestant scriptural scholar: 'In biblical faith, the doing of justice is the primary expectation of God.'[2]

21

PETER KISSEL

14 MAY 2019

Peter Kissel is national president of the Irish American Unity Conference (IAUC), a non-profit, non-sectarian human rights organisation working for peace and justice in a reunited Ireland. He previously served as the IAUC's chair of human rights. Peter's Irish ancestors came from Counties Offaly, Meath and Dublin. He is an avid student of Irish history and has travelled to the North of Ireland on many occasions. He received his degree in political science from Syracuse University and a Juris Doctor from the Washington College of Law. He has written widely on Brexit and human rights.

My father was a Presbyterian – a very active, proud member of the Presbyterian faith. My mother was Irish Catholic. So I was raised as a Catholic nominally.

My interest and that of my wife Sharon in Ireland was in terms of human rights rather than any idealistic longing for what de Valera talked about – 'comely maidens dancing at the cross-roads'.[1] Most of those rights, historically, have been denied to the Catholic population in the North of Ireland. Working on this over the last decade or two, I have come to the conclusion that the English psyche is so prejudiced against Irish Catholic people that there will never be true equality and justice in the North of Ireland without Irish unification. The

English government in particular and their security forces appear to be so bigoted against Irish Catholic people that I don't believe you can get equal justice in Northern Ireland.

We first went to Ireland in June 1991. We'd gone there because we'd heard it was a neat country and a pretty beautiful country. And when we got there, we felt on that first trip that somehow this was where our ancestors came from. That was the fun trip.

The big trip came three years later in June 1994. We'd spent a couple of days in Dublin and we said, 'Let's go up and see what the North of Ireland is like.' So we were cruising up the highway in a hired car, when all of a sudden the road opens up to a huge tyre-eating claw. And there's a guard station there. And British army punks come out with rifles or machine guns in hand. 'Who are you? Where are you coming from? What are you doing here? Where are you going? When are you going back?'

It was stunning. It felt like we were in East Germany. When we got through that checkpoint, we got up the road, stopped the car, looked at each other and said, 'This is outrageous – this is really outrageous!' I mean – waving guns at us – come on! We knew we were in a different place; we knew we were in a very unpleasant place for certain people. And I remember we were thinking, 'My God – if we get treated that way, what do the people up here get treated like?' The trip unfolded with more and more of that. We stayed in a very lovely home the first night up there, and we were awakened at six o'clock in the morning by choppers going over at 100 feet. It was awful.

We got stopped at one impromptu checkpoint, and talk about spoiling an idyllic drive through the lovely Irish countryside. It was such a shock, even more so than the border stop coming up North, because at least then we were on a major highway connecting two major cities. This time we're out in the middle of nowhere. Sharon described one of the guys as looking with his trench-coat like he was out of a movie.

As you know, the Loughinisland killings occurred on 18 June 1994. That day, Sharon and I drove back out of the North into Co. Meath and sought out a pub to watch the World Cup game between Italy and Ireland. We found this wonderful country pub packed with people, and everyone was having such a great time. It was before the age of instant communication and, as you know, the Loughinisland murders happened, and nobody in that pub in Co. Meath knew that the attack had happened. The place was full of joy.

The next morning I got up to read about the game, and even then there was just a tiny blurb, stuck in the upper [portion] of the right-hand page: 'It's been reported that six people were killed in a pub in Northern Ireland.' No detail whatsoever – the communication wasn't fast enough then.

That trip – it was like getting hit on the back of the head by a two-by-four: so this is the real world in the North of Ireland. Sharon and I have been involved in human rights issues in the US for a number of years. Seeing that in Ireland – I don't know whether you'd call it an opportunity or a need or whatever, but that's how we got involved in Irish matters.

Ireland North and South is not analogous to Robert Frost's 'Good fences make good neighbours.'[2] The question in Ireland is, are the folks on one side being treated in the same way as folks on the other side? The answer is a resounding no. Yes, it's better than it was, but it's still a resounding no. To me it's more like what was going on in the south of the US when I was growing up. They had fences to keep out people of a different colour: they had literal fences and they had psychological fences.

Unification, when it comes, has to be about not just getting along but pulling together for a better society: better education, better housing, better employment opportunities, etc. I appreciate that more and more unionists are recognising that. At the same time I think it's impossible to understand what another section of society is going through if you're not part of that section of the population. Protestants – who have ruled that area for so long – can't understand the experience of Catholics who've been discriminated against.

And I don't think all that's over. I met Father Aidan Troy a little while ago. [Father Troy was chair of the Board of Governors of Holy Cross Girls' Primary School. Over a twelve-week period in 2001, four- to eleven-year-old girls faced demonstrations and abuse from loyalists.] When you can't walk little girls to school without having stones and abuse hurled at them, it's not over. When you can't get people housing, when you can't walk into a Stormont Executive, for instance, and have a simple thing that's imbedded in the GFA – an Irish Language Act – that's not equality.

Now when I go up North, I'll get the bus out of Dublin airport and go to Belfast – to Queen's University to courses and conferences up there. And I always like to sit in the bus and look out over the countryside and have a smooth ride up with no army officers or obnoxious signs. You only know you've gone North when you see those signs change from kilometres to miles – and the roads aren't as good! Which is a reversal.

Yes, the border is still there, and there are a number of people to this day who've never crossed the border to go to the other side and are reluctant to do it. There is definitely a border in their minds.

I think the changes beyond the commercial changes with the invisible border are far more important. Forty to fifty per cent of Irish beef goes North; milk and Guinness go back and forth across the border. That's important because it helps build the economy of both sectors. But I think what's more important, judging from talking to people I know up there, is the invisible psychological improvement – freedom to live your life and travel where you want to travel. There are a lot of people who have families on both sides. But just the idea that I'm living in Newry, say, and I want to drive down to Dublin for the day because I've got a couple of cousins down there. I just want to visit, I don't want to buy anything or take anything back. Or maybe I want to take a ride out to Sligo, see what that's like. That psychological impact, that freedom of the mind – it's the most important thing. That's what frees you: that feeling that you can move about, you can visit wherever.

We have a place in Mayo and we visit it quite a bit, get over to Dublin where we have quite a few friends. There's an astounding number of them who still have never visited the North. It's not a fear of anything bad; it's just a sense, a prejudicial sense, that the North is an undesirable place, a hostile place. Personally, I love Belfast. I tell people that they wouldn't believe what a neat, open city it is, and the same for the rest of the North. A lot of people in the South do not realise that – people haven't taken as much advantage over the past twenty years as they could have.

And it's not just people from the South who are reluctant. We have a number of very close friends who are English, who live in Surrey. Most of them have never been to the North of Ireland. There's a sense of 'Why would I want to go to that grubby place?'

But I do think attitudes have improved in the South, because we do meet people who say, 'I haven't been up but I'd really like to get up there.' And we do know people in the South with small businesses and they do go up and back, of course.

Brexit has indeed changed everything. From the standpoint of both the IAUC and a lot of Irish-Americans, Brexit does indeed increase the prospect for reunification. There are two reasons I say that.

One is economics. There is little doubt in my mind that Brexit is going to be an economic disaster for Britain, and for Northern Ireland even more so. Northern Ireland, when I last checked, was the second lowest economic tier in the UK, and I believe it was one of the ten lowest in the EU. So the GFA has opened up a lot of opportunity for international businesses to relocate there, but there's a long way to go. They really need to build their infrastructure in terms of services and manufacturing.

So it's already limping badly economically. I think Brexit carries the threat of dealing a death blow to the economy of Northern Ireland.

The other reason I think Brexit is a disaster is – it goes

back to the psychological thing. Young people in the North as well as in the rest of Ireland feel very strongly that, before any nationality, they are European citizens. I've talked to a number of them, I've been to forums and lectures where the subject has come up, and young people – not kids, but people in their twenties, thirties, up to forty years old, they say, 'We're European – what are you going to do about us?' They don't think in terms of 'I'm British' or 'I'm Irish'. So Brexit is having a terrible effect on those people's sense of commitment to the place of their birth.

I don't know how that's going to play out, but I've seen it and I've heard it, and it's very real. I despair if young minds and young bodies are leaving a country which is already kind of hurting a little bit. Their attitude that they are European reflects that they are much less tribal, much less likely to care what the other person's background or religion or colour or ethnicity is. And if those people leave the North, then the pressure to remove the border, psychologically and literally, will not be as strong as if those people remain.

People who see themselves as more leftist – which is more associated with nationalists/republicans – some of them favoured Brexit because they don't like the EU. They think the EU is too controlling. Some of the People Before Profit (PBP) party felt and still feel that way. But given the disaster that Brexit has been, and how much disaster and fear it has created, a number of my colleagues and I do see the opportunity to push Irish reunification. Had I been over there, I would never have thought of voting for Brexit, knowing how it could hurt the people and the economy. But now that it's happened, been voted through, I think I would be derelict in my duty and my thinking to not take advantage of that. I'm very torn on this, because I've interviewed people on the border, and I know people who live up there close to it, and I know it's going to be terribly painful for people. So do I really want it to happen? No. And yet I do believe that Brexit is going to accelerate reunification.

If the read is correct and Brexit is going to be very hard on the North, then it follows logically that we would want to get rid of the border by reuniting Ireland. I've seen studies done by organisations in England [showing that] the hit to England could be anywhere from 3–8% of GDP. In the North of Ireland, it could be 15%, it might only be 8%. Those are figures produced by economists who know a lot more about it than I do.

I am convinced that the South as well as the North would be better off together in the long run. You have a small island with only 6.5 million people on it, give or take half a million. Five million of them are in the South, 1.5 million in the North. So you have two different entities: an entity of 5 million people that is trying to survive in a global world, and another entity of 1.5 million people trying to survive in a global world, and even though they're part of the UK, people in Britain don't even think of them as being part of Britain.

If you combine the two of them, it's not just economies of scale, it's also the intangibility of businesses feeding on each other – small businesses, mom-and-pop businesses, more interchange, more across the entirety of Ireland than you have when they're different.

I've studied countries large and small since I was in college and how effective they are. If you had one island nation, the diplomatic prowess of that entity would be considerably improved. It would be a more credible entity on the world stage to have an impact on different affairs that it's concerned about and that help it. I am absolutely convinced that that would be a plus for both parts of Ireland.

At present Ireland is economically integrated, but I wouldn't see it as economically united. You have different currencies, you have some different regulations, you have some different red tapes. I understand the argument of duplication of services, but I don't think it's a biggie. We're talking about government services, and there is a one-time saving on them in the event of unity. But I think the integration far beyond that is what would be much more significant. When I talk about economies of scale, I'm talking about distributors and manufacturers in the North and how they are coordinating with somebody in Wicklow or Cork or wherever – and vice versa. I have no doubt that if you had one government, those entities would have a much-enhanced ability to operate efficiently.

The DUP mouths the right words on cross-border trade, but they're just words. They are so insistent on preventing the backstop, so insistent on not having any separation between the North and the rest of the UK in the event of Brexit, that they are sacrificing keeping the border free. I think their view of that is illogical, inconsistent. They want Brexit [to be an even stiffer separation] than it presently is. That's what astounds me. There are regulatory differences right now – phytosanitary [control of crop disease], agricultural – between the North and the rest of the UK. They want to take Brexit as an opportunity to do away with even that, much less take one step of accommodation to ensure that there won't be a return to a hard border. So to me their words are not very well thought out – it doesn't make any sense to say we don't want a hard border and yet we're going to insist on separating totally from the EU but not at all from the UK in any regulatory fashion whatsoever. You can't have both.

I fully recognise that there could be a need for checks between the North and the South. What I have read over and over again is that, according to the EU, there is not currently a technological solution to that. So you're going to have goods produced in the UK that no longer have to adhere to EU regulations, and so when those goods are shipped South – and going South is where the concern is – how does the EU ensure that those goods are consistent?

I had a discussion with the former ambassador to the EU, David O'Sullivan. David has since moved on to another post. But when I spoke with him a couple of months ago, his view of it was that the firms in the UK are currently adhering to EU regulations and they know how to operate that way. So there's not going to be some kind of immediate switchover, and even as time moves on, those firms, no matter what they're allowed to do under UK law, are going to want to continue to comply with EU regulations. So David does not believe there would be an immediate impact where there would need to be checks, etc. Down the road, he recognises that there could be a need for the EU to do something to ensure that goods that now maybe have begun to vary from regulations would have to be qualified in some way. The hope is – and this is what the backstop is about – that we could buy time. That for now you're still within the EU regulatory ambit until at least the end of 2020. In that time, as everything advances – thinking, technology – hopefully there will be a solution down the road. But we're not there yet.

That made a lot of sense to me. Of course the British firms are used to operating under EU regulations, and they're not going to want to change their regulations overnight. They're still going to want to sell to Europe. Business is pretty smart, once something affects the bottom line. And I do have enough faith that the industry, the business associations, will come up with a solution that allows the free flow of commerce. And if you have the free flow of commerce, then you may have openness for people.

When we spoke to people from Border Communities Against Brexit, they did say that if something goes up to obstruct a road, it'll be torn down that night, under cover of darkness. By peace-loving people who want to go back and forth. Maybe they have a business on both sides. In similar circumstances I'd probably do the same.

So I'm afraid of that kind of situation. That's why I'm opposed to a border. I'm a realist and I know that sort of thing could happen. But I firmly reject the idea that you'll have a return to the kind of civil war that you had up there. That is not going to happen, I'm absolutely convinced of that. But you will have a number of people who will be very pissed off. You will also have the dissidents, who are going to take opportunities like this, as they already have in Derry, to create problems just for the sake of creating problems with government. But you'll also have people engaging in civil disobedience – I'd distinguish that from violence. Somebody puts up barriers trying to prevent me going somewhere, then I'm going to go out there and knock 'em down. Yes, maybe it's against the law and maybe I will get arrested – I accept that.

Violence could happen again, but I don't think it will. I'm an optimist. In Ireland in the late 1960s and early 1970s, you had factors much worse than they are today, which affected people. It was a much poorer country then, especially for the Catholic population, who were the object of discrimination. So you had a lot of angry people who were poor and didn't have a lot to lose. You also had a country where people hadn't learnt to deal with each other to the extent that they do now, thanks to the GFA. You also had a country that was poorer – and I'd include Protestants in this. The economy of the country was not as strong as it is now. People now have a lot more at stake. And that's why I can't see it going back to that, I really can't. I see that it could get quite disruptive, and yes, people might die as they did in the US to get civil rights. There might be some of that going on, but I just don't see it happening. The circumstances are not what they were in the late 1960s and early 1970s.

I see human rights post-Brexit as a huge problem. People will not be subject to the European Convention on Human Rights (ECHR). Britain wants to repeal its own human rights act, which requires the ECHR to be incorporated into British law. There's also the Charter of Human Rights, which is separate from the ECHR. The Charter is not a legal document in the sense that the ECHR is. And you have the European

Court of Human Rights, which is not the same as the European Court of Justice.

I see it as a huge problem because I'm involved in legacy cases. I see it with people like the Ballymurphy folks and the Loughinisland folks, trying to get some kind of recognition under the European acts that there has been a deprivation of life and that that has to be acknowledged – forget about compensation. But yes, I see that as a huge problem. I don't have much faith in the English government in particular, or the English government's respect for human rights, even the rights of its own population. I know Niall Murphy has brought a number of cases that rely on the European model and laws for enforcing human rights. Take Trevor Birney and Barry McCaffrey [journalists who investigated the Loughinisland killings] – talk about a violation of human rights. They are getting their office turned upside down, they're getting their computers basically stolen by the PSNI for very little discernible reason. And that's under the existing system. That's the kind of respect I see coming out of the UK for the basic human rights of people. And I'm very concerned that it's going to get worse.

I'm totally in favour of allocating some of those extra MEP seats to the North, and I think the EU should have done it. Varadkar is the leader of a country. If someone says, 'Here, I'll give you two extra seats,' is he going to give them somewhere else? Probably not. But should the EU have allocated the extra seats up there? I think they should, and I know a lot of people are very concerned about that. But it's also a legal conundrum, because that entity will be no longer be part of the EU jurisdiction. One could argue that you may as well give seats to the US. MEPs in the North would be physically resident in a country that is not a part of the EU. I think Leo Varadkar didn't part with the seats because he saw a chance to take a seat away from Sinn Féin. I'm not necessarily criticising him for that. That's just reality – I don't think that it was a concern not to upset the unionists.

Nobody knows under what circumstances a border poll may be called. The British secretary of state decides: how ridiculous a set-up is that? Why have a border poll if you think it's going to be won? But you have no criteria for the calling of a border poll, much less a process for conducting it. What if the secretary of state decides, 'Oh, I think we'll have a border poll,' and some unionists want to challenge that? Do they have a right to challenge the decision? Apparently not. It's crazy. And a lot of nationalists want to have a poll now – right now. Which I think is crazy.

The British have packed their bags and left from other places, like India, with disastrous results. But I think they inserted the secretary of state deciding into the GFA because it gave them complete control. The compromise to the nationalist people was supposed to be that when the people on both sides of the border vote for reunification, that's what will happen. But what does it do? It sets it up in the sole unbridled discretion of one person – a person appointed by the prime minister of England [Great Britain].

But I would say that, today, an awful lot of people in England want to get rid of Northern Ireland, so maybe it will be to their benefit as well.

I think the people who favour reunification – such as

myself – have to be convinced the poll will pass, and I am not convinced of that yet by any means. I keep reminding my American colleagues that you don't get to have another poll for seven years if you've lost the first one. So how would a poll right now pan out? Maybe fifty–fifty. Do I want to take that chance when it's going to be 2026 before we can go for it again? No, no, no! I want to wait a little bit longer. I think the momentum with Brexit means that more people in the North are getting comfortable with the idea of the unification of Ireland. So let's give it another couple of years for this to play out. Let's just see how bad Brexit is going to be for the North of Ireland – the people in the North as well as the economy. Then is the time to hold a poll, in my view.

What needs to be done in the meantime is that the political parties in the Republic have got to get their act together and address that issue and start planning for unification. Britain should probably be involved; certainly the North of Ireland should be involved in it – all segments of it.

In planning for reunification, you have to have studies, you have to have a clear vision of what kind of government you're going to have. Are you going to have just the Dáil? Are you going to have some regional governments? Are you going to have a temporary regional government only in the North, with the idea that eventually that would go away? I don't know what the answer to all that is, but what I'm saying is somebody's got to really have a look at that. We've got to plan, to interview knowledgeable people as well as the person on the street, to get an idea of what people would prefer. There are unionists in the North who feel that if reunification happens, a regional parliament would be important to have. So what would people prefer, and just how would it work? And maybe you'd have a regional parliament in Cork as well, and maybe Limerick. How would that relate to the powers in Dublin? How federated and confederated would the entity be? And would a regional parliament in the North be permanent?

So you'd need to have input from the people, as well as from experts, on how a government should be set up. In the US, you had people who sat down, even as the Revolutionary War was going on, considering: these are the departments we ought to have, this is the kind of bicameral [two-chambered] legislature we ought to have. You really need to put some thought into that. But the ultimate relationship between the different parts of the country – you've got to have public forums about that, you've got to have public discussion about that, you have to give people the ability to comment on it – it's a long process. And I don't see anything of that nature yet coming out of the government in Dublin. Which is a huge disappointment and a terrible oversight, in my opinion.

How long should this planning take before a poll? Three years. But I don't think it'd be appropriate to have American involvement in the process. If they want US advice, sure – we're not slow to give advice when asked! But I don't think it's America's place to be involved in that.

Perhaps the analogy is unfair, but when the US was set up, it only took thirteen years – although it was a much smaller country then, of course. But they had no models for it. Now you've got models – you've got think tanks that know how to set up forums, know how to interview people, know how to engage them in a meaningful way. That sort of thing is done all the time in the US.

You are always going to have people in any situation who are going to be kicking and screaming. But you can't let that stop you. You have to engage unionism; you have to get buy-in from a substantial portion of the unionist community. But you can't be worried about maybe even a third of them screaming. We've still got a third of the people in this country [the US] screaming about integration. Too effing bad! Those people just have to be dragged along kicking and screaming.

I think the 50%-plus-one question is a false question. It's not going to happen. It's going to be 52 or 53% or it's not going to pass. But 53%? That's enough. That's democracy.

22

BRUCE MORRISON

15 MAY 2019

Bruce Andrew Morrison is a former congressman from Connecticut and candidate for governor of Connecticut. In the 1990s he formed the Americans for a New Irish Agenda to support and encourage peace negotiations in Ireland and, with Niall O'Dowd, acted as a key intermediary between Sinn Féin president Gerry Adams, the White House and the Irish government. He is an immigration lawyer, a member of the Democratic Party and an officer of the National Democratic Ethnic Coordinating Committee.

When I was first elected to Congress in 1982, my district was about 15% Irish-American, and I was well aware of the various organisations that had talked to me during the campaign. So I came to the Irish issue more from the direction of human rights and immigration rights in the US than from things that had gone before. My grandfather was born near Enniskillen in the North of Ireland – he was a Protestant – and my maternal family were immigrants from Germany. So I wasn't raised with any focus on Irish issues – it came to me in the form of crises.

In 1987 I was on a trip sponsored by the IAUC, which was an umbrella group of Irish organisations at that time. We went first to Dublin and then we went North.

I was prepared for the militarisation of the border, but I don't think I was prepared for the rest of the North, with its checkpoints everywhere. We went to both Belfast and Derry, and in Derry I was held at gunpoint by the RUC for over an hour because I was in the company of a Sinn Féin councillor. We were pulled over and literally held at gunpoint.

It was frightening and surprising. I was a US congressman carrying an official US passport – not a tourist passport but an official passport. I handed that over. I also tried to take down the badge number of the officer, but he grabbed the paper away from me and said that I had committed an offence, collecting information about the security forces. They held me on the street for an hour. It wasn't a chummy little conversation – they had guns aimed at me. It was a show of force – clearly intimidation was the objective.

In the South we had a few meetings. We went to the US ambassador's for lunch, which was very pleasant. We also had a meeting with Seán MacBride [Clann na Poblachta founder and Nobel Peace Prize winner] – this was shortly before he died – and spoke with him about the MacBride Principles, among other things. We had a meeting with the Department of Foreign Affairs: they were very hostile to the MacBride Principles in particular. 'Dismissive' is, I think, the word I would use.

Then we went North and we stayed with a number of republican families. I had arranged a second round of meetings. The Unity Conference [IAUC] had arranged meetings with Sinn Féin people and, through the consul-general's office, I had arranged meetings with other than Sinn Féin.

So I met with John Hume in Derry and with Alliance people. Alliance were on the rise then. They were really a unionist party, although a moderate unionist party; now they're more cross-community. And I had a meeting with some unionist politicians, none of whom would have met with me if they'd known I was meeting with Sinn Féin.

I had two lives, sort of, when I was there. I had the tour of Derry with Gerry O'Hara of Sinn Féin and I had the tour of Derry with John Hume: same places, different storylines.

I know a lot of unionists and loyalists, and I've met with them over the years. They come in different shapes and sizes like everybody else. They always viewed Americans as green, and that's because most Americans they met were green. But I always found that the most enlightening experiences of my time during the peace process were meetings with unionists and loyalists. We didn't confront them on issues of the right and wrong of partition; we talked to them about peace and the way in which reconciliation could come about. We were for an end to violence all round.

I did indeed learn from them. The most important meeting I ever had was with several loyalists who had been imprisoned for a variety of offences, including murder – Gusty Spence, Billy Hutchinson and others. It was a completely secret and private meeting at the time and could not be disclosed to anyone, for their safety and for ours, I suppose.

We had a very open conversation about the history of the Troubles and about their feeling of being used by unionist politicians. They felt what had happened to them was more consistent with them being victims than heroes of loyalism.

They'd done their deeds and done their time, but this was not the future they wanted.

We had a very respectful conversation. It's not that they gave any ground on their Britishness, but they were for a peace process.

During the period between 1993 and 1998 I must have gone back and forth twenty times at least. After 1998 the border became … nothing.

Today's border is symbolic of something bigger, and that is that the Republic and Northern Ireland have become much closer. Most of the people I met in the South when I was doing my peace-process work had never been to the North. They had attitudes towards the North that weren't necessarily very charitable. When we started going up there, it was seen as a fool's errand. A lot of people in Dublin thought, 'Well, those heathens in the North – a pox on both their houses!' So there was a distance – and the distance now has lessened. People now travel from the South to the North or the North to the South in a way that didn't happen then.

That's partly the lack of a physical border, but it's also partly the opening up of the place. People no longer fear going to the North, no longer fear coming to the South. All kinds of normal economic activities, including milk being produced in the North and sent to the South to be turned into cheese and then sold back in the North – there's all kinds of trade back and forth.

If you try to clothe that trade in a political term like 'unity', you will get an argument. Better to just observe that from an economic standpoint, there's no reason for the two jurisdictions not to benefit from each other's strengths.

Unionism and nationalism/republicanism haven't come closer over the twenty plus years since the GFA. I would say the North is very much more segregated now than when the GFA was signed. People live separately, for the most part. The most integrated area is the workplace, and that's because of the anti-discrimination laws which were just going into effect when I first visited there in 1987. There were businesses where unionists would never have hired a Catholic – that is different now. But where people live, and most importantly where they go to school, is completely separate, and the separation of those communities has not really been addressed.

The structure that came out of the GFA, which was probably the only structure that could have been addressed at that time, is a sectarian structure. Republican parties run for republican votes, nationalists for nationalist votes, unionists for unionist votes. Maybe Alliance is now making some headway, but at that time it had not. Nobody has to win the other guy's votes. Politics is driven by the fear of losing an election, and if you don't need the other guy's vote, you don't need to listen to the other guy.

The exception that proves the rule was Martin McGuinness and Ian Paisley, who got to know each other personally – so much so that Martin was at Paisley's funeral. That would never have happened normally. That happened because the big man [Paisley] had crossed the Rubicon and made peace with himself as only he could, and Martin was probably the most unique republican politician that ever lived.

As to Brexit, I still do not believe it's inevitable. If there was a second referendum, they might well change course.

I think Jeremy Corbyn is a disgrace. If Tony Blair were head of Labour right now, this would be sorted. This socialist Euroscepticism from Corbyn – yes, Brussels is not perfect, but it's not a capitalist plot and it's not 1945 and Britain's not going to renationalise all its industries.

We can accept the likelihood that there'll be some border, but I will not concede that Brexit is inevitable until it happens, because it's a mistake and I think the mistake could be remedied.

The less that the border intrudes on the lives of people, the better. The border was the source of smuggling and illegal commerce in the past and will be again – as every border is – if it comes back into existence.

I don't think violence is inevitable, but there are people around, as we know from the recent killing [of journalist Lyra McKee], who are willing to engage in violence in the name of politics, which no longer has the community support it once did. But it's around on both sides and it could happen. I think the reason that Brexit's a bad idea doesn't have anything to do with violence or the GFA. But obviously the GFA is something that people on both sides of the border are pledged to uphold. Because this has grown into a threat to what has become a prosperous and peaceful situation on both sides of the border, people are going to paint the worst outcome.

It will be what it will be: in other words, Brexit is a terrible idea, a hard border is a terrible idea. The answer is a customs union because then you don't need any of this. There'll be a customs union for a number of years even under the withdrawal agreement that hasn't passed. But it's not imminent, there's time for people to decide that they never want to leave the customs union. The economics of leaving the customs union are terrible for the UK – their own government has said so. So I don't take the view that some people have political motivations for doom and gloom. This is a great argument for a united Ireland, but it won't make a united Ireland happen, because the Republic doesn't want a united Ireland with a fifth column of people in the North who are declining in percentage but are still half the people in the North. You wouldn't want 750,000 discontented people in the Republic of Ireland. A united Ireland is something with which I have great sympathy, but it is a political process, not a gun-to-the-head process. So when people are ready to vote for it, there need to be unionists to vote for it.

A vote doesn't change people's attitudes, and the reason there's partition in Ireland is that that was the easy way for the Brits to deal with the unionists in 1922. They didn't really care about the six counties; nobody in London has ever cared about the six counties. They cared about not having a problem. They were trying to settle the War of Independence, and this was quick and dirty – with the Brits it always is. That rump group of people, however many unionists it is, who say no – Ulster Says No – is always going to be there. But there's going to need to be unionists who say Ulster Says Maybe.

I don't think it's a legal question. Ask the same question about the vote on Brexit. There was a vote on Brexit that was 52–48% in favour of leaving. Has that settled the question? No. The point is, Parliament can't get it done at the moment. When the country is split fifty–fifty, as the North is at the moment, votes matter – who gets the most votes.

But for something to be workable, there has to be more. I don't want your candidate, but I have to say, 'I accept the result.' You've got to get to the point where people see there's a legitimacy to the outcome. I'd say 50.1 to 49.9% will be a mess. I don't say anything about resorting to violence – I say there are a lot of halfway houses between here and a united Ireland.

We're in one of them now. Ireland is becoming more and more of an economic unit. The North wants to lower their corporation tax to be the same as the South's. This is all part of a homogenising of the economy. The UK leaving the EU is a huge shock to a transition that was going on, because it's a statement that a lot of things were being taken care of because everybody was in the EU. But Brexit is an event where the worse it is, the better it is for a united Ireland vote. But is that a responsible view? In other words, should we make it as bad as possible so we force a united Ireland? The GFA, which is about accommodation and parity of esteem and respect for people's different points of view about their identity: the Agreement should be gobbling up Brexit, instead of the other way around. At some level, I fear the political use of bad outcomes, as opposed to the political work of preventing bad outcomes.

There's a difference between organising for a border poll and having one. The unionists always argue that a lot of nationalists would prefer to stay in the UK. But there's no evidence of that. The unionist community's behaviour over the last couple of years has been antithetical to that outcome. (My grandfather was a unionist before there was partition and as bigoted as could be.) If I were a leader of the unionist community and I truly believed that the UK arrangement was better for Northern Ireland as opposed to better for unionists – that unionism was a good thing, separate from my religion – then I would be trying to make Northern Ireland a better place compared to the Republic. I wouldn't be fighting gay marriage, abortion, all these things that make people feel like they are not getting reasonable rights, and I would be working to make the economy better, better, better. I'd be against Brexit because I'd see Brexit as making my case harder to make.

The DUP has done the opposite in its alliance with the Tories and its disastrous governance. So I take it that unionist politicians have a death wish about Northern Ireland as a separate entity. They have a death wish because they have an all-or-nothing approach to everything.

You can't let them hold Northern Ireland hostage. We've got the votes, we take the votes, 51 to 49% … But a democracy is built on conciliation. Winning by one vote – that really isn't ideal. So people who don't conciliate – people like the DUP, who never signed the GFA – they're always a conundrum. Because they sort of dare you to vote them down.

But we need to be smarter than they are; they can be undermined politically. I think a political problem with the GFA is that it locked in a sectarian government and that no one really has an incentive to go get votes on the other side. Nobody really competes for those votes because everyone is seen as waving a sectarian flag, whether that's the way they come at it or not. There are no non-sectarian politics in Northern Ireland worth talking about.

Somebody should be organising for a new Ireland. Not a united Ireland but a new Ireland. Because obviously not everything is perfect about the Republic of Ireland, so this is an opportunity for reform generally. In other words, provoking discussion and looking for leaders who would say after Brexit – assuming it happens – 'Hey, this doesn't make sense any more! I was a unionist, but these people walked out on all these sensible arrangements of the EU, so now I have a different view.' Lots of business people would have that view.

Now that there's a kind of equipoise in the numbers, a cross-community political project is needed. That can be about the reaction to Brexit, it can be about the border poll, but it mostly ought to be about 'Let's get people off the constitutional question for a few minutes and talk about what makes sense in the daily lives of people living in the six counties.'

I have low expectations about Stormont because my experience in politics is that getting things done is hard work. It requires compromise. Stormont by its nature is a sectarian institution in which there is no reward for compromise.

They should be looking across the peace wall. They should be fighting the Catholic Church for integrated education. There are a lot of things going on in the North that are encrusted because of partition and other institutional factors that are impeding the integration of people into a normal society. It's been twenty-one years. A lot of work has been spent on the mechanisms of political office, but very little on what politics is supposed to deliver in terms of the day-to-day lives of people.

So getting Stormont set up again: not my project. People

doing it, people spending a lot of time on it – I don't expect a lot from it, when it gets all done.

People in the South need to participate. People need to suggest that reform can happen both sides of the border. The idea is that we can make both places better by putting them together, rather than 'This is the victory that wasn't won in 1921.' Allowing the British secretary of state to decide the timing of a poll is the brake on the system, for good or for bad.

I think Germany should be involved in planning for a united Ireland – they have actually done unification.

Arlene Foster may say that talk of a border poll deepens divisions, but the border poll is mentioned every day. I mean, whatever damage is done is done. It's in the Agreement – that does whatever damage she sees. Arlene means well but does poorly – she's not to be listened to. If her party wants to listen to her, fine, but I don't think anybody else should listen to her because I don't think she has any wisdom about this.

There's a need to talk to the business leaders or the farmers: what would it take for you not necessarily to support but to be OK with a border poll that voted to reunify Ireland? Let's have that discussion. People will tell you, 'Oh, oh, no!' They said that about the peace process; they said it would never succeed.

I think the sense of a deadline would be good. If there's no deadline people won't do anything. But like everything else, the deadline's negotiable too. In other words, if you say, 'We're not ready!' – all right. But if you just say 'Forever', we know about Ulster Says No. 'No' is compatible with 'forever'.

All agreements are for now. Look at Brexit: the deadline was March 29 – correct? Brexit is not unique. It's only unique in that the UK took a vote that was an advisory referendum and turned it into a Magna Carta. That's what's unique. Because it was nothing but Cameron's little trick to get himself re-elected and it came out perversely. Then the Tories allowed these Brexiteers to paint it like it was a Magna Carta, like it could never be changed.

When people say 'this is a deadline', I say I've never met a deadline that couldn't be moved. If, in the course of negotiating, the deadline becomes a problem, well then OK. But we'll start with this deadline because otherwise people won't take it seriously. March 29 was the deadline for Brexit – it was extended.

Five years would be more than enough to prepare for a border poll. The sad thing about Brexit is that it has created a crisis where there wasn't one. There wasn't a crisis about when the border poll was coming. It was sneaking up on people but there wasn't something awful that was going to happen tomorrow if you didn't do something different. Crises are always useful for making change, but they also are crises and they aren't necessarily handled well.

It isn't the job of political leaders to create hardship. It is the job of political leaders to create progress. I lived through the 1960s when everyone said things would have to get much worse, that that was the only way you'd get the revolution, that you'd get things better.

That's all bunk. When things get worse, they get worse. They don't inevitably lead to this great tomorrow – in my experience. I haven't seen many instances of that in the world.

Brexit has narrowed the mind to contemplate this line across Ireland, which never made any sense and doesn't make sense.

More people are thinking about it because the not-making-sense is coming closer to home.

I never felt particularly susceptible to the charge of being romantic and misinformed about Ireland. I'm not Catholic, I wasn't raised Irish Catholic, I wasn't raised green. My constituencies were green, but I went out of my way to seek out the other view.

Yes, they did say we were interfering. I encouraged Bill Clinton to take a role. After he was elected I went to the British Embassy and I said, 'You got two choices. You can say, "It's a domestic matter and you can butt out." Or you can say, "Thank you, Mr President. This conundrum that we've struggled with, if you can help, we'd appreciate it." If you did the second, he'd really be happy.' They did the first until Tony Blair was elected, and then they did the second and it came out much better. So the point is, you can call it meddling or you can call it the help of a friend. I always thought it was the help of a friend.

In 1991 I went to the North and I met with a loyalist leader in a housing estate. And in 1998 I went back and built a house with Habitat for Humanity. And there was a guy standing just off the worksite. And I went over to him. And he said, 'Do you remember me?' It was the loyalist leader I had met with in 1991. I said, 'I do remember our meeting.' And he said, 'You know, you done all right.'

23

RICHIE NEAL

15 MAY 2019

Richard Neal is an American congressman serving as the US representative for Massachusetts's First Congressional District. He is a member of the Democratic Party and a former city councillor and mayor of Springfield, Massachusetts. As chair of the House Ways and Means Committee and former chairman of the Subcommittee on Select Revenue Measures, Neal is an influential figure in House of Representatives economic policy. He has also dedicated much of his career to US–Ireland relations and maintaining American involvement in the Northern Ireland peace process, for which he has won several acclamations.

I have a grandmother who was from Co. Down, my mother's family is from Co. Kerry and I have a large Irish constituency – particularly when I was starting out. There was Irish literature, the John Boyle O'Reilly Club, the annual commemoration of the Easter Rebellion – plus the fact that we had the last of the Blasket Islands people in Springfield [Great Blasket Island was evacuated in 1953]. They were Irish speakers, so if you went to the funeral homes, it was the Irish language you heard.

I first experienced the border in Ireland in 1983. I crossed it in Co. Down. There was a search there, with long lines. At that time it was a militarised state. I use this comparison all the time: there were 30,000 British soldiers in an area the size of Connecticut. If you tried to move anywhere in subsequent visits, a helicopter circled, the RUC circled and everywhere you went there was a British soldier standing at the street corner.

In 1989, on a bus with Speaker of the House Tom Foley, we were going from Donegal to Derry, and the bus was stopped and searched. British soldiers in full military garb mounted the bus with night vision and heavy armaments, and they searched the bus. Three weeks ago I was there with Speaker Pelosi and we simply walked across the border.

It was indeed frightening that first time in 1983 – you were reminded that the violence consumed 3,500 lives in a pretty small area. It would have been the equivalent of tens of thousands of Americans having been killed.

The border was Strand Two of the GFA – the elimination of that border. The idea was to build all-Ireland institutions, Dublin–Belfast in particular. The accommodation was a pretty simple one: the border was eliminated and the Irish government gave up some of its claim to the North.

I think today, when you consider the tens of thousands who cross that border without being searched or checked, you would have trouble knowing which part of the country you were in. And the border counties in particular are heavily dependent on each other. So I think that that was a sizeable achievement and yes, I felt a sense of accomplishment.

If you were in Springfield, which has a large Irish population, most people thought this was one of those intractable issues that can't be solved. After all, it was the longest-standing political dispute in the Western world – 800 years by some accounts. It was born partly out of geography; Ireland had the bad fortune of being located right next to a world power who decided that they couldn't take the risk of a foreign force occupying Ireland as a threat to them – and Ireland suffered the consequences of it.

I think people felt compelled to have closer ties. Back as far as the Downing Street Declaration in 1993 [which established the principle of consent], the government of the Republic was given a consulting role in the governance of the North, and as time has gone on that has expanded. The genius of the GFA is that for those in the North, if you wanted to be Irish you could be Irish, if you wanted to be British you could be British. The Irish government has said they would accommodate Irish passports for anybody on the island.

My role is to be supportive of the nationalist position, whether it be John Hume, the SDLP or Sinn Féin. We all came to the conclusion that you were not going to bomb unionists into a united Ireland. But I do think economically, the resilience of the Republic of Ireland has now convinced many unionists that maybe their future lies better on the island of Ireland, in the Republic. John Hume used to always say that our job was to reach an agreed-upon Ireland, and I think that's what the GFA did.

In recent times I have met with the Brexiteers. Rees-Mogg and some of the others were there, and unfortunately it didn't go very well. They didn't share our opinion of the border.

I've been hearing forever the line that we Americans are intruding. I would cite Tony Blair. He invited us all down to the British Embassy for his going-away gathering, where he spoke. There were many areas, he said, where America and the

UK were agreed, except for one issue: Ireland. And he added that there was a time when he would have seen the Friends of Ireland [US congressional organisation] as a hindrance, but in fact the Americans helped us get through this.

By way of history, in the difficult days thirty years ago, I pointed out that the Brits were always only too happy to give us advice about Vietnam. You may say that's different, but not to us, in terms of what they'd done on the island of Ireland.

If a border were to be established between the EU in the South of Ireland and the non-EU in the North, there would be no free trade agreement with the UK. We are a guarantor of the GFA. It is our agreement too. The American dimension is what made it possible to resolve that long-standing dispute.

Now I'd qualify that by asking, 'Is it desirable to have a trade agreement with the UK?' Yes, it is. But some things we don't give up for trade agreements. And one of the questions that we would put to them is: what has been more important to you than the GFA? How many British soldiers suffered on the island of Ireland during those decades? I think that they'd be very happy to have that issue resolved.

I've known the unionist community for a long, long time, and despite what they used to say, they were always welcomed here. We've had many, many gatherings with them, and I've met the hardest people. Billy Hutchinson: I've known him for a long time. When David Ervine [former head of the PUP] would come here I'd meet him, and gladly so. They said to David once, 'In principle, could you ever accept a united Ireland?' He said, 'If they'll accept my majority today, I'll accept their majority tomorrow.' We never heard Dr Paisley say that.

I don't think we want to be reminded, through a border, of what it was like for people living in that small area during the Troubles. Just as we were leaving Ireland three weeks ago, that murder [of journalist Lyra McKee] took place. The people who did that have no idea what they're doing. There were a lot of good people who were hurt during the Troubles, and while this appears to have been a random shot, it also was a dangerous act.

I have walked the border with BCAB representatives. The only party that wasn't there for that crossing was the DUP – the UUP was with me. There is nobody in the unionist community that I'm aware of who wants to go back to any sort of border. Yes, they're still cheerleading for Brexit, but the idea that you're going to leave the customs union and the idea that you're going to monitor the automobiles and everything through technology? That technology hasn't been created yet.

I don't think there'll be an escalation into violence at the border because I don't think we're going to have a border. They'll call Brexit something else, I would guess. There's something to be said for nuance but I can assure you of one thing: there will be no return to a hard border.

The meeting we had with the BCAB people was good, and they were enthusiastic about us walking the border with them. We stood there on the bridge. That's what I try to remind people of. When Speaker Pelosi and I were at the border, or the former border, we walked all of ten yards forward and we walked ten yards back.

When the six counties was formed there was no nationalist majority. In a representative democracy, you have to convince people of your point of view, and that's going to be the challenge. As to a border poll, is the electorate ready for something that seismic? I think they're going to have to be convinced first. And I also think that one of the things that Brexit has done is it has reminded many of those unionist farmers that their future lies in selling products in the Republic.

The question is, when do you hold a border poll? The timing is everything. I'd be in favour of a border poll at the right time. When the cake is baked, it'll be ready to be served. For me to say when a border poll should be held would be intrusive. It's up to the people who live on the island.

When we first put together, with John Hume and others, the question of the GFA, that was thought to be a long shot; nobody thought that that could happen. And when it did happen, you'll remember one key element was that the referendums had to happen on the same day, both sides of the border. That was really very constructive.

In the lead-up to the GFA one of the things that nationalists did and unionists didn't do was this: nationalists prepared their followers and voters for what might not happen. Unionists never did that. Unionists were more intransigent, wanted to keep things the way they were. Nationalists said, 'You can't keep things the way they are, but we might not get what we want tomorrow.' And that's what you do when you cross the hallway here in the House of Representatives. There are a lot of days when I don't get what I want, but I'm OK with what I have.

You have to convince unionists that their future is better in the Republic of Ireland. Overall you have to convince the majority of people in the North – that's what the GFA says. That's what everybody understood going in. You don't give up Articles 2 and 3 of the constitution without that sort of a guarantee.

I think that a five-year period would be desirable, during which citizens' assemblies and discussions could be held as to what a new Ireland might look like and what place unionism would have within it.

Where we are now is an extraordinary achievement. I mean, the odds against us being where we are ... I know people today who travel back and forth across that border and they think nothing of it. I was there the day that Ian Paisley came to greet Bertie Ahern at Leinster House. He got out of the car: 'I must take this man's hand,' he said. 'I'm an Irishman.' Wow – we almost fell on the ground, all of us who were there.

Yes, I think I'll live to see a united Ireland. I think we're headed for a confederation right now.

24

MICHAEL JOHN CUMMINGS

16 MAY 2019

Michael J. Cummings, a native of Springfield, Massachusetts, is a graduate of St Anselm's College and New York University (Master of Public Administration). He worked for the state of New York for thirty-six years in various capacities including as assistant deputy state comptroller and director of the Justice Court Fund. He is a former member of the National Boards of the IAUC, the Ancient Order of Hibernians (AOH) and the Irish Northern Aid Committee. He is currently secretary of the American Brexit Committee.

I was in New York City, studying as a graduate student, in 1968 when the civil rights protest in Ireland began, and I think that was the beginning of my awakening of interest. I heard Bernadette Devlin speak in Gaelic Park and was impressed by what she had to say and how she said it. It was from that point that I and many others began to wake up to what the Irish problem was really about.

My visits with my wife and family to Ireland were primarily focused on the Republic. I remember one day after the killing of Mountbatten, when we arrived in London, a neighbour who was a Kerry woman said, 'Oh, you've arrived on our great day of shame.' I said, 'What was that?' 'Oh, the IRA blew up Mountbatten.' I said, 'Maybe it's your great day of shame but it's not mine!' I've always been marked in the family ever since over that!

When I visited my wife's cousin, who was a member of the Dáil, I happened to mention to him about the Dublin and Monaghan bombings and asked why the Southern government didn't take a stand. 'Nobody cares' – those were his precise words in response. That astonished me.

Generally the people I met in the Republic either weren't well-informed or really didn't much care about the North. If you fast-forward to now, a relation of mine heads up an association of farmers. When the subject of the North came up in terms of Brexit, he said, 'You have to understand – these Northern people are very awkward.'

The first time I crossed the border was in winter. Sinn Féin would hold an annual meeting with people from Irish Northern Aid's board. I drove up with my entire family and there were heavily armed guards and checkpoints. I had a van and the soldiers were looking underneath it. They weren't disrespectful so much as officious about anything they asked me. I had no reason to believe they knew anything about me or my beliefs or actions. I just assumed everybody was dealt with in the same way. My wife was kind of frightened and my kids were kind of curious, but I wasn't frightened, no.

In 2002 members of the Hibernian National Board went over for the thirtieth anniversary of Bloody Sunday. We visited the Holy Cross Girls' School in the Ardoyne, where the protest [by loyalists against the children's attendance] was going on. We were given a briefing about what it was like to live under those circumstances at that time, which was quite an eye-opener.

My discussions with people I know there – some of them have been involved in various aspects of the politics of the conflict or in the conflict itself – they think that if the border has to be there, it should be invisible because it's finally getting people at ease with one another, if not loving one another. There are some elements of the loyalist community who want to have that high payroll which peace brings. The North of Ireland has the highest level of public employees in the United Kingdom. Much of it is security related.

There is a hard core, mostly represented by the DUP, that would not want to see the border disappear or even have people fraternising with one another. Their work with the Conservative Party to make sure that there is a customs border is pretty absurd, particularly in light of the vote that the North gave to remain in the EU. Economically, the agricultural sector and the export sector are primarily affected by this. So I think the pockets of people in some of these urban areas in Derry or Belfast won't feel the same economic impact that Brexit will bring.

When the GFA was signed, some things were left on the negotiating room floor that have not been addressed – including the fact that the DUP has never signed the GFA. That signals how willing they are to ignore everything that it means and everything it stands for.

I don't think you can have Brexit and an invisible border, at least in terms of customs enforcement. They don't have to be armed guards but they have to be bookkeeper types or inspectors, and I don't think anybody would complain about that as much as checkpoints with military and machine-guns.

There is always this latent force, some might say a latent gene, that runs through the veins of people who've been involved in this Irish unity struggle for generations. It amounts to 'Well, if we don't achieve it, we'll do our best and then pass on to the next generation.' I think that Adams and McGuinness had hoped that there would not have to be any handing on to another generation, that this would do it. But if the British keep lying, if the Ministry of Defence keeps obstructing the truth, you have to wonder what their long-range plan is.

The thing that would make some people opposed to any change in the border situation, even if it was only to install a customs border, is that the Conservative Party Brexiteers could decide that they want to have guards at this border. There's nothing that prevents them doing that and, given their history, they could very well do it, because as far as they're concerned this is sovereign territory of Her Majesty's government. So I think that the very fact it could change that way at the behest of Conservative Brexiteers leaves people with a bad taste in their mouths.

It comes down to mistrust of officialdom in the North. Even though there is relative calm now, there isn't justice, and there won't be justice until the families of victims get the truth. Unlike the American form of government, where certain policies are agreed upon on a bipartisan basis, particularly foreign policy, and you proceed forward with some of those principles, you have a Conservative Party government that could change anything on a whim because they're the government in power. They don't have any written constitution with a bill of rights. So things that couldn't happen in America could happen in

Britain overnight. I remember someone saying that the reason the British sent so many troops to quell the civil rights protest was that they wanted their troops to have their blood-kills there, and this was a good way to train them. So there's a lot of suspicion.

It's hard to tell, but I'm pessimistic about whether we can avoid further violence, until the British government is faced with the reality of returning those six counties to Ireland in some long-range plan. Maybe Senator Mark Daly's report [*Brexit and the Future of Ireland: Uniting Ireland and Its People in Peace and Prosperity*] would be a starting point. And there are a number of economists who have come up with plans for the costs of reuniting Ireland. So if the United States, in this latest round of Brexit talks, was willing to have talks on what it would take to reunite Ireland, the people who would really benefit are the British taxpayers and the people in Northern Ireland.

Brexit will hasten the day when there will be a reunited Ireland. A man much more thoughtful than me, Richard Haas [former US special envoy to Ireland, now president of the Washington-based think tank the Council on Foreign Relations], when he analysed the vote on the referendum to leave or remain, said, 'This means the beginning of the ending of the UK.' I just hope that is correct. He said that because of the stirring of a nationalist movement in Scotland, alongside nationalism in Ireland, and the fact that even before the EU referendum Scotland had already begun that breakaway movement. It would just make no sense for the British to keep maintaining partition at a cost they really can't afford. They're no longer ruling the seas.

I wouldn't mind a border poll if I had the opportunity to define the question people are going to be answering in that poll. It could at least serve as a benchmark. If nationalists were to lose it would be a guide for how to proceed further and identify issues that would make unification more popular. But I'm not sure the poll is going to satisfy some people.

I was talking to an Irish diplomat one time about a reunification poll. I asked, 'What do you consider a sufficient winning margin? Would 5% more for reunification do? Or 10%?' As long as the trigger is in the British government's hands, there isn't a poll that they can't overcome, because it is the secretary of state for Northern Ireland who deems whether it is a significant enough amount. And then the secretary of state defers to the Department of Foreign Affairs, which determines whether something should be submitted to Parliament. It might take two or three parliaments, who knows?

So I'm very much sceptical on the sincerity involved. And if you look at the qualities of our current secretary for Northern Ireland, she's clueless on so many issues and has stumbled in Parliament several times with some of her comments, particularly on a British soldiers' amnesty bill.

A 50%-plus-one majority for unification in a border poll is the sort of thing the Irish government wouldn't be too keen on. Throughout the history of the conflict, the Irish government has had some spineless Taoisigh and spineless Dáil members. The fact is that they have sat on the investigation of the Dublin and Monaghan bombings, which were no-warning bombings meant to kill as many people as possible and were an act of war against the state of Ireland. So the question for me would be, is the Irish government going to support a border poll?

People in Ireland are so long accustomed to the status quo, they don't want to rock the boat. That's certainly true of some of the people I've met. A vote in the South might not even get a majority for unification, or it might be a small majority for unification.

If you're going to have a border poll, there has to be an education programme beforehand. It's quite possible that people will be voting on a yes-and-no situation, which means they'll vote to not rock the boat. That's the sort of thing you have to worry about.

There have been EU referendums that were put to the Irish people which they first voted down, then it came back and it finally passed with some adjustment. The answer to a lot of these questions will [hinge on] who's going to structure the border poll, what the questions will be, and what kind of campaign is going to precede it.

I think it would be a mistake to do anything as rash as a yes-or-no question without a campaign that explained things in advance. There is also the fact that a united Ireland campaign would be financed by little Ireland, with whatever resources they can put into it, and on the Northern Ireland side by all the resources the UK could swing at it. So there's already a disadvantage for Ireland in getting the result that they want.

Reports like Senator Mark Daly's Senate report and the views of the economist [Gunther Thumann], who was involved in the reunification of Germany, and the Canadian study that was done about Irish reunification [by Kurt Huebner of the

University of British Columbia] – those have to be drilled down into and made into products that can be in every household and in every hand. That information might frighten some people, but I think it would be very successful.

There is the possibility of a hard core of unionists being dragged reluctantly into a reunited Ireland. But I think this period of twenty years since the GFA has minimised the kicking-and-screaming crowd, the hard core of the DUP. There's the Alliance Party now, Sinn Féin of course and other smaller parties. You could handle the matter so that those objecting, those kicking and screaming, were doing their objections in a political forum rather than retreating to the farms and housing estates and starting guerrilla warfare.

We've come a long way from the rejection of the 1918 vote by Ireland for independence. The only recourse then was seen to be an armed struggle to achieve that independence goal for the entire country. I think this time there are enough tools in place and structures and options. They already have an Ireland-wide electrical grid, and there are several all-Ireland bodies that are working together. I think half of the loyalists or those represented by the DUP are willing to accept that. And Arlene Foster said that if Ireland was reunited, she'd be thinking of leaving town. Well, that's another plus for us.

There's always a positive aspect to meetings of civic nationalism. Organising along those lines has been made a lot easier with the Internet. Information can be widely distributed, timely things can be done and responses given. But the view that I have, and one of the reasons I set up the Brexit Committee, is that the only thing that'll change Britain is a big gun like America. The US has the power and the persuasion to get them to move off dead centre. You can hold all the forums you want in Ireland, but Britain's control of the media – at least before the Internet, and even now in terms of the major newspaper distributors – and their willingness to engage in every manner of treachery: that will keep fear growing.

Irish-Americans and others have the ability to bring the issue of Irish unity to the table of Congress and say, 'We've been battling this for so long, from its beginning to its end. The British have corrupted a portion of Ireland for its own political purposes, which nobody voted for in a democracy. You can change that.' Brexit may give us the ability on this side of the pond to change that, because the Conservative government desperately wants a trade deal as the only salvation for them if they leave the EU. At least it gives the case for a united Ireland some leverage. Ireland has no leverage to make things happen. The United States does.

The American Brexit Committee consists of Irish-American activists and leaders throughout the country but primarily in the Eastern part of the United States: the AOH, Brehon Law Society, IAUC people and also people who are activists of their own accord and are not affiliated with any organisation. We have convinced them, and they have shared their conviction by becoming part of the committee, that America has a chance to translate Brexit into something more positive. Two major positives would be to get the British to show full compliance with the GFA and to get testimony before Congress about why this is an opportunity to speak about a reunited Ireland from an economic standpoint.

In the course of doing that, we've had one major letter go to sixty or seventy members of Congress who are in key positions. The two key congressmen on the House side are Richie Neal and Eliot Engel of Foreign Affairs. They have the power to hold hearings and to delay any action on a trade deal, as well as to hold hearings on what the State Department has been doing or not doing with regard to the British observances of the GFA. We'll be using those points of leverage, because the British are loath to get involved in hearings of that nature, so they'll be pulling all of their hidden sources of influence to try to stop it.

But time is on our side. The recent visit to Ireland by Speaker Pelosi and Richard Neal was good, affirming that there will be no deal unless there is observance of the GFA and its promise. I think that message sent over and over again is going to be making it clear that the British don't have the options they once had. And then it would help if there was a change in the British government to one led by Jeremy Corbyn.

There's a prominent attorney in Philadelphia, John Corcoran, who's been involved in a lot of the extradition and deportation treaties. He's the chairman of the American Brexit Committee and I'm the secretary. The principal inspiration for it in New York is the former State Assembly member John Dearie and former congressman Joe Crowley. They have both lent their support to bring this issue as far as we can.

Unfortunately we have a president in the White House who is a train wreck, and he'd be inclined to give a US–UK trade deal to England, even though we have a heavily unfavourable trade imbalance with the British. There would be no point in giving them a trade deal that would be favourable simply because his mother was from Scotland and he loves the queen and he has his golf courses. We believe that the leverage power comes from Congress and particularly from the House of Representatives.

We may have helped spur on Nancy Pelosi's stand through our first letter campaign back in January of this year, and there have been some very successful press conferences.

Just before St Patrick's Day, the parade grand marshal this year, Brian O'Dwyer, the son of Paul O'Dwyer, issued an article in *Legal News* in New York emphasising the importance of that trade deal towards getting some leverage on the British. Several members of his Brehon Law Society are members of our committee, so there's a momentum from the New York leadership. I think that with the next letter going out we will have seen several changes in the situation and we will feel a bit more positive about getting hearings in Congress for this issue. The British hate the idea of going before Congress for any reason on anything – they'd much rather work behind the scenes. Summoning their representatives to give their side of the story is anathema to them.

Unionist and British politicians have not been responsive to the Irish language requirement, not been responsive to the legacy requirements and not been responsive to the human rights requirements. So in the light of that, the border poll is something that could be introduced. And maybe it could act as a stepping-stone to a United States consortium working on a reunification plan. I think that's possible. It all depends on how much turmoil Congress will be in, in a presidential election year. If those hearings are held now, I don't think we want them to be interpreted as opportunities for Democrats to score points against a Republican president.

I'm surprised. I thought the Irish-American response to all this would have some modest beginnings – and yes, they are modest beginnings, when you consider some of the major lobbying efforts that Congress is subject to. But it has survived the St Patrick's Day hoopla and has gathered steam since then. So I think it's structured to be in this for the long haul. Even when Congress recesses in July and when it comes back in September, there'll be things that'll be on the table.

This issue has certainly energised the committee and some of their associates, but the people in the street still need to hear more about it. We just released a letter by three former national presidents of the AOH who are from Pennsylvania addressing this issue. It was distributed widely throughout Pennsylvania as a way of drawing in more people to consider the fundamental issues.

Once you cultivate that audience, there is one other thing you have to consider, and that is that foreign relations are conducted in this country by a very small group of people. It's usually done bipartisan and much of the work is done behind closed doors, in concert with the secretary of state. So while an activist base is helpful, it's more important that we get information into the hands of that small foreign policy base. We're never going to be able to motivate them as people are motivated over taxes or some other bread-and-butter issues, because the country is not structured that way. In fact it gives the lead in foreign relations to the president, with Congress in more of an oversight role. And it's that part which requires informed people like Joe Crowley and Richard Neal. Joe Crowley is in the position to be a lobbyist on this issue, if he wishes. And there are others who know that this is a point where we can begin to exercise that leverage intelligently, with those who would make the most difference.

Brexit is now the focus among the activist Irish-American community. And that's why it's important that we keep getting our issues in the newspapers and so on, because we don't expect – and I've said this at several meetings of the committee – we don't expect to get people up over the barriers or to start writing out cheques for the American Brexit Committee. That isn't the way it's going to work. It's going to be: 'If you read what we have to say, and if you can intelligently make the connection between a trade deal and the GFA, and ultimately the reunification of Ireland, then we want you to meet with a congressman. But not just any congressman. It may not even be your congressman. It's the people who can make a difference in foreign policy in this country who we have in mind.'

There are those who are very much living in the past, and that's the only way I can describe some of the DUP people. They're living in the past, as are Boris Johnson and Jacob Rees-Mogg and company. At some point their colours are going to be shown as so shallow and so subservient and so narcissistic that they'll give up the ghost. So that's my hope.

25

RAYMOND McCORD

24 MAY 2019

Raymond McCord is the father of three sons, the eldest murdered by UVF state informers on 9 November 1997. Due to his campaign for justice the UVF have tried on several occasions to murder him. He believes in Northern Ireland remaining part of the UK but that sectarianism is ruining Northern Ireland and is generated by sectarian politics. In August 2019 he issued proceedings at the High Court in Belfast claiming any move to ensure the UK leaves the EU on 31 October without a withdrawal agreement would be an 'unconstitutional attack on the people of Northern Ireland'.

I was born in York Street and grew up in the Rathcoole housing estate in North Belfast. The border to us at the time would have been a total irrelevance. Politics was never discussed. My father was a member of the Orange Order, of the Black Institution and of the Apprentice Boys, but we were working-class people and we didn't discuss politics. Your mother bought you new shoes and new clothes for the Twelfth of July. And because your father was in the Orange Order, it was taken for granted you'd be in it too. But I had no interest in it.

The first time I crossed the border was with the Star of the Sea football club. Bobby Sands [republican hunger striker] was on the team, and we went down south to play a team in Dublin.

I'd have been about sixteen at the time. You didn't think 'I'm going into another country.' We just went down in a minibus, stopped at Dundalk to get drinks, lemonade or something like that, and used the toilets. We played the match – and won.

My parents used to go on bus runs down south to Dublin, maybe, or Dundalk. It was just a day out for them. It was never a big issue, going across the border then. It was two countries and it's still two countries. People talk about respect: when I'm speaking, I refer to where I live as Northern Ireland. If there was a united Ireland, there wouldn't be a Northern Ireland, it'd be Ireland. But right now Northern Ireland is the name of the country. People who want a united Ireland, particularly Sinn Féin and republicans, they refuse to acknowledge the name of the country. For me personally, that sends a wrong message to unionists.

A couple of years ago, I was sitting in Belfast with a couple of guys having a beer. I'd been up in Derry – I was invited up there by the Bloody Sunday people to speak. I said I'd been up in Derry and this man – he's a great Glasgow Rangers supporter – he says, 'Londonderry.' I says, 'Let me tell you something. My father was in the Orange Order, the Royal Black Preceptory and the Apprentice Boys of Derry. If "Derry" was good enough for him, it's good enough for me.'

When the border was militarised, we didn't see it as a border, we saw it as a security thing, to catch bombers, try to catch IRA ones and all that. Unionists saw the border as a way in which republicans committed atrocities; they went across the border and were safe. What we saw was how lenient the Southern courts were, particularly with extradition.

The time since the signing of the GFA has not been well used. For me, over the twenty years since the signing, the effort wasn't put in to bring people together. It was a waste of twenty years and it's still being wasted. It's a case with the two big political parties of keeping the people divided so they'll stay in power. One wants the link with the UK, one wants a united Ireland. But what these two parties have to remember is, it's not the parties that decide, it's the people.

Both parties are equally to blame, equally guilty. They try to use the number of votes they get, at the European elections, the Assembly elections or Westminster. What they don't tell the people is that it doesn't make any difference. They don't tell people that if one party gets ninety seats, it doesn't make the link stronger to Britain or a call for a border poll stronger. It's the people who vote, not the parties. And the parties would need to start explaining that to people, but they don't because they'd lose too much.

I voted to remain and so did the majority of people in Northern Ireland. The MPs who were supposed to be representing Northern Ireland at Westminster chose to follow the views of the people of the UK, rather than the views of the people here. They come out with garbage that a small percentage of the unionists voted. I don't believe that. Anyway it's irrelevant. The vote doesn't say it's unionist or nationalist. It doesn't say on the ballot paper 'unionist' or 'nationalist'.

Nobody was told the truth before Brexit, neither side – although the ones who voted to leave were told more lies. Unionist people who voted to leave would now vote to remain. They're worried about their jobs, their pensions and all that.

So it's been a disaster, the last three years since the Brexit vote. We've no representation at Westminster. The way the vote was carried in Northern Ireland, most people are being ignored at Westminster.

Arlene Foster is doing what the two political parties do: cherry-picking on who the victims are. She's quite right to say the Brexit referendum was a UK vote. But it's a case of if a vote doesn't suit our party – not our people, our *party* – we're not going to fight for that. You listen to farming people, listen to business people throughout Northern Ireland – Brexit doesn't look good in any way whatsoever. Does loyalty to the crown mean more than a stable country and a stable future for the next generation? It'll also cause more division – more 'them and us'.

To my mind, the DUP is destroying unionism. It's making unionist people look bad. It's making the unionist people look as if they're sectarian, it's making the unionist people look like they don't believe in equality, it's making the unionist people look as if everything is about themselves.

You're going to have unionists going to the DUP camp for the sake of safety. I can never bring myself to vote for it. Its policies and attitude – its self-serving people. I think if it spoke with people who, in the last election, voted for it, many would normally have voted for the UUP. They vote DUP to keep Sinn Féin out, and vice versa.

The DUP has chosen to ignore the representatives of business, to ignore the farmers. I mean, I go to the doctor if I feel ill because he's the expert in medicine. I go to the dentist if I've a sore tooth. These people are the experts. And if you can't listen to the experts, whose businesses are going to be affected, who do you go to, who do you listen to?

I don't think Brexit will lead to a border poll. The Irish government have nothing in place for a border poll in the constitution.

People keep using the border poll as a big stick to beat their people at election time: vote for us or you'll have a border poll. Mary Lou McDonald keeps demanding a border poll. I'd like to remind Mary Lou and Arlene: we live in a democracy. Bully-boy tactics don't wash with me and they don't wash with normal people.

We have a secretary of state who lives on the mainland deciding about a border poll, and she is open to political deals, apart from the on-the-run letters [letters from the authorities to a number of republicans telling them that they were not wanted for crimes], which were a disgrace. They talk about amnesty – that was amnesty. Nobody should have that – unionists, nationalists, soldiers, whatever. If Labour came in, and Sinn Féin was behind the door saying, 'Listen, we'll do a deal with Jeremy Corbyn, make sure you get re-elected. We'll have a relationship with you, give us a border poll,' – or Arlene Foster could turn round and say, 'We'll support you and there'll be no border poll' – what I'm saying is let's have certain conditions put in place, set in stone, that if these conditions are met you call a border poll. It can't be done on the basis of what the secretary of state says.

I've seen, over the years, parties talk about transparency. Politics is anything but that. It's secret deals. I voted against the GFA because, plain and simple, I don't think prisoners should have been released, because they said they wouldn't go away and they haven't gone away.

But in the GFA they talk about a border poll: it's vague, it's really vague. It says the secretary of state can call one, but it doesn't state in what terms. She can say, 'I think that it's time for a poll,' and you say, 'Why do you think that?', and she doesn't have to say why. She's the secretary of state who didn't realise that unionists vote for unionists. And this is the person who's going to say what way the country is going to go. People from the nationalist and republican community think that the Irish government in the South, no matter who it is, are all pumping for a united Ireland – but they're not. There's nothing there.

I want a court ruling that says it's illegal – it's wrong that one person can just say, 'I believe there's a need now for a border poll.'

The barrister wants to see how my case gets on in Northern Ireland. We took it down South and the judge was completely different. It was like watching something from *The Quiet Man*, it was done that quickly. No fuss – the barrister said a few things, that's all right, no review. But I want my barristers to push this. They have to go back to Dublin for a full review and say to the Irish government, 'What plans, what legislation have you for a border poll?' I want proper legislation drafted where all the political parties can sit down and say, 'A border poll will be carried out if and when' – whatever the conditions are.

Ian Paisley spoke to me on the phone and I criticised him in the papers in an open letter. I said, 'See regarding a border poll? None of you have come near me to ask about this – DUP or Sinn Féin. Or any political parties.' The two main parties – they're frightened of it. And it shows you the fear through their fear of legislation that says, 'You must have a border poll under these conditions.'

If there was a border poll today, in my opinion, the people would vote to stay. Voting for Sinn Féin in local elections doesn't mean you're going to vote for them in a border poll. I don't think people would want to escape the damage of Brexit by voting for Irish unity in a border poll. For a lot of the nationalists and the unionist people too, they'll consider, 'What is the lesser of the two evils?'

We hear from Irish America, we hear from Northern Ireland – we don't hear from the South at all about a border poll. You can understand Irish-Americans – they don't live here. I'm not criticising them. But they have romantic ideas of a united Ireland, going back to 1916 and all that. I can understand – people have their own aspirations. But you can't have aspirations where unionist people turn round and say, 'We're not going to accept that.' There've been no debates in relation to this. There have been no proper debates, no consultations. And the consultations need to be done with the people. Events need to be held at Queen's University, where young people can debate, with non-sectarian, non-political speeches.

If it's been talked through and people turn round and say, 'A border poll can and must be held, when these conditions are met' – that's democracy. And if it's in favour of a united Ireland, people have to accept it. I can see some loyalists saying, 'We're not going to accept that.'

At the moment, the bulk of unionist people would say, 'We're not going to accept that.' That's because no one's convinced them that it would be better.

I see Mary Lou McDonald as a peaceful person who looks at it from both sides. For people in Sinn Féin who want a border poll, I'd say, 'Have you learned nothing from Brexit?'

People have to ask themselves, do they want to remain part of Britain and be worse off financially, in terms of education, health and so on? Those are for me the main factors.

Britain wants rid of us. If they could get rid of us in the morning, they would do so.

The policy of the DUP and the fear factor of Sinn Féin – these influence unionist people. A lot of unionist people want to move forward, away from the Troubles, but Sinn Féin has to move forward too. Both sides. Glorifying the past, parades, commemorations for murderers – they may call them volunteers but unionists see them as murderers. A lot of people from the nationalist side would see it the same. Those are big issues for the unionist people. You're sitting in a bar talking, and every so often it'll come up: the park in Newry named after a hunger striker. People will say, 'What sort of an example is that for young people?' There are all these issues. And both sides have to say, 'What can we do, how can we help embrace the other side?'

Supposing I walk up the Falls Road to see a victim's family, or in Divis or the Ardoyne [republican areas] – which I have done – people know me, they know me as a person, nobody insults me. But would they do that with every unionist? Nothing has been laid down by the two parties. It's not just enough to talk about a united Ireland. For me the most important thing is, what sort of united Ireland will it be? Until that's done, I don't want to see a border poll. I believe that Sinn Féin is trying to use Brexit as a big stick. Nobody knows what its policies are. It keep saying, 'Border poll, border poll, border poll.' But what are the conditions? What sort of country is it going to be like?

We're having an event at Queen's University and asking, 'Can we not have a citizens' assembly to deal with the past?' And there are a lot of people for that. Because politics have failed badly here. They've failed even worse in what's become a two-party state; they've failed even worse in their talk about a petition of concern. Because one party likes it and another party doesn't, so nothing gets through. We're worse off than when we started out. So yes to a citizens' assembly to look at a possible united Ireland, without political interference.

The parties could get together as well. I put this to the political parties years ago to deal with the victims issue. They talk about 'legacy' – these fancy terms as if it was university they were at. I said, 'What's "legacy" supposed to mean? These are murder cases.'

The truth is, every political party sitting at Stormont should have a victims officer – Sinn Féin, the DUP, Alliance – and it has to be someone from the other community. So with Sinn Féin, you'd have a unionist victims officer. And the same on the other side. No secret talks, and the victims officer can't be overruled by the party leader.

And with a border poll, have conditions set down which must be met. Let's see if those conditions can be met, and take it forward from that. If these conditions could be agreed, for each election coming up it means the two big parties can't use it as a border poll. They can't turn round and say, 'Vote for us and we'll get a border poll', or 'Vote for us and we'll stay part of the UK.' That means you're taking the orange and green out of elections.

As to a poll which returned a decision 50% plus one? I agree with a majority vote. So 50% plus one – that's a majority. I voted in the election the other day – the European elections. Now supposing a candidate gets 1,000 votes and another gets 1,001 – I'm hoping it's my candidate gets 1,001, because majority rules. In Stormont, the way it's divvied up with all the political parties – that's different from this here that we're talking about. The political process that we have here is different from the rest of the UK. In one way that's good, because it means that decisions aren't sectarian. But it's being abused badly. Still, if you're a democrat and you vote for something, whoever gets the majority vote, you take it on from there.

I've heard about Seamus Mallon's [former deputy first minister of Northern Ireland, former deputy leader of the SDLP] interview on TV. Is Seamus Mallon saying that if you convince enough people up to 50% plus one, that's not enough? He's saying he wants unionists convinced. In one way what he says is good, but in another way he's contradicting himself. He's saying he wants to wait until unionists are convinced. So is he saying he'd wait until unionists are convinced and they'd vote for a united Ireland? But what if that never comes? So I think it couldn't work – it's impossible for it to work.

Seamus Mallon's politics over the years weren't my politics. I wouldn't have been a fan of his, to be honest with you. I've nothing personal against him, but the impression he gave me over the years was that he was anti-unionist. And if he's anti-unionist, he's anti-democratic. So in what way is he anti-unionist – is he anti because of their policies? Because of the statements he comes out with – you have to show respect for different viewpoints. That didn't come from Seamus.

People have seen over the years how easy it is for unionists to come together. We've seen that with Paisley and the big rallies and so on. I really hope that those days are long gone. I don't want to see that again. I don't want it to come to a point where people say, 'You're either in this camp or you're in that camp – you can't sit on the fence.' Is that going to arise because of this?

Let's get something that people can agree on. Let's say, 'A border poll will be called when these conditions are met.' If, as time goes by, those conditions are met, then a border poll must be called.

We've seen in the nationalist/republican community there are dissidents who won't accept things. I think there's a strong possibility the same thing would happen in unionist areas after a poll that voted for Irish unity – and there would be a bigger number of them than there are of dissidents. Because unlike the Provos, who went into politics, these people – loyalist paramilitaries – haven't gone into politics.

I think people have a choice. Do we go along with the democratic system, or do we say there's an element where there might be more conflict, there might be more shootings, and this time it'll come from loyalist paramilitaries? Do we say we'll stand up to these people? Because within the unionist community, the state hasn't done enough against these paramilitaries. They've let them stay in control; they've given them respectability.

We see in the newspaper the likes of Jackie McDonald, a senior UDA man. Unless I'm mistaken, the law states that the UDA is a terrorist organisation that's proscribed. I don't understand how the likes of Jackie McDonald don't get arrested. The state is still pandering to the paramilitaries. To move forward regarding a border poll, you don't round up all these people and put them in prison. You say, 'You're to go away, there's no longer funding for you.' The oxygen for these groups is money.

First and foremost before there's any poll, the paramilitary situation within loyalism needs to be dealt with. The paramilitaries have built themselves into a big criminal organisation. They'll say to themselves, 'In a united Ireland, our powers will be taken away from us.' These people need to be seen for what they are, as criminals. If they're concerned about Protestant/unionist identity, let them stand in elections. They say they're there to defend people against the dissident republicans. Well, let's take it back to 1998 and the Omagh bomb [on 15 August 1998 a Real IRA bomb in Omagh killed twenty-nine people and two unborn babies], let's take it to the prison officer who was shot coming up to work and other cases – loyalist paramilitaries have done nothing about it. They don't want to engage and go down that road because they're making so much money. We've seen the police saying they're only criminal gangs. So they're not wanted in the unionist community.

It would be different if the unionist community was under attack. The unionist community isn't under attack.

If conditions are laid down and people say 'We accept those conditions,' that's when a border poll can be called. A lot of people will object, like Paisley's 'Never, never, never, never,' but those days are gone and we don't want them back.

Suppose there were conditions set up and those were met and a border poll was held and people voted to remain part of the UK – what is Sinn Féin going to do? Is it going to say, 'We're not accepting that,' and in two more years there must be another border poll?

When I spoke to Ian Paisley Jr, he said to me, 'I've no objection to a border poll, but there'll only be one – not another one after.' It may say in the GFA that there can be another poll, but the DUP says it never signed up to the GFA. 'There's the cake, we'll take that bit with cream on it. See that bit without cream? We're not going to take that.'

As for Mary McAleese inviting Jackie McDonald down to Áras an Uachtaráin. What she did was an insult to victims and an insult to the unionist community.

The Brexiteers, especially in Britain among the Tory party – have this idea of the grandeur of old Britain – the old British Empire. Those times are long gone – they have to live in the real world. I took out an Irish passport a year or two ago. I get certain rights now – I've a British passport and an Irish passport.

As to a border poll, if the majority of people are nationalist/republican and are voting for a united Ireland, and the terms have been negotiated and have been met, there will still be people on either side who will object to it. But the main thing is democracy. There's no good in people calling for a border poll, unless they believe in democracy. One of the things I would like to see before a border poll is called is for the two parties to stop using elections to give a false impression that they're going to have a border poll or they're never going to have a border poll – whatever camp you're based in.

Brexit and the border poll are two divisive issues which are used by the two main parties here to keep the people apart. I've experience of that working with victims. If victims work together, they've unity and strength. If the two parties get into a room, the victims wouldn't agree with their policies. The two parties don't want that. They want people there just to agree with them.

As for Brexit, the people are still unsure what's going to happen. Are we going to leave? Is there to be another referendum? A lot of things have been said. There's talk of Boris Johnson – that he's going to take over, that he will take them out. But if he gets in, we'll see the way he changes his mind back and forward, flip-flop. He's the old-type Tory. But if you're talking to people, most of them will say what I say – that they don't understand it. No one has explained it to us. So are we going to have the same thing with the border poll?

They haven't learned their lesson. To eradicate a lot of these fears, what's being organised is civic forums – but for only one side. That isn't helping things.

I was involved in setting up a charity – a victims' charity – and there are cross-community people in there. We were operating five, seven days a week. Ones from the Shankill are meeting ones from the Falls in June, to talk about the Twelfth and all. And then we're going to meet again in November and talk about forums and that kind of thing that are taking place daily. So let the forums be dominated by local communities – not the politicians. Take it away from the political people.

26

BILLY HUTCHINSON

5 JUNE 2019

Billy Hutchinson was a member of the loyalist paramilitary UVF and was imprisoned in the Maze/Long Kesh from 1975–90. During this time he was influenced by UVF veteran Gusty Spence, who believed that loyalists needed to develop a political strategy. While in prison, Hutchinson took a degree in social sciences and a diploma in town planning. He was elected to Belfast City Council in 1997 and to the Northern Ireland Assembly in 1998. He is currently a member of Belfast City Council and is leader of the PUP.

I grew up in the Shankill. People back then would have talked about the border, about the Free State. Many of them would have crossed the border, done a bit of smuggling. I particularly remember the smuggling of silver lighters – ones with cotton wool and a wick in them.

I was born into a mixed marriage: my father was a socialist and my mother was a unionist. [*Laughs*] My father would have taken me to Dunville Park, to Clonard pictures – we lived in Conway Street. All his friends were Catholic. He ran an illegal bookie's for the bookies, who are now all millionaires.

But people went to Southern Ireland for a whole lot of reasons. Holidays, for example. I can remember my mother's brother and his wife – they used to go to a place in Omeath, to a farmer called Willie. He had all this farmland and a wee cottage and he rented it out every year. They went down and stayed there, and I went down too a couple of times. I was very young but I remember when you came to the border there was customs and garda and so on. You knew you were entering a different place. I don't think I had any sense that it was hostile or anything like that. The people weren't different: they were farmers, they did the same things. We didn't have any contact other than with the farmer, or maybe when we went to a shop about three miles down the road. That was when I was about eight or nine years of age.

People in the Shankill would have talked about the Free State and the things Paisley would have been talking about in the early to mid-1960s – fire and brimstone and snowballs and all the rest of it. And some people became more acutely aware of what the South was. It was seen as a priest-ridden state.

Thinking changed when the militarised border emerged. Because of IRA attacks from across the border – it was perceived that the Irish government were in some way involved in all of that. So a big sea-change occurred in people's thinking.

And yet I grew up in the Shankill where people did Irish dancing, I went to primary school with a sprig of shamrock in my jumper. All of that was great until the Troubles came, and then it was a totally different mindset. People who were doing it then backed off. People blame this on the Provos, and there was an element of that, but I think there had to have been more than that. There was the whole notion of using the Irish language as a weapon, Irish culture as a weapon. And I think that has a lot to do with people's thinking around an Irish Language Act: what is this about?

I don't think anybody welcomed the militarised border. It was there for negative reasons, those being that attacks were being made across the border. People saw militarisation as necessary to prevent those things happening. But look at the border and how long it is, how many roads were closed, yet still the IRA were able to operate. They were operating in border counties and they were active on both sides. And despite the militarised border, the IRA continued to do what they did. So a judge coming across the border after a holiday gets murdered. You don't do that unless somebody gives you information.

I never crossed the border during the time it was militarised. I never had any cause to cross the border at that time – the conflict was going on here. On one occasion a senior republican was asked by an international group, 'Did you know Billy?' And he said, 'Yes, but we didn't know it was Billy.' And they asked, 'Was he your enemy?', and the republican said, 'Yes. If we'd got him, we'd have killed him.' Which I thought was pretty honest. [*Chuckles*]

When I got out of prison, I met a guy called Christof de Baróid, whose son Ciarán wrote the book about Ballymurphy [*Down North: Reflections of Ballymurphy and the Early Troubles*]. He was a very strong republican and he was working with some people from the Shankill, bringing people from disadvantaged backgrounds down to a centre in Cork called Between. I'd been approached by them, and they said, 'Look, if you've any prisoners' wives or families, bring them down.' So I went and spoke to the UVF and the UDA and they took the families down. We did that for a few years.

I felt OK about doing it. I was a different person at this stage. I'd done a lot of Irish history and met republicans face to face rather than in a different life. So I was OK with it. I thought it was a genuine offer: he didn't need to make it, but he did.

The border had eased up quite a bit by then. We were all part of Europe, and I think at this stage the authorities had enough intelligence, they knew who they wanted to stop and who they didn't.

I knew the border was there but I knew because we were in Europe, we were all Europeans. I knew that I lived in the UK; I knew that I wanted to be British and was pro-British, I wanted to be part of the UK. But I had also learnt that there were people who had aspirations of a united Ireland, and those aspirations were great to have, as long as there wasn't physical force. There was still a lot of bloodshed when I got out of prison, but I knew it was going to end. Within the prison both the UVF and the IRA were on a road to calling ceasefires, and they were in negotiations with people to get that to happen.

It was the people of Between who changed my mind. I knew they were republicans, but they were no threat to me. And that was different to up here, because here there was always a threat against you.

At this stage, I had started work on a cross-community project between the Shankill and the Falls, on the Springfield Road. This would have been around July 1990. So I was working with people who I knew were republicans. The conflict was still going on and I had a bit of nervousness around that.

I had a guy who worked for me called Tommy Gorman. Tommy escaped off the prison ship *Maidstone*, and he would have been one of the key Provos at the time and was well respected. On one occasion me and him went to Conway Mill to hear speeches around how we have peace.

It was very interesting because Tommy was one of the people who challenged those present. He said, 'Oh right – is this all about out-breeding people? Then why don't you just tell us to stop using contraceptives?' He started this whole row and I was with him. Everybody was looking at me and I'm looking round the room and wondering who knows my background and who doesn't. But those sorts of things gave you life experiences that you'd never had before.

As to Brexit – I read a document in 1983 from the PUP while I was in prison. They had this part in it about how we keep middle-class Catholics in the UK. And their argument was for equality. Catholics needed to feel that they weren't being discriminated against and that they would do well in the UK in terms of the economy.

I read all through it and I said, 'This is a brilliant idea.' Because what they were actually doing was trying to ensure that Catholics could be British and Irish at the same time. They could hold dual nationality; they were in Europe; they were happy with it. So why then would they want to go into a united Ireland?

It's a very economic argument, I know, but if you're not attacking someone's Irishness, then people can feel secure. But you have to follow it up by deeds, not just by words. At the time there would have been people for it and people against it. But I suppose it's how you give leadership, how you show people this is the right thing to do. It's very hard for people to argue against giving people the same rights as you. When John Finucane became lord mayor of Belfast this year, he was talking about equality. I said, 'John, you're very welcome, I'm very glad you're here. But do you see when you get to equality? Make sure I get some of that.'

That's what worries me about Brexit. I would be worried about middle-class Catholics living in Northern Ireland who have actually done well – they have worked hard and progressed in this society. They have positions in this society that they wouldn't have had in the 1960s and 1970s. It's great that that happened, but my concern about it is that they always felt safe within the UK because we're a part of Europe.

We need to be careful in Northern Ireland what we do about Brexit, because we could poke the bear – middle-class Catholics. We have seen how middle-class Catholics will lend their votes to Sinn Féin – and maybe their votes will go somewhere else.

The GFA has never been implemented in full – a lot of things have been missing. When we got to 2007 we had the St Andrews Agreement, which turned things around. The first and deputy-first ministers had to have cross-party support, direct rule not being implemented when Stormont falls, and now we've got all these departments sitting there with permanent secretaries who can't make a decision because they might find themselves going to court. It's easier taking a permanent secretary to court than it is a minister.

The other thing we didn't have was the civic forum. The civic forum was part of the GFA and was never implemented. Unionists didn't want it implemented because they saw it as some sort of left-wing idea that would stifle them from doing anything. But it was never like that. The civic forum was never intended to be decision-making, it was to be a touchstone. And there was to be people from the trade unions, community centres, churches, from business – it was to be well-balanced. And I think if we had had the civic forum, there'd have been fewer breaks in government than we've had.

As to a border poll, I believe if there was one tomorrow, unionists would win it. I'm not so sure about a second or a third one, given the demographic change. They tell us that by 2020 or 2021 there'll be a Catholic majority. That doesn't mean all Catholics will vote for a united Ireland. In terms of the GFA and the protection it gives, the union would be safer if we were all in Europe. But we're not going to be there. They made a decision, they had a democratic vote, and Leave won it. So I think we'll be coming out and we'll have to see what deal is done in the end. It looks right now like there's not going to be a no deal, but we'll see who is prime minister. I think Boris Johnson will do just what he wants to do, irrespective of who it affects.

In democratic terms, Arlene Foster is right – Brexit was a UK-wide vote. When they had the abortion or pro-choice referendum in the South, Donegal voted against it. Does that mean Donegal doesn't have abortions? You can't break this down. The fact is the UK is the UK, it has a number of regions, and those regions have different levels of government, with Westminster as the parliament.

At the end of the day, we know who calls the border poll: it's the secretary of state. And while it's the Tories, I don't think they'll see any conditions where they would call a border poll until there is some sort of condition where they think they need to call it. But there will be a border poll at some stage.

I think the first poll unionists will win, but I'm not so sure about a second or third. The reality is, [because we're] leaving the EU, nobody knows what's going to happen. We knew what was happening while we were in the EU. We know Westminster is a shambles because they haven't done what they were asked by the electorate.

If you were a rock star or a very wealthy barrister and you were going to get a divorce from your wife for whatever reason, you'd get somebody to represent you. And they'd go to your wife's representatives and say, 'What does she want out of this?' Then once you know, you go back to the divorce and you know what you're going to give her. Whereas what they did with Brexit was they jumped in even before they had any deal and signed Article 50, which meant we were running out of road. These are all supposed to be very clever people.

It's hard to tell if most unionists are pro- or anti-Brexit. I think it's a margin of around 2% either way. The Ulster Unionists stood in the EU election [2019], and before they stood they told me privately that they were pro-EU. Jim Nicholson [UUP MEP] was pro-EU – he was there for forty years. He was definitely pro-EU and always talked about it. But you do need to tell people this and the UUP didn't – they fudged it. They did exactly the same thing as the Labour Party did and they fudged the thing.

With the PUP, it's a free vote because we don't stand in Europe. And there was probably 51% of our membership wanted to leave and 49% who wanted to stay. That's probably the same among the unionist community generally.

I don't think Brexit has hastened the day when there'll be a border poll. It has made Catholics/nationalists uncomfortable – unless we see some sort of major benefit from the union [with Britain] in terms of quality of life. Whether Catholics/nationalists are pushing for a border poll, I'm not even sure that they would vote because as I say to nationalists and republicans all the time, 'Wrap the green flag round me, but not just yet' – St Augustine.

Pressures on the secretary of state from nationalists for a border poll may have an effect, but as to how long before a border poll is called – how long is a piece of string?

If Brexit happens on 31 October, I think that the British government will be engaged in talks. We hear that Trump is going to give them a deal. That'll be good – we'll see what he's going to give them. Allegedly, Trump has been the best president yet in terms of the US economy. I'm not so sure that's true, but their economy is booming. We'll see about all of that – there are too many imponderables at present to know when a border poll might be called. They're not going to call it in 2021, for the simple reason that both sides of the border have got something to talk about – here, we have the anniversary of the first parliament on 22 June.

In my view, Sinn Féin has done a deal with the DUP in Belfast City Council. It doesn't want to be in office in 2021 because then it would have to meet the royals. I've no evidence of this, but watching it pick its people, it seems it doesn't want to be in office. Its office ends in June, and on 22 June it will be 100 years from the first parliament in Northern Ireland. These people are not sitting idle; they're talking to each other and they're choreographing it.

I'm asking political unionism, 'Have you thought about a border poll and what follows? I'm not saying you're agreeing with it, but no matter what happens we have to manage it.' I want to see where political unionism is going if it ever happens. I personally don't think Irish unification will happen the first time, because unionism will win. I may not be here for the second or third time because I'm getting old, but as I said on *The View*, political unionism needs to at least have an internal discussion about a border poll. And if there was a united Ireland vote – I don't think there will be but if there was – what does that look like? What do we need to talk about, does it work for us, does it not work for us, is everybody going to just emigrate? I favour political unionism actually telling me where it's going to go. I think political unionism is going to bury its head like an ostrich and say, 'What is the point? It's not going to happen.' I don't think there's a need to rush, but I think those debates need to happen.

We need to learn lessons from 1921 – the hurt from then around the six counties. They were left behind. People need to have practical discussions or even academic debates, I don't care. But somebody needs to be talking about it. Where is unionism going to be in ten years? I don't know if they're having these discussions; if they are, they haven't told me.

No unionist is ever going to say that they would support a united Ireland. But I think we need to consider a number of scenarios. If it was to happen, what do we want? Nothing concentrates the mind like a hanging, but I don't think we've got there yet. I don't know when there'll be a border poll, but the British government can only hold on for so long.

What needs to be concentrated on is that people are registered so they can go out and vote. That will be the first tactic. Before the council elections, some people interpreted a spike in the registration to be about people coming out to vote in Europe and locally. But it wasn't – there were low turn-outs. It had to be that people were registered to make sure they could go out and vote on a border poll. Because they'll not be voting for a party in a border poll, they'll be voting for or against a united Ireland.

The first thing unionism needs to talk about is, why does middle-class unionism vote for Alliance? We're moving to a new world and we need to get real about this. I think unionism needs to have a talk, not about the parties but about what we do to convince people that unionism is still something worth voting for. Traditionally unionism didn't need to do this – they were the largest party for years. Now the DUP and Sinn Féin are doing the same thing. They're saying to vote for them, make them the largest party. And that's fair enough. The problem is, because we use the single transferable vote, those votes need to be transferred, and there needs to be a viable unionist party to take those votes. Whatever it's called – it could be called something totally different, but it would be unionist. So we need to think about how we attract voters in the future.

We also need to be looking at policies. Are these social policies that millennials would vote for, and where are these millennials? If it doesn't happen by 2030, there'll be no unionists other than the DUP alongside Sinn Féin, and I think that would be a shame. People think that you need one party. We've had one party before, and did that work? No – what we need is a party that's on the right and another one that's centrist. I think that we need to learn lessons. And that lesson is that we need to be doing things now. I would never suggest or ask a Catholic to vote for a unionist party, because that's somebody's own decision. And it doesn't matter about your religion – you could be a Catholic and unionist, you could be a Protestant and a republican. But we do need to be looking at this.

The DUP isn't going to do it. It's the biggest party, and that's what scares people, because it's so far right. Middle-class unionists can't vote for the DUP because they don't agree with it. So they look for another party. In Belfast they didn't vote for the Ulster Unionists. I think they don't vote for the DUP because they see the DUP as being far right. Which it's not – it's on the right but it's not far, far right. So they want a party that wants to remain in the UK; they also want a party that is actually going to deal with issues on the ground. And those issues are about equality, about poverty, about all of those things.

We know there are people out there on both sides who clearly want a united Ireland or they want to remain part of the UK. Once things come to the point where they need to negotiate, they'll want to negotiate. Unfortunately political unionism doesn't want to negotiate around a united Ireland, and neither do I, but I want to hear what political unionism has to say about all of these issues.

The border poll was put into the GFA for a reason. If we look at that border poll element, part of that was to make sure that violent nationalism didn't exist. Now it still does exist, but it exists in a different form. And it looks to me as though both sides of the border have got control over that. Yes, people have lost their lives, but more people would be dead if it hadn't been for the cooperation of Ireland and the UK. So why not have a border poll as part of the GFA? I'm a confident unionist – there's not many of us about [*Laughs*] – and I'm confident in my Britishness and will make that argument. But politics is politics and if there's a border poll there's a border poll.

Seamus Mallon's point about the need for a majority of un-ionists to favour a united Ireland is just common sense. It's not what the GFA says, but when the ceasefires were called and the Agreement reached, I thought, 'This is it. It's over now, we've won it, let's get on with things.' Do you honestly believe that the spirit of the Agreement is being supported by the last two first ministers? No, because they've got into these argu-ments about things that weren't in the Agreement.

The reality is – and I think Seamus is right – you can't do this over a large minority. I'm not sure they were that smart to not make that clear in the Agreement. They were more in-tent on fudging it. But the reality is, people thought with the Agreement things were going to work. And it hasn't worked. So we need to do it in the here and now. And we know that you can't have a minority of republicans either. Unionists have to think about what it is they need to change.

I can't say if there would be violence or not in the case of a nationalist majority in a border poll, and I'm not going to start giving someone the excuse to carry out violence. People in this country who were never involved in ceasefires or anything else are flying round the world telling people how to do it. And one of the things they talk about is this whole thing around cultural intelligence. If people don't realise that there needs to be cultural intelligence here, on both sides of the border, there's something wrong with them. By cultural intelligence I mean [understanding between] people living in different communities, having different cultures. And it can't just be British or Irish – we have all sorts of different cultures here, and we need to be working on those things, building relationships. It seems to me the Assembly isn't doing that at the minute.

You could say the same thing about violence if we were to remain in the UK after a border poll. Would the IRA or anybody else give up and say, 'OK, politics didn't work, back to war.'?

There are a number of things that need to happen before we get there, and I want to hear what political unionism says. The problem is we had a conflict that some people say started over 600 years ago, while others say the 1960s. What we need to consider is what came first: polluted politics or the paramilitaries? Polluted politics came first. So if we pollute the air in terms of politicians and put people against each other, then we're leaving a vacuum. Politics needs to work. We know what happens when we leave a vacuum. On a point of principle, I'm not going to predict what others may do. We need to work through politics and make sure politics is working. If we do that, we don't create a vacuum.

For years, I was a unionist. Fifty per cent plus one was good enough. But I'm saying somebody needs to look at this. If there's a big minority, then they need to look at how to handle it. That's all I'm suggesting. If they want to go 50% plus one, we go 50% plus one. I'd have to accept that as a democrat. But the point I'm making is the consequences of 50% plus one either way.

Brexit, irrespective of whether you're pro or anti, has left the UK a divided country. If Brexit happens, if we end up leaving, it depends on how the economy goes. If the economy is going well, people will forget about it. If it's not going well, then we'll be on a life-support machine in terms of keeping people in the UK together, getting the right things done. As far as I'm concerned, no one knows what's going to happen until it's done. It could have a destabilising effect on the whole UK; it could also have a very stabilising effect. The economy makes the world go round.

Optimistic or pessimistic? I always see the glass half-full. Despite everything. People say Britain doesn't want us. In my opinion they do. If they didn't want us they could have got rid of us years ago. You could say that about the Irish government – they don't want us. But people have aspirations. It doesn't matter what country you live in, the politicians will always do something you don't agree with.

ENDNOTES

Preface

1 King George V, speech, Belfast, 22 June 1921; printed in *The Belfast News Letter*, 23 June 1921.
2 *The Parliamentary Debates (Official Report)*, vol. 16, House of Commons, 1933, pp. 1,094–96.

1 Martina Anderson

1 Martina Anderson, speech, European Parliament, Brussels, 13 May 2017.
2 Leo Varadkar, *Belfast Telegraph*, 11 December 2017.

12 Ray Bassett

1 Bruno Waterfield, 'Barroso Hails the European "Empire"', *The Daily Telegraph*, 11 July 2007.

14 Diarmaid Ferriter

1 Edward Carson, speech, House of Commons, December 1919.
2 Paul Murray, *The Irish Boundary Commission and Its Origins, 1886–1925* (UCD Press, 2011).

19 Niall O'Dowd

1 Jack Lynch, speech, RTÉ television, 13 August 1969.

20 Sean McManus

1 Reverend Walter Brueggemann, 'Voices of the Night', in Brueggemann, Thomas Groome, and Sharon Parks, *To Act Justly, Love Tenderly, Walk Humbly: An Agenda for Ministers* (Wipf and Stock, 1997).

21 Peter Kissel

1 Taoiseach Éamon de Valera, Raidió Éireann broadcast, 17 March 1943.
2 Robert Frost, 'Mending Wall', in *North of Boston* (David Nutt, 1914).

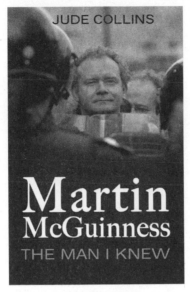

ABOUT THE AUTHOR

Jude Collins is a retired university lecturer. He has broadcast extensively on CBC (Canada), BBC Radio Newcastle, BBC Radio Ulster and BBC Radio Five Live, as well as appearing on BBC NI, BBC World News, RTÉ and PRESS TV. He has written four works of fiction: *Booing the Bishop and Other Stories* (1995), *Only Human and Other Stories* (1998), *The Garden of Eden All Over Again* (2001) and *Leave of Absence* (2006), as well as three collections of interviews: *Tales Out of School: St Columb's College Derry in the 1950s* (The History Press, 2010), *Whose Past Is It Anyway?* (The History Press, 2013) and *Martin McGuinness: The Man I Knew* (Mercier Press, 2018). Jude writes a weekly column for *The Andersonstown News* and blogs at www.judecollins.com.